ACHIEVING PERFORMANCE EXCELLENCE IN UNIVERSITY ADMINISTRATION

ACHIEVING PERFORMANCE EXCELLENCE IN UNIVERSITY ADMINISTRATION

A Team Approach to Organizational Change and Employee Development

Manuel London

PRAEGER

Westport, Connecticut
London

Library of Congress Cataloging-in-Publication Data

London, Manuel.
　　Achieving performance excellence in university administration : a
team approach to organizational change and employee development /
Manuel London.
　　　　p.　　　cm.
　　Includes bibliographical references and index.
　　ISBN 0–275–95246–0 (alk. paper)
　　1. Education, Higher—United States—Administration.　2. College
administrators—United States.　I. Title.
LB2341.L66　　1995
378.1′00973—dc20　　　　　95–14427

British Library Cataloguing in Publication Data is available.

Library of Congress Catalog Card Number: 95–14427
ISBN: 0–275–95246–0

First published in 1995

Praeger Publishers, 88 Post Road West, Westport, CT 06881
An imprint of Greenwood Publishing Group, Inc.

Printed in the United States of America

The paper used in this book complies with the
Permanent Paper Standard issued by the National
Information Standards Organization (Z39.48-1984).

10　9　8　7　6　5　4　3　2　1

For Dr. John H. Marburger III
and Dr. Stan Altman

Contents

Preface

This book helps university administrators think about how they can improve performance in their institutions. The idea for the book stemmed from my experiences helping administrators in a fairly large state research university during the last five years. These were times of technological change, resource constraints, external pressures from multiple constituencies, internal conflicts, and continuous challenges to do more and do everything well. The university became quality conscious and got into the habit of always looking for ways to improve. Human resource management and organizational development were keys to administrative effectiveness, and we viewed ourselves as change agents. We were in the business of facilitating and evaluating change and helping others learn how to do the same.

This book documents our efforts to improve administrative efficiency and manage the university well in tough times. Overall, the book demonstrates methods to maintain and enhance organizational vitality in an environment of tight resources and external pressures. It shows how to extend the university's community of learning beyond faculty and students to create a continuous learning organization in the administration.

This book encourages administrators to think strategically about their decisions and actions before events overwhelm them. We present ideas to make change happen. Some changes are frame breaking in that they involve a major redefinition of the institution—its mission, goals, products, and clients. Such wrenching changes are less common. Other change is incremental. It happens a bit at a time, without a clear direction and unified purpose. Such change may seem more like muddling through. The challenge is to make such changes less like muddling through and more deliberate and self-enhancing, from the perspectives of individuals, work groups, and the university as a whole.

This work is for academic administrators and students of administration to help them understand change process as well as means to create, and cope with, change. The book suggests key leverage points for change—work processes, interpersonal dynamics, and programmatic interventions—that facilitate and prompt change. The book considers a university administration's vulnerability (areas of weakness) and resilience (areas of strength and resourcefulness). It presents a frank picture of a university's struggles to establish and gain commitment to goals. The book provides examples of methods, programs, and interventions for making change happen through people.

We are grateful for the assistance and contributions of many valued colleagues. We persevered through times of steep budget cuts, interdepartmental conflict, and management transitions. We learned to be experimenters and facilitators, pushing a bit here, pulling a bit there, to convince and cajole people to be team players. As lead author, I am especially grateful to the two people who contributed the most to this book: Emily Thomas, university planning coordinator, and Douglas Panico, director of performance management. Other administrators and students whose names are mentioned throughout this book also joined the creative process. I am also grateful to Dr. John H. Marburger, former president of SUNY-Stony Brook, and Dr. Stan Altman, who preceded me as Dr. Marburger's deputy. Their insight, resilience, and encouragement fostered creative management, directed lasting organizational change, strengthened employee development, and resolved conflict constructively. We all learned from their leadership and benefited from their friendship.

PART I

AN INTRODUCTION TO UNIVERSITY TRANSITION

1

Directions for Change

The notion of change in universities is not new. Nor is the recognition that their administration must be as effective and efficient as possible. Critics of university management abound. Barrett and Greene (1994, p. 38) typified the observations when they wrote:

What do you think of this company? It is the recognized national leader in many of its markets and employs hundreds of the nation's best minds. It has more potential customers than it knows what to do with. What's more, it has about $3 billion in income-earning investments and an Aaa bond rating from Moody's.

Now the bad news: This same institution was forced by escalating costs to more than double its prices over the last 10 years. Its services are not more expensive than most of its competitors' and it offers deep discounts to many clients. There's been recent turnover in its top jobs, and it has had operating deficits in excess of $40 million over three years. Professional estimates of deferred maintenance on its plant and equipment several years ago exceeded $500 million (though corporate officials won't—or can't—confirm that figure). . . .

Truth is, it's not a company we're talking about—it's Yale University.

Barrett and Greene suggest that such a scenario is not atypical. Furthermore, it is a symptom of "root rot in the way the nation's colleges and universities are managed" (p. 38). They haven't changed enough to respond to changing conditions.

University administrators, similar to corporate executives, now often search for best practices and apply total quality management (TQM). Such change may come from the top of the institution and occur after considerable attention to direction and design. Alternatively, it may be more haphazard and reactive, with most of the effort coming from grass roots—the departments feeling the most pressure and pain.

Reform in higher education management will require containing administrative growth, streamlining processes, eliminating duplicative effort, clarifying priorities, revamping reward systems, and supporting teamwork (Bruegman, 1992). McGuinness and Ewell (1994) argue that universities should set goals for substantial and lasting change. Moreover, they stress that marginal change will not be enough. They recommend change within current structures. They observe that consensus management has extended beyond the faculty to administrative and support personnel. As a result, decision making is slower and more costly. Moreover, they argue that administrative and support services have expanded and, because they are more professional, they are increasingly detached from the institution's core missions of teaching, research, and service. They recommend that universities follow the example of major private corporations by focusing on improving services to clients. Quality management processes rely on team input to understand and respond to customer expectations. The teams focus on, and redesign, core work processes.

SOME UNIVERSITY EXAMPLES

Tulane University

Some universities are undertaking major redesigns in response to changing student composition, decreasing research support, and increased costs. For instance, Tulane University embarked on such an effort starting in the spring of 1992 with a consulting firm's analysis of its budgetary problem and ways to rectify it without creating negative impact on academic quality (Kelly, 1993). Subsequent analyses of the academic base indicated that faculty resources were stretched by competing demands with the result that inadequate attention was devoted to undergraduate and graduate education and research. Recommendations included continuing the highly competitive environment by reducing the number of freshmen admitted each year and lowering the annual tuition increase to 3%. On the administrative side, this would require eliminating redundancies and paring back the growth of personnel that had occurred during the prior seven years. Tulane's President Eamon Kelly opened these recommendations to extensive campus discussion and debate led by the university senate. After considerable revision, a set of recommendations was adopted by the senate. Senior administrative officers worked with their managers to determine how to reorganize their areas. The results limited the number of required layoffs to only 22 following a successful voluntary separation plan that led to 219 employees leaving. The restructuring concluded in March 1993 with the redeployment of staff and achieving financial equilibrium.

The University of Maryland

Another example is the University of Maryland at College Park. The institution cut its budget by $45 million between 1990 and 1992 (Falk & Miller, 1993). It did so by following several key principles: avoidance of across-the-board cuts, maintenance of commitments, faculty involvement, openness, and ongoing communication within the institution. Numerous groups played a role, including the institution's Academic Planning Advisory Committee chaired by the provost, the college senate, and off-campus lobbying groups (e.g., through letters and meetings of contacts among state agencies and legislators with university officials and in open hearings held by two independent, predominantly faculty committees. The process showed the fairness of the deliberations' ultimate decisions. Losing $29 million and 183 positions during the first year, virtually every unit was affected. A key to the procedure's success was the willingness of the senate and administration to view the budget situation as a shared problem that required cooperative effort to resolve. Existing processes for evaluating programs and resource allocations worked well during the fiscal crisis, demonstrating the importance of effective systems and procedural structures.

The University of Tampa

President David G. Ruffer of the University of Tampa recently described the "administrative reinvention" of this private university (Ruffer, 1994). The school's "Quality Process Management" began by identifying a number of tasks (e.g., expansion of financial support base, development of budget priorities, enhancement of a sense of community, and creation of a long-range planning process). Overall goals were to improve the effectiveness and efficiency of the administration, move decision making to the level of those affected, direct resources to student programs, and involve as many persons as possible. The quality process action plan was announced in September 1992. Teams were formed to examine and improve key operations, such as the registration process. The teams were to identify major users of the work process, gather suggestions for improvement, communicate with others, and implement changes. Team members were trained in group process and team facilitators were assigned. A "quality coordinator" and a "quality council" monitored progress, looking for significant, measurable changes in key university operations. The quality council members identified the following general benefits of quality process management: 'It provides participants with a broad base knowledge of other operational units, it enhances communication among team members, it allows university decision making to be shared broadly, it generates staff commitment to working cross-functionally, it lends objective perspective to teamwork through facilitators' involvement, and it documents the complexity and interrelationships among functions (Ruffer, 1994).

While this book is not devoted to structured quality improvement programs, these programs and university "reengineering" efforts in general depend on effective structures, clear processes, employee development, and teamwork. The importance of these structures, processes, continuous learning, and opportunities for employee participation in decision making are emphasized throughout this book.

STRATEGIES FOR CHANGE

Tight budgets and changing marketplace demands in higher education have made administrators attentive to alternative ways of increasing productivity, including the above examples. For further ideas, see a useful edited volume by Anderson and Meyerson (1992) sponsored by the National Center for Postsecondary Governance and Finance. In that volume, Massy (1992) discusses *factors that reduce productivity in administrative and support areas* (growth of support costs, too much organizational slack or "fat," unnecessary tasks and functions); presents a *process for problem diagnosis* (a process by function matrix; process flowcharts; and diagnoses of function importance, reliability, redundancy, and use of technology); and lays out the *elements of an effective productivity improvement strategy* (strategic thinking regarding vision, plans, and measures; incentives, recognition, and rewards; individual and group empowerment; and recognition of constraints on available resources).

Also in that volume, Kaiser (1992) outlines a procedure for managers to evaluate the effectiveness of their own maintenance organization with an effectiveness rating system to measure *productivity* (the proportion of a worker's time that is directly productive), *performance* (how well an individual works), *quality* (characteristics of the work product), and *priorities* (whether the priorities set by management are appropriate in the eyes of relevant constituencies such as faculty, students, and staff).

For another interesting focus on ways to improve productivity and quality in higher education, see McGuinness and Ewell (1994). They outline three strategies for change: (1) setting goals for substantial and lasting change (not marginal change) and rewarding departments on their demonstrated commitment to the mission and the change process, (2) transforming core processes through methods for continuous quality improvement, and (3) enhancing learning productivity through faculty, student, and course management.

We take the view that all administrators are change agents and human resource managers. While administrators have functional areas of expertise, they accomplish their goals through people in their own departments or in other departments. A central element of their jobs is managing change through people in ways that promote organization effectiveness and goal accomplishment. Change management skills and creating opportunities for human resource development become a source of management power in addition to the administrator's formal role and responsibilities.

The types of changes occurring in one university are likely to be similar in other universities and institutions of higher education. In general, dimensions of organizational culture (e.g., innovation, stability, and orientation to people, teamwork, and detail) are fairly stable within types of industries (Chatman & Kehn, 1994). As such, the problems and programs discussed throughout this book are likely to generalize to a variety of universities and colleges.

Consider the following changes:

Moving to all-funds budgeting. This refers to instituting a process that recognizes the multiple sources of money and incorporating all sources in the funds management and planning process. As the accuracy and timeliness of financial information systems increase, administrators have more complete financial information. They can recognize one-time and recurring (base) sources of funds, and cannot easily protect funding sources. This provides a more accurate picture of how departments are funded, including the resource limitations or enhancements.

Determining information systems needs in the face of changing computer technology (e.g., distributed systems and local area networks, and the disaggregation of academic and administrative computing). Local computer technology increases administrative flexibility while changing allocation of resources, expertise, and control. Administrators need to be more knowledgeable in systems costs and capabilities. Also, they need to implement the systems in a way that generates employee cooperation, learning, and acceptance of new responsibilities.

Improving relationships between principal investigators, provision of laboratory maintenance and operations by the campus services department, and investment in research infrastructure. Researchers may view their role as essential to the university's success, and, indeed, research development funds may be invested in hiring world-class investigators and the brightest young scholars who can attract research funds. However, this might be at the expense of investment in facilities. Moreover, researchers who are not responsible for facilities maintenance may feel that campus services do not operate efficiently. Establishing a research facilities users group with representatives of principal investigators, campus services, the vice president for research, and vice provosts responsible for facilities is a way to focus on problems before they become catastrophes.

Managing processes rather than functions. Key functions in the institution are really part of larger processes across departments. For example, consider the enrollment process that may involve recruitment, admissions, undergraduate and graduate studies, publications, residence hall operations, the continuing education division, facilities operations, and the finance department, not to mention the academic departments providing educational resources. Financial and facilities operations are important other processes. Administrators in each component of a process must think of themselves as a link in the process—a customer or a supplier. Being part of a process (or several processes) means having multiple bosses, an awareness of the broader goal and how one's job contributes to this goal, and a desire to contribute to the success of the entire process, not just one individual's job. Communication and cooperation become keys to success of the enterprise.

Establishing top-down university plans without creating a useless bureaucratic exercise. Instead of creating a planning department, the university uses existing resources to form a planning team chaired by a planning coordinator. The team's function is to spearhead annual department plans stemming from the university's mission and overall goals. The plans demonstrate interdepartmental objectives and interfaces and provide a foundation for establishing priorities and reallocating funds accordingly.

Formulating service agreements between departments that recognize interdependencies, cross-department funding, and the value of an internal market economy. Departments annually negotiate with each other to determine the level and type of services provided and cross-charges. Service departments can then plan their staffing. Also, they are forced to operate competitively, recognizing that client departments can go to the community for similar services. However, this means that services that are in demand and make money can no longer easily subsidize others that are needed by the school but are not self-supporting. This focuses attention on cost and profit centers and forces the question about whether to continue operating unprofitable enterprises.

Creating a performance management function and reorienting management control programs to promote performance excellence. A new department called "performance management" conducts administrative department reviews, develops and distributes key indicator reports, and coordinates with management engineering and internal audit to help departments establish ways to reduce costs and improve customer responsiveness.

Investing in employee training and development as a key to the continued viability of the institution, especially in tight economic environment. While the university is a seat of learning, resources may not be devoted to improving the functional and managerial knowledge of its employees. To change the situation by drawing on existing resources, the president creates a steering committee for employee training and development. The committee conducts a training needs analysis and creates an annual series of special courses preceded by a training kickoff celebration. This supplements already available training and calls attention to the importance of continuous learning for all employees.

Implementing an upward feedback survey process to provide supervisors with anonymous feedback from subordinates. The idea for the process comes from the campus advocate (ombudsman) who hears one complaint after another about incompetent supervisors. The upward feedback process, along with supervisor training, increases employees' awareness of, and supervisors' attention to, cogent elements of boss/subordinate relationships, such as goal setting, coaching, evaluating performance, giving feedback, and supporting training and career development.

THEMES IN THIS BOOK

The changes just described are more than procedural. They are strategically oriented moves aimed at managerial effectiveness and excellence—doing more with less and doing things better. They evoke the following themes that are discussed throughout this book:

- There are many internal and external forces for change (competition, globalization, economy, technology). However, change happens through people.
- Many endeavors require interdepartmental cooperation. Work processes that cross departmental boundaries and organizational levels need to be recognized and established.

Process leaders need to emerge or be appointed. The administrative team is really a mini-organization or system (Neumann, 1991). Collaboration, teamwork, and conflict resolution are keys to process management.

- Existing resources can be deployed in new ways to do more with the same or less.
- Planning can be proactive and interactive, not reactive and bureaucratic. It should be based on a clear articulation from the top of the institution's character and vision for the future.
- Issues of empowerment, enfranchisement, and inclusion need to be addressed explicitly. Employee involvement generates commitment to decisions, especially when employees need to live with the decisions and when they have the knowledge and ideas to contribute productively to the decision process.
- Organization development is evolutionary. Each new program (e.g., quality improvement, team building, training, or performance management) builds on prior programs and moves the institution a step toward increased effectiveness.
- Employees need skills in group process management and participation, communication, conflict resolution, negotiation, teamwork, and team building. Administrators become educators, coaches, facilitators, and experimenters.
- Comparative data from other institutions along with good internal data and management reports can be a source of policy analysis and directions for improved operations.
- Quality principles apply to university operations even when there isn't a formal quality program. These principles include recognition of external and internal customers, responsiveness to customers' needs, and opportunities for employee input and involvement, which are important to commitment to work goals (Melan, 1993). Total quality management is not discussed here in any depth because there are many other publications dealing with TQM in higher education.[1] TQM is a structured approach that requires extensive training and facilitation as well as commitment throughout the institution. The process, team building, and customer/employee feedback examples described here accomplish many of the same goals as TQM.
- There are opportunities to grow a *community of learning* for staff and administration as well as students and faculty. This includes a sense of identity, place, and belonging that leads to commitment, involvement, and motivation.

These themes lead to some general ideas about human resource management:

- Change requires strong and visible commitment from the top of the organization.
- Employee participation is key to increasing commitment to change processes and benefiting from employees' knowledge and ideas.
- Working in teams can result in more innovation, less interdepartmental conflict, and faster implementation of decisions. However, people have to learn how to work productively in teams—including how to listen to others without being judgmental and how to raise and resolve conflict.
- The nature of management is changing from control, monitoring, organizing, and evaluating to coaching, facilitating, educating, giving feedback, and managing change.
- People need to be recognized and rewarded for their achievements even when incentive and merit pay increases are not possible.

- Measurement and feedback are critical to management insight. Collecting and imparting performance information to individuals and groups helps set realistic, achievement-oriented goals. Departmental evaluation is important to continued success.
- Performance management can be facilitated by various control mechanisms that are participatively oriented (self-studies).
- Human resource activities and programs need to be integrated and mutually supportive. These include formal programs from the human resources department (e.g., selection, performance appraisal, and compensation) as well as administrators' implementation of these programs and, more generally, how they treat their people.
- Planning and work processes and their outcomes should be documented and communicated widely throughout the university.

The topics covered here focus on directions for organization development in higher education administration, the importance of leadership or facilitating roles, planning, managing key processes (councils and forums for financial planning, enrollments, and capital facilities councils), and using collaborative methods to solve organizational problems (such as designing and introducing new information systems). Organizational structures (e.g., teams), functions (e.g., performance management and measurements), and team-building efforts drive toward performance excellence in administration and facilitate managerial transitions. Interventions for performance excellence include total quality management, training, and methods for program evaluation and performance feedback.

OUTLINE OF THE BOOK

Part I conveys directions for administrative transition. Chapter 2 shows the importance of leaders and their emissaries in directing and implementing change. A case study shows that the leader's competence as a communicator and visionary sets the stage for effective change or, alternatively, becomes a barrier to change and a force for organizational dissolution. The chapter also highlights the role of the executive assistant, which we call deputy to the president. The deputy's job involves all aspects of university operations, just as does the president's. The deputy, working with others, designs and facilitates plans for work process and outcomes. As such, the role can be pivotal in bolstering and maintaining comprehensive and systematic change processes. The chapter also shows the importance of effective mechanisms for communication within the organization.

Chapter 3 shows how the human resource department can be a vehicle for change and how human resource professionals can be change agents. Human resource programs have the potential to inform and direct university strategies. Key human resource problems include the need for retraining and cross-training, fewer advancement opportunities and fewer chances for bonuses and salary increases, an imbalanced workforce, continued requirements for clerical personnel, and support for employees' understanding the implications of university changes. Human resource professionals are experts in organizational research, communications, negotiation, training, and change strategy. Moreover, they understand the importance of creating and being role models. The human resource department is responsible for establishing a comprehensive, integrated, goal-oriented set of programs (e.g., human resource forecasting and planning, career planning and development, compensation and appraisal, performance management, feedback and measurement processes, and employee training and development).

Chapter 4 opens Part II on setting the course for organizational change. The chapter describes methods for university-wide planning and goal setting that build a sense of teamwork, belonging, and unity of purpose. Most universities have planning and priority-setting processes, and the procedures described here are not unique. Our purpose is to emphasize the necessary tie between broad university objectives and departmental action plans and to avoid having planning become a meaningless bureaucratic exercise. The university's planning staff (representatives from the major departments) works with the president, provost, and vice presidents to establish overall university goals and objectives. The plans demonstrate that different units contribute to the same goal in different ways. The chapter gives examples of general university objectives, departmental contributions to those objectives, special departmental initiatives, and annual reviews as a basis for the next planning cycle.

Chapter 5 provides scenarios for financial, enrollment, and capital facilities planning. These processes demonstrate process management, teamwork, and the need for regular calendars of planning events. The processes all rely on user input, expert judgment, and shared decision making. They are a way to set priorities, evaluate success, and make corrections along the way. The outline of facilities planning is an especially comprehensive approach to setting general objectives, assessing conditions, and establishing plans for specific locations. All of the processes indicate the need to relate functions to university-wide objectives.

Part III moves from planning to operations. In particular, it focuses on ways to manage performance—that is, evaluate and enhance the quality and cost effectiveness of campus operations. The theme is managing for effectiveness. Chapter 6 shows how internal audit and performance management functions can provide constructive input and consultation to develop more effective work structures. The chapter describes an administrative review process that provides opportunities for feedback and self-reflection, involving the department's employees, customers, and outside experts in the process. The chapter concludes with a proposal for integrating these functions under an organizational effectiveness unit. The chapter emphasizes that control functions don't have to be watchdogs of bureaucratic regulations but can be promoters of organizational analysis and continuous learning.

The concept of a market economy can be applied to university operations as a way to enhance the quality of administrative services and products and reduce costs. Accurate and timely information is needed to adjust to changes in demand, competition, and modes of production. This helps to ensure market share and provide maximum operating flexibility. Chapter 7 shows how quality measurements coordinated by the performance management department are used to examine unit effectiveness, make comparisons with similar operations at other institutions, and make improvements. A variety of service quality measurement methods and applications are described. The chapter begins with a discussion of how to negotiate interdepartmental service agreements for charge-backs. Cost analyses and management engineering studies are ways to improve efficiency and lower costs. A case example shows how poor planning and little communication in implementing self-sufficiency and internal market economies can cause disruption and user dissatisfaction. Next, key indicators of university effectiveness and management reports are described as ways to track, compare, and improve organizational effectiveness. Ways to collect and analyze comparative "benchmark" data are described. Finally, methods for obtaining user input and satisfaction are shown. In all, the chapter suggests how an administrative unit can use information to increase quality and reduce costs of production.

Part IV considers human resource strategies for organization development. Chapter 8 describes team-building methods for improving communication and reducing interpersonal conflict among university administrators. The chapter begins with sample agendas from planned retreats to discuss university goals and to establish common objectives. The mission is presented for an ongoing customer-oriented focus group. Then the chapter concentrates on the formation of a team of top administrators for the purpose of improving interdepartmental relationships. The top team can be a forum to discuss external changes that impinge on the university and analyze the need for change. It is an attempt to make ourselves into a "learning organization" focusing on the processes by which we work together such as how we resolve conflict, develop our people, and involve our people in decision making.

Chapter 9 shows how support for employee training can be an organizational development tool—actually a way to change the organizational culture. It describes how the university at first did not perceive training and development as important areas of investment when dealing with nonfaculty. Environmental changes suggested that employees need training to be capable of operating in a more fluid, less-well-defined environment. However, tight finances made it impossible to add more resources to the training department. Rather, the president decided to take advantage of the existing resources on campus that would also enhance employee involvement in training and development. Specifically, the president created a campuswide steering committee on training. The chapter details how the committee designed special events and training sessions to communicate that investment in staff development was critical to the institution's continued vitality. The chapter outlines a master plan for employee training and development at a university.

Chapter 10 suggests methods for enhancing attention to employee development through appraisal and feedback. Several new techniques are discussed. The first is a "ratingless" appraisal as a way to reduce the threat of performance feedback and to increase its constructiveness. The chapter describes how to implement such a system in an environment used to evaluating performance with numerical ratings or scores. The rest of the chapter describes survey feedback methods—ratings from subordinates (termed upward feedback) and ratings from peers, subordinates, supervisors, and customers (termed 360 degree feedback). These processes allow collecting performance information from diverse sources—sources that are likely to have different views of the employee's actions and effectiveness. The method provides regular flow of information to support continuous learning and improvement.

Chapter 11 focuses on problem performance—ways to deal with, and hopefully overcome, marginal performance and ways to deal with abusive managers. Marginal performance is likely to increase as job expectations increase with more demands placed on the organization and fewer resources to handle them. Marginal performance can be overcome by increasing employee competence through training and development and enhancing employee motivation through job challenge and changes in job responsibilities. Employee abuse by managers is another matter. It should not be tolerated. Different forms of employee abuse, some subtle and some not-so-subtle, need to be recognized and managed immediately.

The concluding chapter offers some reflections on implementing the policies and programs for employee development and organizational change discussed throughout the book. This includes owning up to the frustrations experienced in implementing some of the programs as well as the benefits and pleasures. We end the book by offering directions for creating transitions and enhancing human resource practice in academic administration.

CONCLUSION

This is a book about change management. It suggests that all administrators, regardless of department or functions, are managers of people and agents of change. The pressures for change in academia are many—making the job of manager more complex and challenging. Key challenges include visionary leadership, team development, customer sensitivity, cost effectiveness, process design and management, and proactive planning. Another challenge is just being a good manager—evaluating employees' performance, providing feedback, and giving opportunities for development.

NOTE

1. As a few examples of TQM, see Stuelpnagel (1989), McKenna (1993), and the monthly newsletter *TQM in Higher Education* edited by Robert Cornesky, 489 Oakland Park Blvd., Port Orange. FL 32127. The American Association for Higher Education, One Dupont Circle, Suite 360. Washington, DC 20036, has a "continuous quality improvement project" that offers resources and publications supporting quality management. IBM sponsors TQM partnership awards for colleges and universities (Seymour, 1993). Also, a firm called the International Quality & Productivity Center, P.O. Box 43155, Upper Montclair, NJ 07043-7155, runs an annual conference entitled "TQM in Colleges & Universities."

2

Leadership Roles in a Changing Environment: The Roles of President and Deputy to the President

One task of the university president is to create a team setting that elicits the best capabilities of team members, in the hope of expanding their capabilities (Neumann, 1991). This chapter begins with a description of how the university's president influences change strategies, positively and negatively. The example describes a university (not my own) that recently experienced a merger along with image and enrollment problems. A consultant provides the president with some honest and direct upward feedback and offers suggestions for improving communications and resolving interpersonal conflicts. The next section outlines the role of the deputy to the president. The role is viewed as a facilitator of organizational change. The outline shows how the deputy intervenes, expedites, and experiments to improve coordination and teamwork. The examples show the diversity of university issues in line for continuous improvement. The final brief section suggests ways communication can be improved, and used to foster change, through better use of internal media.

LEADERSHIP STYLE AND ORGANIZATIONAL CHANGE

The following case was adapted from a consultant's organizational analysis of a troubled institution. It describes a small, private university that recently merged with a liberal arts college. The issues were raised during individual meetings with the school's president, provost, vice presidents (VPs), and the administrative department directors under the VPs.

Conflict about Operating Philosophy

Objectives of the school have changed with the merger. The institution used to be run by the seat of the pants with little technical know-how and little understanding of costs. Today, there is far more functional expertise in the administration. However, there is a divergence of opinion about how the university should be guided. The parent university and president want a market-driven enterprise that develops new programs and attracts a variety of full- and part-time graduate and undergraduate students. The old guard (principally admissions staff from the liberal arts college) wants to maintain a university based on personal relationships with students.

Communications Problems

Attempts to address relationship issues among the executive staff have not been fruitful (referring to quality improvement meetings held six months earlier). Partly this was the fault of how the meetings were structured. Rotating groups discussing operational issues failed to provide continuity and commitment to quality improvement. In general, insufficient time was devoted to the process.

Current Status of the University

The university is still experiencing growing pains. The top administration has little management experience, coming from the faculty. Lower-level administrators have substantial experience in their technical areas of specialty, but they also have little management experience.

The admissions and publications staff do not communicate well, yet they need to talk the most. This is the weakest link in the management team. The finance and campus services VPs and their staffs work well together.

The school is small and the responsibilities blend, making it difficult to maintain distinct lines of authority. While job descriptions exist, people get involved in others' areas. This leads to friction. Work needs to be done to more clearly delineate job descriptions. For instance, the finance VP, the admissions VP, and the publications manager seem to think they have some responsibility for setting tuition levels and pricing for noncredit programs.

The school is overcoming a poor public image. Before the merger, the school seemed to run with the philosophy of "doing business at any cost." This meant low tuition levels to attract students and reacting to student requests rather than creating programs that brought in more and better students. The school was relegated to trying to be the low-tuition private school with several popular and reasonably strong academic majors (e.g., business management, social sciences, and nursing). The emerging goal is to develop more and better programs that appeal to a wider variety of students with different needs. However, the school is still caught between new and old goals. Unfortunately, new programs have been slow to develop and enrollments have increased at a slow rate.

Reasons for Recent Enrollment Problems

The slowdown in admissions may be due to many factors:

- the recession
- poor decisions about some programs (e.g., starting programs with academic prestige but little student demand)
- too rapid increase in tuition
- slow development of programs
- low morale in the admissions force
- insufficient recruitment coverage (some recruiters responsible for too broad a geographical area)
- lack of action on marketing and public relations strategies
- recruitment director new to this area (coming from the position of registrar) and is not spending sufficient time in the field

Perceptions of the President (Some "Upward" Feedback)

The president does not give administrators a chance to do the jobs for which they are responsible and should be held accountable. Often the president assigns the same project to more than one person. Some VPs see this as a result of the president's distrust or lack of confidence in his people. Others see this as a result of the president's desire to get things done quickly. When one person doesn't come through, the president goes to someone else. Alternatively, some believe that the president doesn't recognize each manager's specific responsibilities. This creates confusion and erodes morale. Some people feel the president is undermining their authority and sets up competition among the executive staff. The president is handing them mixed signals (giving them responsibility on the one hand and taking it away behind their backs on the other).

Other perceptions of the president: First, on the positive side:

- He is simply doing what needs to be done to turn the school around given the top managers currently with the school.
- He has faith in his managers and leaves them with things to do.
- He doesn't take sides. He tries to let managers work out their problems.
- He is very definite and specific about what he wants done.
- He listens to reason, but you have to do your homework.

On the negative side:

- He demeans and humiliates people in front of others, making it difficult for them to save face.
- He manages by threat.

- He micromanages, getting involved in minute details and making others suffer through progress reports (this is alternatively viewed by some as necessary to get people to follow through and by others as a total waste of time).
- He undermines agreements made with others.
- He fails to tell some managers when a decision is made that affects their unit.
- He does not let others do their jobs.
- He is not open to input (he may occasionally say he wants to know what others think, but he really doesn't).
- He doesn't want to deal with performance problems (firing managers would show that things are out of control).
- He avoids confrontations. He may dislike an action, but he doesn't reverse it. He doesn't face up to others. He prefers to dress subordinates in public.
- He is quick to blame others for failures and take credit for successes.
- He changes priorities in midstream. To some, this is being responsive to students. To others, it is undermining their authority.
- He doesn't have confidence in his management team.
- He is too controlling. He makes directives and even carries them out himself.
- He has definite ideas, and he intends to get what he wants.
- He is not interested in developing the management team (by seeking and using their ideas and letting them carry out their responsibilities). He doesn't leave it to the managers to determine what is needed.
- He can be overzealous because he wants things done quickly.
- He asks whoever is around to solve a problem, not necessarily the individual who has formal responsibility.
- He has the most confidence in the one administrator he happens to know the best.
- He responds quickly to problems at hand, but does not share problems and ask for ideas before making decisions.
- Saying no to him is unacceptable. Everything is a priority, and priorities are constantly changing.
- He micromanages. He believes that if the little things get taken care of, the big things must also get done because they are so important.
- He says he wants people to be open and honest, but he has been known to "shoot the messenger."
- He promises more than he is willing to deliver.

An open question is whether the president is behaving this way because he doesn't trust his people and he believes the people can't change or because his management style and background lead him to be authoritarian and controlling. Another open question is whether there is truth to the above perceptions of the president. The provost and VPs tend to emulate the president. As a consequence, administrators below them are insecure about their jobs. There is a lack of interpersonal trust.

Another problem is that there is not uniform agreement about what needs to be done. Priorities change constantly. In part this is a function of a tight financial climate, a desire to expand the university and enhance its reputation, and a need to be responsive to students. The publications and admissions managers have different views about strategies for the university.

Some department directors see the publications manager as highly political and divisive, yet responsive to directives from the top. Also, she appreciates the expanded role she has working in a small university. She can get a fast decision on an idea and act on it tomorrow. She recognizes the need to understand the financial implications of her role. She feels she does everything she is supposed to do, but others don't understand her role. Regarding the admissions manager, the publications manager believes she is expected to influence him when he doesn't report to her. The finance and campus services VPs meet every morning to review their progress. They are trying to be responsive to students' needs. They both seem to be of the "old school" in this sense.

Consultant's Views of What's Needed

- Get the right people in the right jobs.
- Make sure each person is clear on expectations.
- Let people do their jobs.

Teamwork will follow naturally from the above.

- Need for the management team to recognize they are not a peer group. They are at different organizational levels and have different responsibilities. Alternative strategies include:
  —Decide how the university will be run and go to it!
  —Orchestrate self-assessments and co-worker feedback
  —Development planning for each manager
  —Help the president understand his management style, communications, and decision process
  —Role playing to help top administrators understand each other

Summary

This section showed that a university leader can be a barrier for change. Some upward feedback and consultant suggestions might alleviate the problem, *if* the president listens and is open to change. The situation might have to worsen before the leader is able to break his frame of reference and see the need for personal and organizational change. The consultant serves the role of sounding board. Being external to the organization makes the consultant less threatening than internal university officers, who also would not risk being aboveboard. Indeed, the consultant's interviews were necessary to reveal the extent of the problems, although the president had the insight to bring in the consultant in the first place.

Another strategy presidents use is to have a trusted executive assistant or deputy. Coming from the ranks of the tenured faculty, the deputy is able to be open with the president and with the top administration. As such, the deputy assists the president in setting and accomplishing university objectives through constructive conflict resolution, process management, and team building. The examples show the range of areas for organizational change, and raise topics that are discussed in more detail later in the book.

THE ROLE OF DEPUTY TO THE PRESIDENT

This section demonstrates the scope of activities and the ways a deputy becomes involved in administration in support of presidential initiatives. It shows that the deputy can be a negotiator, facilitator, and team builder. I will return to many of the topics discussed here in later chapters. Overall, the charge of the deputy to the president is to work wherever necessary to enhance the internal operations of the university and improve interdepartmental relationships. A list of specific functions is included after a description of current issues. This outline is based on my position as deputy to a university president.

Involvement in Current Operational Issues

Planning Processes

In 1992, the president formed the planning staff and appointed a university planning coordinator. (This is a part-time job. The coordinator's other job is a policy analyst and assistant to the vice president for health science center.) The president's intention was to establish a meaningful planning process without creating a bureaucratic entity, and he did this by bringing together existing resources and personnel. As a member of the planning staff, I work with the planning coordinator as she establishes the annual three-year program plan and helps the provost and VPs to evaluate last year's accomplishments and develop their annual plans. (Planning processes will be described in Chapters 4 and 5.) I track the development of three major university planning processes: the budgeting process (the planning coordinator is "staff" to the priorities committee chaired by the provost), the enrollment process (the planning coordinator also staffs the enrollment issues forum chaired by the provost), and the capital facilities planning process.

Campus Budget. I follow the budget process as it moves through the priorities committee and the cabinet to the president. My role is to ensure that the president and cabinet address budget issues as the process unfolds. I coordinate with the vice president of finance and management, the provost, and the university planning coordinator to encourage communication, deal with uncertainties, and encourage contingency planning. The process now works fairly smoothly after several years of refinement. However, work is still needed on developing a meaningful, policy-oriented three-year financial plan in parallel with the narrative three-year program plan.

While the state budget is the principal focus of the priorities committee and the budgeting process, the president has an all-funds budgeting philosophy. The VP of finance and management publishes an annual all-funds budget. This combines budget information from various revenue sources such as research grant indirect cost (IDC) revenues, contributions and endowment income, the clinical practice management plan for the medical and dental schools, and miscellaneous revenue from revocable licenses, rentals, royalties, fines, fees, and other payments. The IDC budget is managed by the VP for research under the provost. In an effort to incorporate the IDC budget into university financial planning, the president has been striving for better communication between the office of the VP for finance and management, the provost's budget staff, and the VP for research (including the campus office of research services).

We are hampered by poor expense tracking systems. Financial information from different sources does not come together easily. The university is working on an improved accounting system that will accommodate the state and research budgets, but it is not likely to be available in the immediate future. Meanwhile, financial information is late and not coordinated by source except through various work-arounds. For instance, the provost's office invented an on-line system called "Project" (as in projections), which helps the academic divisions do some coordinated financial tracking. However, the system has many imperfections, and it is not available to other departments.

Enrollment Planning. In 1993, we faced a possible enrollment crisis. This was precipitated by a drop in student enrollment the prior year (which we attributed to a newspaper series on the state university system) coupled with a change in the state funding mechanism that increased the tie between enrollments and campus revenues. To avoid losing several million dollars, we established an emergency enrollment management group with representatives from all relevant departments. When the provost assumed his position in late spring 1993, he took responsibility for the enrollment process and established the enrollment issues forum and the enrollment executive committee.

Our coordinated effort during the spring and summer was successful in keeping the loss in revenue to a minimum. We had one-time increases in financial aid revenue to help attract students. The effort continues under the provost's leadership, and we have been watching application and enrollment figures closely.

Capital Facilities Planning. Since 1992, the planning staff has encouraged the assistant VP for facilities in the campus services department to establish a meaningful planning process. He chairs the facilities planning council, which responds to the state system's annual call for a list of rehab and construction priorities. Unfortunately, the process tends to be fragmented. The plan focuses on a variety of projects that are important but don't provide a sense of campus needs in different major areas (e.g., research, classrooms). The council is currently working on a revision of the campus facilities master plan last done in 1990. Here again, the problem expressed by members of the council is that the process is disconnected from the university's strategic initiatives and does not convey a sense of the whole. (These three processes will be reviewed in more detail in Chapter 5.)

Research Facilities

A continuing issue is the adequacy of funding for research facilities operations and maintenance as well as for rehabs. A number of problems occur because principal investigators perceive that the campus services department is not responsive to their needs—for instance, that they don't do repairs required by federal granting and regulatory agencies (a particular problem in the animal labs) and that they don't maintain facilities efficiently. On the other hand, campus services is underfunded. I chair the research facilities users group, which tries to identify and solve these problems before they become crises.

Performance Management

Performance management is a new department. It is directed by a bright young manager who was previously an internal auditor in the university. He supervises four management interns from the management school. He conducts the administrative department reviews, produces quarterly key indicators reports to summarize important dimensions of university performance, works on various planning initiatives (e.g., the creation of administrative department profiles), coordinates the campus response to the benchmarking study conducted by the National Association of College Business Officers and analyzes the results (a project that compares administrative departments at our institution to other universities), and serves as staff to several committees.

I am directing an analysis of the relationship between performance management, internal audit, and management engineering. These three departments are closely aligned and together form our response to the state's internal control act (legislation that specifies that state agencies must have a plan to ensure adherence to policies and financial controls). The performance management and internal audit functions report to me. The goal of the analysis is to determine how these functions can work together more productively to support a coherent quality improvement effort in our administrative departments. (See Chapters 6 and 7 for a more in-depth discussion of performance management.)

Health Care

I follow the progress of evolving management issues in the health sciences center, which includes the university hospital and medical, nursing, and dental schools (e.g., managed care contracts, cost reduction efforts, and a performance improvement initiative called "operation excellence"). This entails attending meetings, setting up briefings, and generally keeping in touch with the vice president of the health sciences center and his administrators.

Computing

I have spent quite a bit of time monitoring the progress of the computing task force commissioned by the provost after initial work by the planning staff. The goal of this project was to examine administrative computing, academic computing, and computing infrastructure issues. I am a member of the instructional computing task force that is attempting to clarify student computing needs, consider funding mechanisms, and ensure a coordinated approach to advanced technology learning (with the hope of avoiding the creation of "white elephants," such as a "high-tech classroom," that are not connected to university goals). The planning staff continues to be concerned about campus system needs. The vice provost for computing and communications is a member of the planning staff.

Service Agreements

I am involved in discussions on the provision of security and other campus service operations to the hospital. Concerns center on level of service, control, and cost. This is being done in conjunction with memoranda of understanding (MOU), which are service agreements between the hospital and various service providers. We also have MOU between other major income-generating entities, such as the office of research services and service departments, such as campus services and finance and management. The associate VP for finance chairs the MOU committee and the director of performance management, who works for me, staffs it. I often get involved in disputed areas, such as whether the office of research services must purchase training from the human resource department. (See Chapter 7 for more details about service agreements.)

Parking

I follow the union negotiations on parking. Our goal is to increase the fee structure to make it commensurate with the debt and maintenance requirements. The requirement of self-sufficiency for parking structures doesn't work because we don't have control over the rates set—rates are set by union agreement. If bargaining does not succeed, we will go to impasse, and an arbitrator will decide. In the long run, our parking problems may not be solved unless we somehow modify the process for funding parking structures.

Several of us in the president's office get involved in parking enforcement complaints that are escalated to the president. The president wants the enforcement staff under campus services to strike a balance between sensitivity to the community (e.g., special guests, visitors, and patients who park illegally, often in frustration after not being able to find a space) and the need to avoid parking havoc. The parking hearing office is a part of finance and management, not campus services. This achieves independence but is also a source of contention between the campus services and finance and management departments.

Other Interdepartmental Concerns

As you can tell from the above, many of the problems I deal with have cross-departmental implications. They occur because of lack of communication, poor coordination, or divergent (or at least independent) goals.

Scholarships. One recent issue dealt with the process of assigning scholarships and planning for next year's scholarships. This entailed working with the vice provost for undergraduate studies, the dean of admissions planning and management, the university affairs development office, the university's nonprofit foundation, the comptroller, and the budget office to develop a coordinated scholarship planning and allocation process.

Licensing. Another issue dealt with reaching agreement on licensing the new university sports team logo. There was disagreement about who should handle the licensing arrangements, who should monitor the process, and where the royalties should go. The outcome was that a licensing firm is being tried under the direction of the general institutional services (a department in campus services). The president decided to allocate royalties after campus expenses to athletics.

University Senate. I meet frequently with the senate president, the senate executive committee, and the senate committee on campus environment to improve communications between the senate and the campus services department. The senate members feel that they are not consulted before decisions are made about trees, parking places, bookstore operations, and the like.

Bookstore. The need to reissue the bookstore contract precipitated another disagreement. The faculty-student association wanted an opportunity to manage the contract in hopes of one day taking over management of the store. Up to now, the contract had been managed by campus services' office of general institutional services. The campus services department wanted to retain the bookstore revenue, which they use to support several unrelated responsibilities. The president didn't care who managed the store as long as it was managed well and adequate campus consultation was sought to determine ways to improve the bookstore operations. Obvious areas for improvement included more responsiveness to faculty orders and more trade book selections.

Computer Store. The management of the computer store (a money loser up to this point) was another issue. After considerable negotiation between the faculty-student association, the department of general institutional services, and the VP for finance, we reached agreement that the faculty-student association would manage the contract for the bookstore and the computer store, returning to the campus 5% of gross sales from the bookstore and 1.5% of gross sales from the computer store, with the assumption that, if necessary, bookstore sales would subsidize computer store campus obligations. Currently, there is disagreement about whether the request for proposal process will produce a realistic contract and whether the agreed-to percentage of gross revenues is fair. The president decided to maintain the course rather than change it in midstream. However, we will develop specific criteria to evaluate the bookstore and computer store operations.

Campus Businesses. Some time ago the president asked the VP for finance and management to form a group representing campus businesses (e.g., the undergraduate student organization, the faculty student association, the management school, which has a student-run cafe) to review and implement campus business policies. This hasn't happened, although the VP has been actively involved in campus business decisions, such as the bookstore and licensing. Such a group is still a good idea.

New Research Labs. I have had numerous discussions with the chair of a science department and the provost's office about construction and budget issues in building a new research center. The center is housed on the third floor of an existing academic building that houses a science department. The new center reports to the provost, not the science department. The problems here are major cost overruns and poor cost tracking systems. Commitments to the academic department and the research center were made by the former provost. The parties involved are unhappy because the commitments were financially unrealistic and cannot be fully met by the provost.

Residence Halls. Another disagreement focused on use and pricing of residence halls for summer conferences. After considerable cost analyses, a price was worked out between the office of conference services, student affairs, and the comptroller. We are following the success of the agreement and will revise it if necessary.

Currently, the student affairs department manages facilities operations and maintenance for the residence halls. Campus services would be willing to assume responsibility for this function. However, according to campus services, the student affairs department is not willing to transfer all the financial resources needed to carry out the function. Unfortunately, a lingering question is: who is responsible for residence hall grounds maintenance (student affairs or campus services)? Neither department owns up to the responsibility.

Team Building

When I started as deputy to the president in 1992, the president asked me to initiate a team-building effort that would extend meetings he conducted two years earlier with the cabinet. At that time, the goal was to enhance communications and working relationships among the vice presidents. The president held monthly day-long retreats during that academic year. A consultant helped the group work through issues of organization structure, interpersonal relationships, mutual trust, and leadership. This seemed to help, but eventually its value wore thin, and the meetings were discontinued. The president's intention for the renewed team building was to start with the level immediately below the president, provost, and VPs. This group (dubbed the "Top Team") consists of about 35 senior managers, including the vice provosts for undergraduate and graduate studies and the university counsel, who are also on the cabinet. I began meeting with the group soon after I began as deputy to the president.

Our meetings have taken different forms—some all-day meetings and, lately, a series of two-hour meetings every two to six weeks. We focus on "soft" topics (e.g., identifying barriers to effective work relationships, conflict resolution, management style, and decision making). We also examine more concrete topics, such as disagreements about interdepartmental charge-backs (fees imposed without warning by service departments to cover their budget cuts but make it difficult for customer departments to meet their responsibilities with declining budgets). In addition, we use the group to deal with current issues (e.g., implementing recommendations of the recently completed "visitors committee"—a task force chaired by the president's wife on how to improve information accessibility to campus visitors). Also, the team is a vehicle for information dissemination. So, for instance, the Top Team met with the three finalists in the presidential search. (See Chapter 8 for more details about this effort.)

Employee Training and Development

In 1991, the president established the president's steering committee on employee training and development. I was appointed to chair the committee (I was then a faculty member in the management school). This was a way to organize and apply existing resources to an area that needed to be expanded. At that time, as today, we were talking about the importance of investing in our people. The viability of the institution depends on the development of its human resources, especially given institutional goals to solve financial constraints, improve quality of operations, and enhance customer focus. The president asked the committee to develop ways to make employee development salient and rewarded and to arrange training on needed topics.

The result was "July Is Training Month"—a kickoff celebration and a month of special courses on such topics as "reading financial statements," "all funds budgeting," "supervision," and "total quality management." Several very popular and much-needed computing courses are offered. (The computing and communications department discontinued its training in a budget cut several years ago.) These special training activities are announced in widely distributed flyers and a special issue of the campus newspaper. The kickoff celebration is a showcase of about 20 campus departments. This is a fair-like event. Departments display brochures, give demonstrations, and answer questions. The president makes a speech, and awards are given to managers and departments for excellent local training programs.

The event is now in its fourth year and is called "Summer Is Training." The kickoff is in June and courses extend through August. The president's office allocates about $7,000 for the program.

The training committee meets biweekly throughout the year to discuss training policy and spearhead special programs, such as customer service training. The committee is now cochaired by the director of training in the human resources department. (The strategic reasons for this effort and details about program content will be described in Chapter 10.)

Personnel Problems

I am often involved in discussions about various personnel difficulties and management problems.

Involvement in Standing Committees and Groups

Serve as Chair to Several Groups

President's Steering Committee on Employee Training and Development. We oversee training policy, encourage employee development, plan and run annual "Summer Is Training" events.

Research Facilities Users Group. This includes representatives of the office of research services, facilities operations, and the provost's research advisory group. We try to solve facilities problems before they become major concerns.

Top Team (35+ key administrators who report to the president, provost, and VPs). This is our attempt at team building. We have tried to improve interdepartmental communication and work processes, focusing on such topics as crosscharges and the viability of a campus services market economy. We meet every two to six weeks as needed. We have held several one-day retreats.

Member of Several Groups

"Gang of Four + 1" (includes the president, provost, vice president health sciences center, vice president finance and management, and deputy to the president). This group meets every week, sometimes skipping a week or two depending on need. We discuss current issues and do not have a formal agenda.

President's Cabinet. Cabinet members include the president, the provost, all the VPs, the university counsel, the associate vice provost for undergraduate studies, the associate vice provost for graduate studies, and myself. I plan the agenda for our weekly meetings, lasting one to two hours. In the fall of 1993 we held a cabinet retreat to review department plans for the year. Also, I arranged several cabinet meetings during the year to discuss "the university as regional resource" with special briefings on engineering, linkages to the business community, athletics, and the center for performing arts.

Meetings with Provost and VPs. I have periodic (weekly to monthly depending on need) one-on-one meetings with the provost and VPs. Also, to ensure continuity during the transition to the new president, I sit in on the president's periodic meetings with the provost and VPs. The president wants to be sure that issues and decisions are noted and remembered for future reference.

Planning Staff. Chaired by the university planning coordinator, this group develops the annual three-year plan, facilitates the development of departmental plans at the provostial and VP level, and conducts special projects (e.g., producing academic and administrative departmental profiles) and analyses that inform policy decisions (e.g., analyses of personnel and enrollment data over time).

Sensitive Issues Planning Group. We meet every Monday for an hour to review and anticipate problems that might be viewed unfavorably in the press. The group is chaired by the associate VP for public relations and media services, and it includes the dean of students, the campus public safety officer, the campus director for government relations (who reports to the president), the assistant vice president for general institutional services, the assistant dean for public affairs in the medical center, the associate vice president for university affairs, and myself (in my role as deputy to the president).

Instructional Technology Task Force. Established by the provost, the group resulted from a recent report of a campus computing task force. The project was conceived in 1992 by the planning staff. Recently the provost commissioned the task force to examine administrative and academic computing and campus computing infrastructure needs.

Hospital Internal Audit Advisory Group. Meets quarterly with hospital administrators to review goals and accomplishments of the hospital internal audit staff.

Hospital Reengineering. Weekly meetings with top hospital and health sciences center staff on hospital restructuring and cost savings initiatives.

Enrollment Planning Forum and Executive Committee. Meets monthly, chaired by the provost.

Capital Facilities Planning Council. I meet with the council as needed to review the annual capital budget and campus facilities master plans.

University Foundation. Board meetings and committee meetings, special committee on foundation business office operations.

The Deputy's Supervisory Responsibilities (functions and outputs)

1. Performance Management. Functions include:
   - Departmental Profiles
   - Benchmark Data Coordination
   - Administrative Review Process (review 5 administrative departments annually with a process analogous to an academic department review; coordinate with the senate's administrative review committee)
   - Upward feedback survey trials (library, finance, institutional services)
   - Management Efficiency Studies
   - Quarterly Key Indicators Reports
   - Staff to MOU Committee and Research Facilities Users Group (described above)
2. The president's management intern program, which includes four full-time graduate students supported by the vice president health sciences, provost, and vice president finance and management to work on performance management projects.
3. Internal Audit. The internal audit staff consists of a director and three auditors.
4. Serve as the campus's internal control officer. My role here is to ensure that the campus is in compliance with the state's internal control act. This is a combination of internal audit, performance management, planning, and management engineering functions.

Current Situation

I serve at the pleasure of the president. The president asked that I stay in the position as deputy six months into the new administration to assist with the transition and then return to the faculty.

Summary

This section has outlined the role of deputy to the president. It suggests that the deputy can be a key resource to the president in identifying salient issues and keeping change moving. The deputy can be an emissary, sometimes conveying a tough, unwanted message in a tactful yet forceful way. The deputy can orchestrate team efforts, encourage communication, and negotiate solutions to problems that seem intractable. The deputy can afford to push, and in some case force, movement, keeping at an issue until a resolution in line with the president's goals is achieved.

The need for change, of course, touches on more than the top university officers and administrators. Therefore, effective vehicles for communication are necessary to be sure all university members understand and contribute to the president's objectives. The next section provides some helpful guidance from the officer in charge of university communications.

COMMUNICATIONS

The following is a letter written by the campus vice president in charge of media services and publications. It points to the functional and dysfunctional effects various communications vehicles (or the lack thereof) can have on administrators' and faculty members' attention to university priorities. Also, it suggests some actions to enhance communications effectiveness to accomplish organizational change (printed with permission of the author).

I understand that at the cabinet meeting [the weekly meeting of the president and his top administrative staff] on July 14 there was discussion concerning the difficulty in communicating major items of interest to faculty, staff and students. I am sorry to have missed the meeting, but am taking this opportunity to comment because I believe that the professional communicators in publications and media services have suggestions to add to the discussion.

There are, first of all, several reasons that we cannot get people's attention when important communications are disseminated:

—There is a proliferation of administrative "junk mail" so that many on campus make it an article of faith not to read anything that comes from an administrative office, including the president's office. This "junk mail" may range from notices from Graphic Support Services about a new complaint and suggestion phone line to a letter from the president announcing a new academic program. These communications are all treated equally by some recipients, i.e. they go unread, with no discrimination as to what is important.

—There are many, many departmental newsletters on campus that are read, but do not carry major, campus-wide news items. Some employee newsletters are team-building, morale-boosting efforts, but they do not transmit information about issues such as budget problems, etc.

—The inability to reach many faculty and others via e-mail severely limits the fastest way to disseminate important administrative communications. In the best of all possible worlds, all faculty would have access to e-mail, or at the least, voice-mail on their own phones.

There are some obvious solutions to the problem, but they are not necessarily achievable immediately.

—Beginning with the Fall Semester, there will be a weekly electronic "newspaper" with major news items available on all systems used on the campus.

—We should consider changing the campus monthly newspaper to a weekly publication that contains administrative news, other news of interest to the campus community and the weekly calendar. Similar weeklies are used with great success on a number of other campuses (Harvard, Stanford, Buffalo, Wash. U.) and are looked forward to by the campus community as the definitive "word" on what is going on in the university. A weekly should be addressed to individuals and delivered via campus mail on the same day of the week every week.

We do not now have the resources, human or financial, to produce a weekly, and we would have to create another publication for our off-campus constituencies who now receive the monthly campus paper. We will be changing the paper to include regular up-dates on the programmatic initiatives, and a feature from the Human Resources Department called "Workplace" that will include news about benefits, training, etc.

—We will try to institute a system of "departmental correspondents" (probably administrative assistants) who will be responsible for sending in news of general interest and will also be responsible for distributing the weekly electronic newspaper in their departments. We hope that this distribution will be more than putting a piece of paper on a pile by the departmental mail boxes.

—I have investigated an electronic kiosk system such as that used at Boston U. This method is ideal for reaching students and others as they move across campus, but, again, is beyond current resources.

I suggest that, as we begin the look at the three-year planning process again, we consider if we should allocate resources to improve the communication infrastructure on the campus. We should also work down through deans, chairs, service department administrator, directors, and campus governance groups to enlist support and commitment to minimizing the "junk mail" and making sure that administrative communications are properly disseminated to all of their colleagues.

The people responsible for mass communications on campus would be happy to work with others to change the ways in which news is now delivered to the campus community. I would be happy to hear your reactions.

CONCLUSION

This chapter considered the importance of effective leadership in the context of needed change and interpersonal disagreements and ineffective communication. The chapter showed how a consultant and a deputy to the president can be key resources to the identification of directions for change and means to accomplish it. Such change agents enhance communication among the team of university officers and top managers. Other communication methods may be needed to spread the word across the university.

The next chapter considers how the human resource department and human resource professionals in the university can be change agents as well. The department's purpose is to support effective people management. People are critical to accomplishing any organization's objectives, especially when talent and creativity are needed to overcome fiscal constraints and use advancing technologies effectively. Moreover, human resource professionals are often trained in organizational development techniques. Their job is to facilitate change in line with university objectives and to influence these objectives by an understanding of how to select, develop, and reward people.

3

The Human Resource Function as Change Agent

This chapter will consider how changes in universities influence human resource management in these institutions. As such, we emphasize the close tie between evolving university missions and the contribution of employees in administrative departments to bringing about change. We review key human resource problems, including the need for retraining and cross-training, fewer advancement opportunities and fewer chances for bonuses and salary increases, an imbalanced workforce, continued requirement for clerical personnel, and support of employees' lack of understanding about the implications of university changes. Drawing on experiences in other organizations that have undergone similar changes, we describe alternative human resource policies and programs that facilitate organizational transition. The chapter emphasizes the increased role of the human resource function in developing policies and programs that meet the changing strategic directions of universities.

CHANGES AND HUMAN RESOURCE CHALLENGES FACING MANY ORGANIZATIONS

Universities confront a number of changes that are likely to result in negative behaviors and outcomes. For example, changing task demands lead to the need for fewer people in some university departments and possibly more people, or those with different skills and knowledge, in other departments. As such, some employees need to be cross-trained in new skills to prepare for different assignments. Further, there are likely to be fewer opportunities for advancement and salary increases. Unfortunately, many employees do not yet understand the implications of these university changes on their career prospects.

This situation is typical of that experienced by many organizations during the late 1980s and early 1990s. Although brought about for different reasons, these organizations can provide a benchmark for comparison and ideas for actions.

During the last five years, many organizations faced the need to restructure and downsize in response to increased competition, an emerging global marketplace, rapid technological advances, and a weakened economy. Levels of management were cut, hiring was curtailed, "survivors" were expected to do more with less, advancement opportunities were fewer, and salaries stagnated.

On the positive side, employees in these organizations were expected to do new and different tasks and assume more responsibility. Quality improvement programs were implemented, requiring employees to learn group participation and leadership skills. Employees were cross-trained so that they could do different tasks. As a result, they could be assigned where they were needed, providing them with increased employment security and providing the organization with increased flexibility. Mastery paths specified higher levels of competency and provided directions for training and on-the-job learning.

As these changes emerged, employees were kept informed about how the organization was changing and what these changes meant for their career development and advancement opportunities. The organizations recognized that withholding information until all plans were set would be risky. Employees would waste valuable time discussing rumors and sharing anxieties. Research showed that employees who were previously most loyal to their organization were those who reacted most negatively to surprise layoffs and job changes that were perceived as unfair (Brockner, Tyler, & Cooper-Schneider, 1992; Hartley, Jacobson, Klandermans, & Van Vuuren, 1991). Negative reactions included lower work effort and the desire to leave the organization.

Career development programs were formulated to inform employees that they were in charge of their own careers. Employees needed to understand how the organization was changing and what they needed to do to make a contribution to its success. Their employment security depended on their continued development at a time when the stability of any given job could not be guaranteed. The organization would provide the enabling developmental resources, such as information about job vacancies and career opportunities, training, and supervisors who were expected to be coaches and developers.

The following sections review human resource issues in universities and examine alternative initiatives of the human resource function to accomplish organizational goals in changing times. Programs that other organizations found successful for implementing organizational change are discussed in detail.

REVIEW OF UNIVERSITY HUMAN RESOURCE ISSUES

In this section, we consider five major human resource issues facing universities. These are interrelated concerns that emerge from current and anticipated changes in domestic and international conditions. The shifting world order and the search for a peace dividend have personnel implications for universities. There is the need to cut costs and reduce hiring. However, there is the concomitant need to maintain technological expertise at a time when communications and office technology are advancing rapidly. Given the uncertain future of geopolitical events, university preparedness continues to be critical.

The human resource issues resulting from these changing conditions are reviewed along with possible positive and negative outcomes and ideas for action. These ideas are expanded later in an examination of possible human resource policies and programs.

Need for Retraining and Cross-Training

University hiring has been curtailed while the workload and the variety of work to be done remain high. Employees who leave cannot be replaced. Technical changes mean new skill requirements and new types of jobs.

A prime example of the need for retraining is the change in computer environment from mainframe to distributed network platforms. Employees who work in the old computing environment need to be retrained as systems administrators/network managers and repositioned to support local department networking and workstation needs.

Overall, more university personnel should be cross-trained to increase their value to their schools. This will help universities to continue to meet their varied responsibilities in increasingly complex areas of expertise. An example of the need for cross-training is software training of information systems analysts. A related need is for current computer experts to learn more systems in light of emerging distributed computer technologies.

This cross-training and retraining will significantly enhance a university's flexibility in making assignments. Simultaneously, such cross-training will increase employees' employment security by increasing their usefulness to universities.

The people available for cross-training do not necessarily have the capability to learn the new required skills. Also, employees who are capable of being cross-trained are not necessarily interested in cross-training.

Labor force management programs will be needed to resolve the imbalance between the available labor force and job requirements. Such programs redesign and restructure organizational units, identify people who are wanted for the available positions, and then retrain or reassign the surplus employees.

An additional step is to expand and clarify communications about the retraining opportunities and the importance of taking advantage of them—importance to universities and importance to the employees' career prospects. Specifically, employees need to be informed about career opportunities, the need for training to take advantage of these opportunities, and the consequences of ignoring the university's requirements for new and different skills.

Fewer Career Opportunities

In addition to far less hiring, especially in nonmission-oriented/administrative areas, there are fewer advancement opportunities. Salary increases and bonuses are fewer and far between. There is an oversupply of clerks who now have few options for further advancement.

This is a radical change from conditions during the mid-1980s, when a large proportion of university personnel entered the organization. They experienced more abundant rewards, often tied more to service longevity than performance.

This is tantamount to a change in the "psychological contract" between employer and employee. Universities will no longer provide the same advancement opportunities and the same chances for salary increases. Longevity alone will not be enough to receive a bonus.

The few promotions and bonuses that do occur will be increasingly tied to performance, because managers will have to present clear cases for their recommendations. In the long run, this is better management. For instance, bonuses become a way to recognize people who develop on their current jobs by learning and applying new skills and increasing their effort and productivity.

In the short run, it means employees face changed expectations and what they might perceive as unfair treatment.

Employees in growing organizations learn to expect frequent rewards. When growth stops and the size and scope of the organization declines, the meaning of career development changes. Employees in such organizations as AT&T found this a bitter pill to swallow.

When AT&T emerged from the Bell System divestiture into a more competitive world, the compensation system and promotion process were changed to reflect the leaner environment. In the days of regulation and expansion, all new entry-level managers could expect pay increases and promotions on a fairly predictable schedule as long as their performance was acceptable. High performers would be on a fast-track development path. After the Bell System divestiture, the revised compensation program essentially froze salary base rates. Pay increases were no longer automatic. New managers no longer advanced to higher pay grades as a matter of time on the job. Across-the-board cost-of-living increases were stopped. Salary increases would be paid as bonuses based on merit, and only the top performing people would receive substantial amounts of money. The reward for fully meeting performance expectations became keeping one's job. The fast-track development program for young managers was downsized substantially given fewer anticipated promotional opportunities, and the time to advancement increased substantially.

As a consequence, some managers who felt they had better opportunities elsewhere left the business. Others retired early, often taking a financial incentive to leave. Some managers were asked to leave even though they were not retirement eligible. The survivors had to quickly change their expectations. They now worked hard to keep their jobs, recognizing that their employment security depended on making the organization successful. Development was no longer synonymous with promotion. Rather, development (being trained, retrained, and cross-trained and taking new assignments) was to increase one's value to the business and, as a consequence, stay employed.

In this new corporate environment, employees could not count on the company to look out for their career interests. The company supplied the resources for development and helped employees understand what level of performance was expected and the types of people it needed. This message was communicated through supervisors, training curricula, and a variety of communications vehicles (e.g., newsletters, bulletins, special messages from the chairman). While such support was available, employees had to assume responsibility for their own careers. They needed to understand the changing business needs and what it meant for them (what they had to know and how hard they had to work). Those who were not up to the challenge learned the hard way. They left the company on their own accord, were invited to leave, or were demoted or transferred to less responsible assignments. Employees who accepted the challenge took advantage of the available resources to prepare themselves to do better in their current jobs and be ready for the future.

Employees must understand the environment in which universities operate, the shifting demand for different skills, and the need to adapt to these changing requirements and different job expectations. Communications programs should highlight role models—for instance, people who have tackled new and different assignments after being cross-trained. Employees should be clear about the knowledge and skills that are desired. Training curricula should be developed or revised to offer courses in these knowledge and skill areas if this is not already the case. Employees should work with their supervisors to formulate annual development plans, agreeing to new assignments, job moves, and/or training for the coming year.

Employees should recognize that the purpose of this development is not for salary increases or advancement but to meet the current and anticipated demands of universities. The well-worn phrase, "ask not what your country [university] can do for you, ask what you can do . . . ," is apt here. The burden of career planning and development shifts from universities to the employee. The university's obligation is to communicate where the opportunities will be and to provide the resources for development. This includes advice for career planning, opportunities for training, placement in assignments that match employees' new skills and desire to learn new areas, and options for leaving universities for those who no longer fit in.

An Imbalanced Workforce

The changing world order has led to an imbalanced workforce with too many people in some organizations and disciplines and too few in others. As a result, there is a need for movement of people between departments.

Universities have begun to address this issue by holding job fairs. Employees in organizations with too many people are invited. Managers with position vacancies describe the openings and job requirements in hopes of attracting qualified and interested candidates.

Correcting labor force imbalances as they emerge will help keep employees fully utilized and broaden their experiences. This will increase their motivation and alert them to the need for continued adaptation to change. From the university's standpoint, it will generate an organizational climate of flexibility and responsiveness. Universities will be perceived by their constituencies as meeting the needs of the nation in a cost-effective way.

Employees do not take advantage of the job opportunities just because there is a job fair. They have no incentive to switch jobs, and they perceive changing as risky. However, universities cannot sustain an imbalanced workforce—particularly one that is getting worse over time. Eventually, work will not get done or people will be hired in one part of the organization while employees in another part are underutilized. Being underutilized is a demoralizing experience that breeds lasting resentment, low commitment, and possible insubordination. In all, this can be a financially and emotionally costly process for employees and universities.

Unfortunately, using job fairs to correct labor force imbalance is a haphazard process if not handled systematically. On the supply side, not enough eligible people attend, perhaps because they don't believe there is a problem or that they will be adversely affected. They may not understand the possible negative implications of staying where they are, and the idea of learning a new job and working in a different department with new co-workers may be viewed as uncertain and risky. On the demand side, a job fair announces vacancies that happen to be open at the time of the fair. It does not recognize the emerging job families and ways to ensure that sufficient numbers of well-trained personnel will be available over time.

A variety of mechanisms should be applied to resolve and prevent labor force imbalances. Such imbalances are not one-time occurrences. As such, ongoing methods are necessary to analyze changing workloads and associated skill and knowledge requirements, track the skills and experience levels of employees in universities, and identify the skills and education levels of available people in the external labor market.

An outcome of such systematic analyses should be the design of appropriate cross-training programs and procedures to facilitate job rotations and transfers. Job fairs may work well when employees with the needed skills and experiences are targeted to attend and when the reasons for training and transfer are explained clearly.

Another procedure is a computerized or manual job matching system that links vacancies to employees with the required background.

An additional mechanism is to announce job vacancies and invite supervisors to nominate qualified and interested subordinates. Involving supervisors in this way engages them in the career planning process. They will encourage subordinates to learn about changing university career opportunities, consider the value of different job moves, and plan ahead for training and job changes.

Self-nominations should also be allowed as they are in job fairs. As employees take charge of their own careers, they should have the chance to suggest themselves for job opportunities and discover their competitiveness for choice positions. In the process, they will recognize the value of taking on new and different job assignments, even those that are not choice, as a way to prepare themselves for better opportunities in universities.

Continued Requirement for Clerical Personnel

Secretarial and clerical personnel continue to be needed even with advancing record-keeping and word-processing technologies. There has traditionally been attrition from these jobs as individuals move from general clerical to more technical and specialized types of assignments. While the need for clerical personnel remains, universities are not hiring in this area.

There is already considerable movement of personnel within universities between and within clerical fields (for instance, between secretarial, records, and travel positions). This gives employees exposure to different clerical functions, different parts of universities, and different co-workers. It builds expertise and fosters mutual understanding and effective working relationships. The continued need for clerical workers will cause managers to generate work environments (challenging jobs and effective work group structures and relationships) that attract and retain excellent workers.

Clerical and secretarial jobs have limited prestige within universities, and so they do not attract current employees who might move into these areas. Current clerical employees do not want to stay in these jobs.

Consideration is being given to the increased professionalization of clerical positions by adding a higher level and higher paying clerical job title. However, there may be relatively little call for people at such a level. Consequently, clerical jobs would continue to have few advancement opportunities.

Employees in existing secretarial and clerical jobs need to know that their jobs are important and valued by universities. This can be accomplished through recognition programs, spotlighting special accomplishments of clerical personnel in newsletters, implementing and providing training in new office technologies as they emerge, and continuing to make available opportunities for cross-training and transfer between and within clerical available and between clerical jobs and other types of positions.

Employees' Lack of Understanding about University Changes

The changes in universities are just beginning to emerge. If universities' experiences are similar to many private corporations, the pace of change will increase, and universities will have to adapt continuously to the changing world order and national expectations. Furthermore, universities will need to adapt *quickly*. This can happen only if universities' employees understand the changes and are flexible. As indicated above, they have to be aware of the changes and what they should do to prepare for them.

A concerted program to communicate and discuss university changes and their effects of career opportunities will highlight the importance of the changes and make employees feel a part of their evolution. Employees will be more willing to adapt and meet shifting performance expectations. As a result, universities will be better able to meet their objectives.

Currently, many university employees do not understand the effects of the changing organizational mission and conditions on their career prospects and the need for continued development and possible job movement. This leads to complacency and the feeling that it is possible to "wait out the tide." The prevailing attitude may be (or become), "Why take a risk or be bothered learning new skills if there is no incentive to do so? Let the top executives worry about these problems. I'll still get paid. I'll be needed here eventually. For now I can relax." This "It's not my problem" syndrome would result from a failure to engage employees in the process of re-creating universities.

If we agree that the pace of change will accelerate and that employees must learn to adapt and contribute, then a complacent attitude would be dysfunctional to say the least. Universities will fail to adapt and employees will suffer the consequences in the form of more dead-end jobs, fewer opportunities for professional growth and learning, and decreased earning potential. The very survival of universities, at least in its present form with its present personnel, may be at risk.

There may never be another time when university executives can project a static picture of university work and job requirements when future directions are clear and opportunities are evident. Universities can't wait for another period of stability, or even a time when such a period can be anticipated, to communicate information about organizational transition. Employees should be told what is known about universities' changing goals and the need for different skills and expertise. As suggested above, mechanisms should be developed to communicate these changes, provide necessary retraining and cross-training, and facilitate new job matches.

The next section considers how the human resource function should respond to the changes described above. The final section examines a number of specific human resource policies and programs to implement changing university objectives.

RESPONSES FOR UNIVERSITY HUMAN RESOURCE ADMINISTRATORS

Expanded Roles for Human Resource Directors

The human resource department plays an increasingly *strategic* role in organizations that have undergone similar changes to those facing universities. In these organizations, the human resource department contributes to establishing the direction and mission of the organization. New organizational goals have human resource implications, and human resource preparedness cannot be an afterthought.

In changing organizations, human resource policies and programs become strategic interventions to support change and accomplish goals.

Human resource professionals have multiple roles in generating human resource strategy integral to changing organizational objectives. Human resource professionals become

- *researchers* uncovering information about the workforce and organization needs;
- *experimenters* trying new techniques;
- *communicators* explaining directions for change and implications;
- *facilitators* prompting interdepartmental cooperation and negotiation;
- *educators* applying adult learning principles and knowledge of behavior/reward contingencies to the design of instruction, jobs, and compensation systems;
- *organization and job design experts* helping to restructure units with the required numbers of personnel and then managing labor force imbalances;
- *experts in what other organizations are doing* so as to benefit from others' experiences in similar situations;
- *partners with officials in other university departments* in formulating organizational mission and strategies; and
- *role models for quality service* providing timely services that meet the expectations of employees and other university departments.

Human resource professionals are *not* merely

- payroll processors and benefits purveyors,
- record keepers,
- regulators and monitors of rules and regulations, or
- support staff.

The Need for a Proactive Human Resource Department

A cautious response to uncertainty is inaction—the tendency to wait and see what materializes. Resistance to change is a common and natural tendency for both employees and their organizations. However, in the current environment, inaction may be more risky. From the organization's standpoint, and from the perspective of the human resource department in particular, inaction may be counterproductive—leading to rumor, anxiety, feelings of job insecurity, perceptions of unfairness, and low productivity.

Private organizations confronting change have experienced periods of uncertainty that led to employee disorientation and low productivity. Rumors of impending change contributed to hand-wringing anxiety. Some employees pictured the worst. Others failed to see the handwriting on the wall, denying reality. Others derided top management, and unfairly or inaccurately blamed executives for organizational predicaments. These symptoms of ambiguity and change preceded definitive programs and choices. This occurred at AT&T following divestiture and before specific programs were announced—programs that involved employees in restructuring work and organizations, that clarified performance expectations, and that provided career options.

Similar events have occurred in public organizations experiencing or anticipating change. Public universities faced changes similar to those facing corporations in many ways. These universities had to deal with severe financial constriction in an environment with entrenched departments and tenured staff and faculty. Departments were cut, personnel shifted, and nontenured personnel dismissed. Union contracts and the collaborative governance structure (whereby numerous committees have a say in almost any action) made the process more cumbersome in many ways than the restrictions imposed by Congress on universities. The morale of faculty and staff plummeted.

Despite the trauma experienced by these organizations, rash actions are not necessary to clarify the situation and achieve stability. Rather, the examples suggest that employees should be apprised of events and their implications and that employees should be involved in confronting the situation, suggesting courses of action, and implementing them.

The human resource function can avoid negative outcomes by being *proactive*. Strategic human resource initiatives become a series of communication and performance management actions. They *evolve* as the organization changes, new information becomes available, and expectations become clearer.

Foster a Can-Do Attitude

Bureaucratic, regulated organizations prompt a control-oriented mentality. People are cautious and find it easier to say no or assume something can't be done. Organizations have found that change demands prompt action. New organizational structures, job changes, pay systems, and performance evaluation processes may be needed. Clearly private-sector organizations have more flexibility than public organizations. Nevertheless, the general mentality should be "can do." The human resource function should be viewed within the organization as a *proactive initiator of action*, not a monitor and controller of behavior.

EXAMPLES OF GOAL-ORIENTED HUMAN RESOURCE POLICIES AND PROGRAMS

Organizations develop deliberate, comprehensive human resource programs to address changing missions. Human resource strategies are a way to help accomplish organizational objectives by ensuring that employees understand the changes and career implications. The result is a *comprehensive set of interrelated programs*—what may be termed a *human performance system*.

The following are areas for human resource policy and program development that tie to university goals and objectives. These policies and programs build on each other rather than exist in isolation.

Employee Communications Programs

Universities should adopt a policy of frequent communications of current and impending challenges facing universities. This should include information about the likely implications of these challenges for employees, both in terms of the changing nature of projects and responsibilities and in terms of job security and career development. Frank communications can address the uncertainties of university direction, the pressure to cut costs, and the need to reduce the numbers of employees in some areas. They can focus employees on the disciplines that still are in demand, new skill requirements, and disciplines that will increase in demand. *Since personnel requirements will change over time as university objectives change, plans should be made for a regular series of communications.*

In general, employee communications programs are important when employees

- need to know the present state of affairs,
- need to realize that the situation will change,
- may be required to make a decision or take some action, or
- may be anxious and waste time discussing and worrying about rumors.

Organizations facing radical shifts in corporate strategy have found that such communications programs maintain employee trust in management and avoid wasted anxiety and concomitant losses in productivity. A good communications program focuses employees' attention on what is important to the organization. A *regular series of communications* from a department chief to all personnel in the department about impending changes helps employees be a part of these changes and allows them to make decisions and take actions that are in line with the changes, rather than contradictory to them. Moreover, employee understanding builds over time. The alternative is to wait until there is a need for a single "blockbuster" announcement that is likely to shock employees, create dismay, and exacerbate existing anxieties. Communications should be frequent, consistent with each other, and come through a variety of media.

Communications should meet several objectives and cover a number of topics. *Statements from executives should address universities' changing mission and directions.* These statements should include implications for employees—that is, "What this means to you," and "What you can expect." The human resource function can help executives write these statements and produce appropriate communications vehicles. The goal is to be sure these messages are consistent with overall university objectives. While the situations in various departments may differ, departmental communiques can explain these changes in the context of overall university changes and adjustments. Employees in one department will hear about what's happening in other departments. Messages that provide a partial or incomplete picture of university change may generate further uncertainty or suggest to employees that their chief doesn't know what's happening.

As indicated above, *personnel requirements will change over time as university objectives change*. As a result, plans should be made for a regular series of communications.

Communication should have real content. Sometimes it is too easy to communicate in general terms. University executives should be direct in communicating elements of their mission that are changing, skills that are (or are anticipated to be) in demand, retraining and cross-training that are available, the extent to which the organization is over- or understaffed, and the opportunities available to employees within the department and in other departments.

This information can be revised and updated over time. Indeed, employees can be made aware that the situation will change. Change is one thing that is certain. Rather than be paralyzed waiting to see what will happen, employees should be encouraged to take actions that increase their knowledge and value to their schools. This is why communications should be specific about the available options and support.

The above communications should include descriptions of employees who have transferred, received retraining or cross-training, or are considering early retirement. The importance of having role models was mentioned earlier. Such descriptions help executives convey the meaning of change. Employees are not left to their own imaginations to interpret what is meant or how changing circumstances might affect them. Role models clarify opportunities and suggest directions for action.

Having a communications plan, such as regularly scheduled communications, will make it easier to decide what should be announced and how. Also, employees will know to anticipate communications and will know where to look for information.

Today's communications technologies offer a variety of engaging and sometimes inexpensive media for one-way communication and two-way interaction. Communications programs should use a mixture of media, with some methods reserved to announce and explain important issues and others used for more routine communications.

Consider the following media:

1. *Newsletters*. Regular issues of in-house publications (e.g., newsletters) may have a column about university directions and related career development issues.

2. *Bulletins*. Special one-page bulletins can be issued by department heads or the central staff (e.g., the university's human resource department) to address particular events and/or decisions. Care should be taken to clarify what is known and what is still uncertain. Announcements should be clear that additional information will be forthcoming when it is available.

3. *News hotlines*. Many organizations use touch-tone, menu-driven telephone recordings to update employees about current events and implications. Such a line can include choices for daily news, job openings, and special upcoming training programs, such as an announcement of an opportunity for cross-training in a particular field. Such information can be targeted to individuals with special interests

or capabilities—for instance, saying that clerical employees should listen to the message about certain types of job openings, or analytic experts in certain geographical areas should listen to a message about language retraining. This service is flexible, with the possibility of frequent updates. It could be called the school's "News and Career Hotline." Weekly bulletins can be issued to inform employees about what will be on the hotline during the coming week.

4. *Videotapes*. Top officials of organizations often use videos to address employees in a more personal way than can be done in print. Some officials use videos to describe a momentous event. Others prepare weekly or monthly video messages. The videos are distributed to local departments, or they play periodically on closed-circuit networks. When distributed to local departments, supervisors are often asked to play the video during staff meetings and allow opportunity for discussion.

5. *More personal forms of communications*. Directors and corporate officials may have special telephone numbers for employees to call them or their staffs. One president of a large organization actually announced his home telephone number (probably a specially installed line devoted to this purpose). He stated that he welcomed calls, and he meant it.

6. *Forums*. A critical issues forum could be held periodically for all managers at a certain level and above. The forum would last one day or longer, and would be an opportunity to hear directly from university top officials about organizational and technological developments.

7. *News conferences and open panels*. Decisions can be explained in news conference formats with employee audiences participating in question and answer sessions. These can be taped for other employees to view later. Or telephone linkages can be established for employees to listen to the meeting as it occurs and even phone in questions. This works well as a vehicle to explain new human resource programs that have wide applicability across the organization and do not require security.

Role of the Supervisor

Special communications can address the role of managers as interpreters and reinforcers of corporate information and as coaches who counsel employees about feasible alternatives. In particular, discussion aids should accompany communications so that supervisors understand how to approach the issues in group meetings and one-on-one sessions with subordinates.

Human Resource Forecasting and Planning

Making assumptions about human resource needs without systematic determination of these needs and obtaining agreement among executives is dangerous. Executives often believe that they know what types of people are needed in their department and the organization as a whole without specific data. However, not having accurate and up-to-date information could lead to encouraging people to leave when they will be needed later, hiring the wrong people, or training employees in the wrong skills.

For instance, the executives in a large manufacturing facility were startled to discover that more than 76% of the employees were eligible for retirement within the next five years. Retirement eligibility varied considerably in other units of the firm, indicating the need for different labor force management strategies in different departments.

Making assumptions about human resource requirements can lead to hiring and training people who meet immediate needs but have little long-term value to the firm. For example, people might be hired because they have a specific skill that is required now, but not a skill that has lasting value or broader applicability. Or people who are hired may not have the capacity or desire for cross-training. Equal employment opportunity (EEO) concerns are often cited as reasons for focusing exclusively on immediate needs when selecting employees. However, this is not necessarily an issue. Broader requirements can be used if EEO concerns are taken into account in making personnel decisions—that is, if job and training opportunities are offered and provided to women, minorities, and other protected groups.

Human resource forecasting and planning covers *external* and *internal* analyses. A central staff can produce regular forecasting reports based on available public information (news media, the Department of Labor, and the Bureau of the Census) as well as internal personnel databases.

External Analyses

Environmental Trends. This refers to tracking issues in the media that influence university activities and personnel. It may be as simple as tracking employment trends in the area, such as openings or closings of large facilities that affect labor force availability and job openings. Other relevant information would include numbers and types of degrees granted annually from selected universities. A panel of labor force experts, including one or more labor economists, demographers, and industrial and organizational psychologists, could be established for periodic input about key trends potentially affecting universities. A program to track environmental trends would begin with an analysis of the types of information that should be gathered and likely sources of the information.

Demographic Labor Force Analysis. Relevant information should include readily available data and projections about labor force availability from the U.S. Department of Labor and the Bureau of the Census. Analyses of this information are often published in demographic journals and institute reports (e.g., the Hudson Institute's famed recent report, "Work Force 2000"). State agencies also provide local labor force data and analyses.

Internal Analyses

A regular set of periodic studies should be conducted on the university's personnel databases. Relevant information that could be obtained by division would include retirement eligibility based on tenure and age; and skills resident in the organization based on training records, educational background, and skills surveys:

(1) skill requirements based on "future job analyses" that ask top managers to describe the types of skills they believe will be needed in the next five years; (2) training gap analyses reports on the difference between skill and personnel availability and future skill needs.

Reporting and Using Human Resource Forecasting and Planning Information

Human resource forecasting reports should be issued on a regular basis, at least annually. They should include the data mentioned above with integrative and interpretive statements about implications for university actions. Scenarios can be developed to depict different future environments—say five years hence. The panel of experts could meet with university executives annually to discuss trends, identify implications, and suggest and evaluate alternative actions. The goal should be to respond to trends and create a desired future that is consistent with the university's changing mission.

Forecasting information can guide the following human resource activities personnel selection (the numbers and types of people hired); curricula for training, retraining, and cross-training; methods for efficient, cost-effective delivery of training; new management and leadership skills that are in line with the university's desire to deliver quality services that are responsive to different constituencies; the speed at which new technology can and should be implemented within universities; criteria for appraisal, compensation, and promotion; and planning these activities to meet future requirements. In short, human resource forecasting and planning touches most if not all human resource functions and helps contribute to human resource policies and programs that are consistent with, and supportive of, one another.

Career Planning and Development

Organizations under threat of downsizing not surprisingly find that employees are very dissatisfied with career opportunities. Rather than ignore career development, some firms in this situation have designed explicit career development programs that do the following:

- Convey information about areas of the organization that are growing, areas that are stable, and areas that are declining. This information includes descriptions of skill requirements and available training. These programs also emphasize that it is every employee's responsibility to understand organizational changes and to take advantage of available resources to support their career development.

- Encourage (or require) that every employee have a career plan. A process can be established whereby supervisors meet with subordinates individually to develop a plan that meets the needs of the university and is in line with the individual's capabilities and interests. The plan should include training to improve on one's current assignment, training to prepare for future requirements on one's current job, and training for a different assignment. These opportunities should emphasize the university's policy of supporting *continuous development* for employees.

The career planning and development program can be conveyed in a binder of material. Orientation sessions can be held to describe the program, the employee's role, and the supervisor's role. Supervisors can be trained to explain the program and provide the needed counseling. Information on organizational change can be supplied to the career resources center.

Revised Appraisal and Compensation

Performance appraisals should be based on the technical and management skills that are important to universities today and in the future. This suggests that the existing appraisal methods should be modified to ensure that these skills are communicated to employees and are used by supervisors as a basis for evaluation. This is a way to communicate changing organizational culture and expectations and a way to reinforce these changes.

A guideline can be offered to help employees and supervisors establish their key duties and goals. The guideline could suggest and define several skills that are especially important to universities in the changing environment. For managers, these may include "encouraging employee development," "fostering networks and alliances between departments," "building a team spirit in the work group," or "designing challenging tasks and work group structures." For technical experts, these may include "being cross-trained in an area of value to universities," "demonstrating creativity/being innovative," "making effective decisions," and "clarifying expectations of those who use the technician's services."

As indicated earlier, the limited resources for pay increases and bonuses should enhance the link between performance and reward. This should be stated clearly and be evident to employees. They should be keenly aware that the amount of money they receive will depend on their performance, and only the best people will be rewarded for the results of their work.

Individual and Team Rewards

A reward system should be comprehensive in recognizing and rewarding individual and team accomplishments in a variety of ways. Stanford University has a "Reward, Recognition, and Incentives Handbook" published by the institution's controller's office that offers criteria and suggestions for rewards. It includes a number of reward criteria as typical examples of an employee's willingness to "go the extra mile." Examples of accomplishment deserving reward are (from Massy, 1992, p. 78):

• Developed a process that improved the quality, service, and/or productivity of work.
• Developed a process for work-simplification.
• Assumed additional responsibilities during a period of staff shortage.

- Increased job knowledge by voluntarily participating in cross-training.
- Exhibited tact and diplomacy in dealing with faculty, staff, or the outside community on a sensitive issue beyond the normal scope of job.
- Made a difficult decision by using sound judgment and reasoning and carefully weighing alternatives.
- Consistently promoting teamwork by help and cooperation outside of requirements.

The Stanford handbook also lists a menu of rewards and notes that this list should be a catalyst for ideas for new rewards (also from Massy, 1992, p. 78):

- Recognition party or dinner.
- Lunch at the faculty club.
- Permission to attend seminars, workshops, and classes outside of standard university staff development training.
- Tickets for two university performing arts or athletics events.
- Attendance at special lectures, presentations, or other university events.
- Behind the scenes tour (perhaps with family) of university facilities.
- A gift from the university bookstore or gallery shop.
- Personalized office supplies (pen, etc.).
- A handwritten thank-you note.

Critical Issues Forum and a Human Resource Strategy Team

Having an ongoing setting for discussing university strategy and human resource implications is essential. Two groups may be necessary. One group consists of the top university directors and chiefs from all relevant departments. The goal of this group is to set university direction and track progress.

Apparently, such a critical issues group already exists. *This group should consider whether all parties recognize the strategic nature of the human resource function and the importance of employees to accomplishing university objectives.*

The human resource chief's role in such a group is to

- raise human resource implications of decision alternatives under consideration;
- provide information about the labor force (i.e., the type of data described above in the section on human resource forecasting and planning);
- describe human resource policy and program alternatives;
- report on progress from a human resource perspective.

The second group should consist of top human resource managers meeting as a strategy team. They would address the general university issues arising from the critical issues forum and formulate human resource policies and program recommendations. Once programmatic directions are established, the strategy team would track progress and make suggestions for improvement.

The human resource strategy team should recognize that university strategies will change, and human resource policies and programs should evolve accordingly. New human resource programs will be the foundation for a renewed organization and a basis for subsequent human resource initiatives.

IBM and AT&T are examples of how the profile of the human resource department was raised in times of change. The human resource departments in these firms increasingly worked with line units to identify and manage labor force imbalances, communicate organization restructuring, identify requirements for new managerial and technical skills in light of the changing business environment, lead quality improvement efforts (especially training and facilitation of group dynamics and quality improvement team leadership), assess employee attitudes, and design new career planning and development programs in the downsized organizations. These efforts were guided by human resource strategic planning groups that met to consider changing business requirements and suggest human resource initiatives. Moreover, the senior human resource vice presidents met regularly with the executive officers of the organization to discuss business strategies. The human resource VPs are expected to understand the business needs and contribute to them by (1) *pointing out the human resource implications of business decisions* (e.g., whether people with the right expertise would be available if the firm entered a new market or provided a new type of service), and (2) *identifying business decisions that were driven by human resource concerns* (e.g., the need to take action because of low employee morale or high turnover of top talent).

In general, the human resource function should be as expert in guiding strategy as it is in conducting personnel transactions. Discussions of human resource strategy in relation to university mission should occur regularly among the top human resource managers. Also, the human resource function should be represented in key university strategy groups.

This means that the human resource director must be armed with necessary information about the internal and external labor force. The director must be ready to produce creative, timely programs and clear policies. Further, the director must have appropriate communications vehicles available to employees directly and/or through department directors.

The human resource function can be viewed as an interpreter and conduit of information to and from executives, employees, and current developments in human resource procedures. This enhances the profile of the human resource function in universities. It also increases its responsibility to be aware of the best human resource practices in other organizations and be up-to-speed on what is happening in all parts of universities.

The expanded role for the human resource function requires that the human resource director and human resource professionals in the department recognize and enact this expanded role. They should not wait to be called on by department heads and the university officers to provide a strategic perspective. The value of this perspective will be realized only when it is provided. The perspective must be based on clearly explained, systematically derived information; a demonstrated understanding of university mission and functions; and cost-effective, responsive, and timely human resource programs.

Performance Management Initiatives

Performance management initiatives are another way to communicate changing expectations and provide guidance for development. An example is AT&T's "Managing for Excellence Library," which was designed to communicate what the organization expected of its managers in the increasingly changing environment and to announce human resource programs (training curricula, goal setting, performance appraisal, and compensation processes) that supported this change. The "Library" was a series of booklets distributed in a box (rather than the ubiquitous corporate binder). The central message of the "Library" was that managers were expected to enhance their excellence in designing meaningful jobs and work group structures, foster interdepartmental networks and alliances, and focus on the quality of their outputs, not just on their activities.

360 Degree Feedback

People need feedback to know how they are doing, recalibrate their behavior, and feel recognized. The concept of 360 degree feedback rests on the idea that every employee has multiple constituencies, and supervisors are not sufficiently knowledgeable to provide meaningful feedback to subordinates on all relevant elements of these relationships. Multiple sources of information also provide more reliable data on which to base development decisions than would be available from only one source.

In 360 degree feedback, peers, subordinates, co-workers, internal customers, and supervisors rate the employee on behaviors important to universities. A central staff designs the survey method, collates data, and produces reports. The reports are generally used solely for development (as opposed to making salary, promotion, or job placement decisions about the individuals rated). Also, the information is provided anonymously and only when there is a sufficient number in each group (e.g., four or more subordinates) to guard anonymity. Results may be aggregated across employees to diagnose general problems in the department.

Alternative Employee/Job Matching Systems

A variety of systematic mechanisms can be used to match individuals to jobs after appropriate communication about the reasons for change and expectations that individuals will take action and make decisions. Methods include job fairs, computerized matching based on skill databases, manual matching, vacancy announcements, and nomination procedures (with supervisory or self-nomination options).

Employee Attitude Surveys

Large firms have regular employee attitude surveys to track reactions to human resource programs and the quality of management. Survey questions are comparable from year to year and between departments. The companies belong to consortia of other organizations (e.g., the "Mayflower Group") or they use outside vendors to provide a common set of questions for interorganizational comparisons. Areas for questioning include attitudes about career development opportunities, the work environment, job and employment security, supervision, job requirements and characteristics, pay, benefits, and other initiatives (such as child care support). This provides a tracking mechanism and an *early warning system* to highlight problem areas before they negatively affect productivity and turnover.

Organization Restructuring and Downsizing

Organizations facing cost cutting usually conduct an organizational analysis and redesign before implementing a labor force management plan. This may lead to restructuring jobs and/or shifting reporting relationships. The office of human resources can provide assistance to departments in analyzing labor force loads and a system for tracking and announcing job vacancies. Methods for analysis include helping to establish the types and numbers of positions required, match individuals to jobs, and determine gaps between current skills and needed skills (with implications for training and methods of efficient training delivery to close the gap).

EAP and Stress Management

Threats to job security and the nature of work can be psychologically damaging both to those who leave the organization and those who "survive." This suggests that appropriate counseling and referral should be readily accessible and confidential through employee assistance programs (EAP).

Employee Development for Cross-Training and Retraining

Universities have certification programs in some career fields and may have a management development program. These are ways to implement university strategy and communicate organizational change.

Retraining refers to upgrade of skills to be prepared for the future of one's current job; *development* is training that prepares the employee for another job; *cross-training* provides employees with added skills so they have the flexibility of doing more and different assignments and have the potential to move into other jobs. As suggested, human resource forecasting and training gap analyses can determine the amount or type of retraining, development, and cross-training needed for today and the future.

While much of this training will be specific to job families, a systematic approach can be taken to highlighting the importance of continuous learning and providing guidance for training. Such programs include

Mastery paths for specific job families specify the required level of skill development and accomplishment to perform the job. It is expected that employees will achieve this level of competence after a certain amount of training and job experience—usually after 12 to 18 months on the job. Mastery paths indicate the training curriculum, the types of job experiences needed over time to gain mastery, and the supervisor's role in evaluating performance and coaching the subordinate along the way.

Certification and professional development programs, such as AT&T's "Network Professional Development Program," specify that every employee should have a certain level of knowledge in several key areas. These areas may include organizational mission and purpose, people (interpersonal relationships, and management), quality improvement, and emerging technologies. Other areas may be developed for a large job family (for example, all clerical workers). The program recognizes that different employees need different levels of working knowledge in these areas. Introduced in a set of booklets with a classroom orientation, the booklets (called modules) explain each key area for development, provide self-assessment questions and guidelines for supervisory discussion, and contain listings of training and job experiences that will increase the individual's competence in the area. The performance appraisal process asks supervisors to evaluate each subordinate's accomplishments in the professional development program.

Such a program is another way to communicate how the organization is changing, what this means for employee development, and what employees must do to be sure they are prepared to make a continued contribution to the organization.

Labor Force Management (Downsizing) Program Alternatives

Organizations have found a variety of options for labor force management depending on how drastic the need is for downsizing:

- financial incentives for voluntary early retirement
- financial incentives for voluntary termination (applicable to people who are not retirement eligible, with the amount of incentive usually pegged to years of service and current salary level, such as two weeks' pay for every year of service up to one year's salary)
- payment for involuntary termination (a rating system is used by supervisors to classify employees as those the organization wants to stay, those who can have the option to volunteer to leave, and those the organization wants to leave and who will be forced to leave if they cannot find alternative employment in the organization)

The last type of program has the advantage of ensuring that the employees the organization cannot risk losing (probably those who are most marketable) will stay with the organization—or at least will not be paid to leave. Companies relying strictly on voluntary programs have often found that they lose the wrong people.

Civil service restrictions in public universities may limit program options unless approval is obtained. Approval should be sought for programs that best suit the university's needs. Organizations often undertake a series of programs, starting with several early retirement offers, followed by incentives for voluntary termination applicable to employees who are not yet retirement eligible, then moving to involuntary terminations. Sometimes these incentives apply to everyone in the organization. Other labor force management programs are more targeted, offering the incentives only to employees in overstaffed departments.

TOWARD AN INTEGRATED HUMAN PERFORMANCE SYSTEM

The programs discussed in this chapter, when taken together and developed in tandem, comprise a human performance system. They are integrated and mutually supportive. This suggests that concentrating on one program is not likely to be enough. For example, a communications program will not be effective unless there is information about future job requirements and data about skill gaps in the school. Employee attitude survey data will not be valuable unless universities are prepared to respond—for example, with a career development program that recognizes employees' dissatisfaction with developmental opportunities, if this is one of the findings.

Given these linkages between human resource programs, the human resource function should analyze current human resource policies and programs to determine the extent to which they contribute to university strategies. What new programs need to be established? What revisions should be made to current programs? What information is required to guide these changes? How can the human resource director and top staff capture the attention of other university executives and demonstrate the strategic importance of the human resource function in today's rapidly changing world?

This analysis should lead to a human resource plan, first for the human resource function in how it manages the function and relates to other departments, and second for the university as a whole. Establishing the first plan can begin immediately. Establishing a human resource plan for a university can occur only after engaging university executives in discussion of human resource objectives and initiatives in the context of revising university directions.

CONCLUSION

This chapter showed the strategic role that the human resource function, and human resource professionals, can play in shaping and accomplishing university objectives. The human resource department deserves a seat at the planning table, and the head of the human resource department should participate in the forum of top officers in managing the university. Human resource policies and programs facilitate organizational transition. Human resource professionals serve as expert organizational researchers, communicators, negotiators, educators, change strategists, and role models. The university's human resource professionals should be proactive in creating an integrated set of goal-oriented programs. These should form a "human performance system" encompassing employee communications programs, human resource forecasting and planning, career planning and development, compensation and appraisal systems, strategy-setting forums, and methods for performance management, such as feedback and measurement processes and employee training and development initiatives. Human resource departments usually have a major role in organizational redesign and cost-saving efforts.

The next chapter begins a section on setting the course for organizational change. Specifically, it describes methods for university-wide planning and goal setting that foster teamwork and common understanding.

PART II

SETTING THE COURSE

4

Planning and Goal-Setting Processes

Planning should be proactive and interactive, not reactive. Planning doesn't require a separate staff, and it should not be a regimented bureaucratic enterprise. Moreover, planning should be iterative and flexible, changing as the issues and the environment shift. The planning horizon should not be too long to require speculating on totally unforeseeable events and not too short to be trivial or merely operational. Establishing campuswide goals and objectives demonstrates the interdependencies between departments and how each department contributes to common goals.

Universities initiate strategic planning efforts to respond to changing demands and resources. Colorado State University provides a good example ("The Future of Colorado State University: The Context for Planning, 1992). In 1991, the school established a strategic planning committee with broad representation from all areas of the university community. The result was a document that outlined the future of the institution with sections focusing on the evolving land-grant heritage, the university's mission, and the university's culture (including such values as excellence, academic freedom and integrity, high-quality undergraduate experience, public service, multiculturalism, and shared government). The committee outlined major aims and underlying goals. They also established five judgmental criteria to guide decision making and priority setting: quality, centrality to mission, need, cost, and government policies. The annual planning process begins with a scan of issues, threats, and opportunities conducted by the emerging issues committee. This input is used by the strategic planning committee as it initiates and facilitates an annual planning exercise. During the fall semester, departmental plans are rolled up to the college and division level, then to the offices of the provost and vice presidents, culminating in the university strategic plan approved by the president. This serves as input to the annual university budgeting process during the spring semester conducted by the executive budget committee. Budget proposals are reviewed with respect to departmental achievements and outcomes and university aims and goals. Every four years, the strategic planning committee conducts a comprehensive review and update of this strategic planning framework to ensure that the planning process is working.

What follows in this chapter first is a quick planning process that accomplishes these goals. It shows how a mission statement, goals, and departmental action steps can be formulated in a simple team process. The chapter then outlines a university-wide planning and goal-setting process, demonstrating how overarching university objectives can guide department goals. Moreover, it demonstrates that planning is a *process* that links top university officers and requires a process coordinator. Taking a three-year planning horizon, the planning process must be tied to other key university processes, especially financial planning. The chapter should be useful to administrators in ensuring that the planning does not become a useless bureaucratic exercise. Seeing that multiple departments contribute to the same objectives should be a guide to introducing strategic university planning. The specific calendar of events indicates practical ways to merge objectives and activities across university departments.

BUILDING A MISSION AND SETTING OBJECTIVES

This section describes a very simple process for establishing an organization's mission, cross-departmental objectives, and department-specific action plans. The initial process took place during a single meeting of the management team, all professionals, in the organization—in this case, a community library with 45 full-time professional staff and more than 200 part-time employees. The process was facilitated by a consultant who began by eliciting reasons for having a mission statement. The 25 participants eagerly suggested reasons and the consultant elaborated. The first flip-chart was quickly filled with reasons, such as communication of purpose to multiple audiences, setting a common direction, understanding important yet currently unmet needs, building commitment from the staff and patrons, and socializing new employees.

Generating the Mission

After this first ten-minute session, the group was split into interdepartmental subgroups to spend 30 minutes brainstorming potential components of their mission. Here are the results:

Brainstorming Ideas for the Mission

- Serve the public—residents, taxpayers, and the larger county community via direct and interlibrary loan access.
- Be a community center.

- Meet the informational, recreational, social, cultural, and educational enrichment needs of the community by providing access to a broad range of current and useful materials, resources, programs, and services.
- Provide up-to-date technological resources, programs, and services for people of all ages and abilities, including individuals and families in a welcoming, comfortable, neutral, nonthreatening environment.
- Develop a leadership role and provide unique and innovative services and programs based on responsiveness to a changing community.
- Be committed to the concept of life-long learning.
- Be linked to the larger community through networking and outreach.
- Reach individuals of all ages and abilities in our local district as well as the community at large.
- Identify and supply informational needs and interests, educational enrichment, recreational and cultural activities and services, programs and materials, and technology.
- Provide quality services via a well-trained and educated staff committed to the concept of life-long learning.
- Play a leadership role in the development of library services.
- Serve as a family/community center, an informational and technological center, and a life-long learning center.
- Be user focused, and encourage involvement.
- Be committed to continually finding new ways to enhance our service to the community.
- Be the technology center of the community.
- Have facilities that are modern, attractive, physically accessible, and well-maintained.
- Satisfy the needs of the community by providing a comprehensive up-to-date collection, well-trained congenial staff, excellent patron service, diversified programs and activities, public relations and publicity (inform community of the offerings), in a comfortable, safe, and clean setting.

The leader of each subgroup read out the group's results as indicated above. After the meeting, this was woven into the following statement by the consultant for the senior staff's review and revision:

Our Mission

We are the community's center for informational, cultural, recreational, social, and educational enrichment. We are committed to life-long learning and meeting changing community needs. We do this by providing access to a broad range of useful, current, and technologically up-to-date materials, resources, programs, and services. We serve people of all ages and abilities—individuals and families—in a welcoming, nonthreatening, comfortable environment. We have a well-trained, congenial staff committed to excellent patron service and diversified, innovative programs and activities. Our facilities are modern, attractive, physically accessible, and well-maintained. As community leaders, we reach out to patrons in the immediate district and county by encouraging their active involvement and linking our services to county, state, and national networks.

Generating Objectives

The brainstorming of mission components was followed by another half-hour brainstorming session on objectives. These were to follow from the ideas generated in the mission brainstorming, realizing that the mission would need more work, especially wordsmithing. Meeting as a group-of-the-whole to keep everyone focused on general objectives applicable across departments, the group brainstormed and then refined the following objectives:

1. Support technological literacy (information, resources, education, and access) for the community and the staff.
2. Provide current resources for the community's needs.
3. Promote and foster literacy.
4. Take a leadership role and participate in networks, to enhance the library's resources for the community.
5. Continuously develop and improve diverse and comprehensive services that meet changing community needs.
6. Promote and market the library's services.
7. Ensure continuous staff development.
8. Provide a well-maintained, barrier-free, modern, and easy-to-use facility.
9. Reach out to nonusers.
10. Provide cultural, educational, and recreational programs to all residents.
11. Serve as the community center (a hub of activity, information, and resources) for the district.
12. Connect with, and involve, users in the development of library services.
13. Develop sound fiscal policies and provide stable funding to achieve library goals.

Action Planning

After agreeing to the above objectives, each natural work team met to generate possible action plans for the objectives that applied to them. The following are the results for one department choosing to respond to most of the objectives. (Action items are listed by the above objective numbers.)

Circulation Department

1 Put innovative computers in our district schools.
2 Ensure circulation supervisors are familiar with dial-in ports. This will help "circ" staff to answer questions and make patrons feel like it is a user-friendly service.
3 Have a library card drive (using stickers and pins bulletin board, and pictures).
4 Attend user group meetings for innovative ideas. Networking within innovative system will improve our system to our community.

5 Clarify the staff's understanding of services available at other nearby libraries (e.g., videos, talking books).

7 Give staff more training in computers, supervision, leadership, and customer service. Provide this training to both full- and part-time employees.

8 Make sure automatic doors operate properly. Follow up patron messages (e.g., when they tell us the lobby floor is slippery, call the custodian).

9 Make people feel welcomed. Greet them when they walk in. Personalize our services. Realize that we are the first people that patrons see when they come in.

12 Keep patrons aware of any changes in procedures (e.g., fine increases). Communication methods include bookmark reminders, posted memos, and messages on printouts of returned items.

The administrative departments listed actions for multiple objectives, and they distinguished between some immediate and long-term actions. (Again, items are listed by applicable objective numbers.)

Administration

13,1 Acquisition systems.

Immediate action: Streamline acquisition systems and procedures within next fiscal year.

8 Facilities.

Immediate actions: Landscape the front of the main building; retrofit the lighting in the ceilings.

Long-term: Purchase and install auxiliary power supply; replace air conditioning units for main building; replace main building roof; renovate the employees' women's room in the main building.

5,6 Publicity.

Publicize user survey results.

7,8 Provide employees with "right to know" training on hazardous material in accordance with OSHA regulations.

Provide Lotus training for business department staff.

Develop a safety plan for the cultural center.

7 Identify and provide more training workshops for the staff.

Develop a new employees packet and orientation program.

Conduct employee evaluations.

5,11 Create a young adult area.

5,6,7 Encourage and develop interdepartmental planning activities.

Design a long-range plan.

Review processes with other state libraries.

Improve personnel policies and procedures.

Develop a public relations program.

Continue publication of the library newsletter.

1,4 Work with the county library system to develop central services.

13,4 Develop a funding stream directly from the state.

13 Ensure proper fiscal management.

Oversee the budgeting process.

1 Create a database for incidents and suggestions from the patrons and staff.

5,6,12,13 Develop a "friends of the library" group.

Continue to work with the patron focus groups to understand and respond to patron needs and desires.

The other major departments developed their own lists. Each department described the results of their discussion, and all the flip-charts were later typed by the consultant and sent to the library director for review with the staff.

Summary

This planning process took just a morning. Of course, follow-up was anticipated for revision, adoption, and progress checks. All full-time department managers participated in the event, which was held as a rare retreat in pleasant country surroundings away from the library facility.

Planning in more complex organizations requires far more integration, involvement, and systematization. However, there is a danger that such a process will become a useless bureaucratic exercise. The process for university planning outlined below maintains officer and staff involvement. Rather than create a central planning staff of full-time employees, staff members are assigned the task of being part of the planning staff. In this way, existing resources and knowledgeable individuals are brought to bear on planning. The result is a comprehensive process linked to other key processes (in particular financial planning, discussed more in the next chapter).

A PARTICIPATIVE, FINANCE-DRIVEN UNIVERSITY PLANNING PROCESS

This planning process identifies strategic priorities and promotes a shared understanding of the overall direction of the university and its major current initiatives.[1] It integrates specific projects into a comprehensive design that includes both the academic plan and support-service initiatives. The program plan is developed through a participative process, and it is broadly disseminated. Planning is linked to the budget process to insure that resource allocation decisions support strategic priorities.

The planning process integrates strategic priorities established by the president with program plans developed by the administrators and managers responsible for the university's academic departments and administrative services. University-wide planning is supported by the university planning coordinator and other members of the planning staff under the direction of the deputy to the president.

Planning Documents

The university's strategic plan is documented in statements of the campus mission and a three-year program plan. The president identifies strategic priorities and elaborates on this vision in an annual convocation address. The three-year program plan identifies university goals, initiatives of university-wide significance that address the goals, and the projects through which those initiatives are currently implemented. The president establishes goals that articulate the university's missions. Planning initiatives are the major efforts through which the campus will work toward those goals in the next three years. Projects are specific activities or achievements that contribute to these initiatives. Projects can generally be completed in one to three years. The three-year program plan also identifies the vice president or vice presidents responsible for each project.

Development of the Three-Year Program Plan

The three-year program plan is updated annually. Planning begins at the vice presidential level with an update of the academic plan and other vice presidential plans. These plans are developed through internal discussion to build consensus about university-wide and local priorities. The vice presidential plans are synthesized by the planning staff into a draft document. This draft is refined by the president's cabinet, finalized by the president, and broadly distributed.

Progress toward completion of all projects included in the three-year plan is assessed annually. A status report is prepared by the planning staff for review by the president's cabinet and distribution to the campus community.

The status report on the three-year program plan is completed during the summer and early fall. The updated three-year program plan is completed during the fall semester in order to provide a basis for the campus budget process, which begins in November.

Roles and Responsibilities of the Planning Staff

The planning staff coordinates university planning efforts, develops strategic planning, establishes a more explicit linkage between planning and budgeting, and enhances the reporting procedures that provide information on the outcomes of the planning and budget process. The members of this group all have other jobs at the university, and they bring a variety of skills to the planning effort. They are the deputy to the president, the director of the office of institutional studies (the keeper of faculty and student head counts), the director of performance management (a function mentioned in Chapter 2 and described more completely in

Chapter 6), the associate provost for communication and computing, a management engineer, the assistant vice president for campus facilities, the human resource director, and the university planning coordinator. The deputy to the president coordinates the integration of planning with other university activities, including performance management. The university planning coordinator is the team leader for planning activities and staff to the priorities committee—the group that reviews budget allocations and makes annual budget recommendations to the president. This committee represents the administration's accountability to the university community for resource allocation ("Communicating Financial Data," 1993).

The planning staff has seven principal responsibilities:

1. *Develop and implement a university planning process.* This includes establishing an integrated planning and budget process in cooperation with the vice president for finance and management.

2. *Produce university planning documents under the direction of the president.* These documents include the university goals and objectives and a three-year plan.

3. *Participate in university planning and system-development activities as directed by the president.* For example, members of the planning staff have a central role in the establishment of interdepartmental memoranda of understanding (service agreements for cross-charges) for general and administrative services and in the development of new transaction-processing systems.

4. *Coordinate the development and implementation of management reporting.* Most of these reports are produced by other areas. The planning staff assists in the development of standard formats, supports the annual update of departmental profiles, and produces reports that document the extent to which planning objectives are achieved. The planning staff coordinates with the budget office in reporting on the results of the distributions made in the budget process.

5. *Serve as staff to the campus priorities committee.* The planning staff will work with the budget office to provide financial information to the committee and with the vice presidents and other senior administrators to provide the information used by the committee to make recommendations to the president in the budget process.

6. *Support the university's performance management program under the direction of the deputy to the president.* The planning staff assists the president and his deputy to establish university performance management objectives and initiatives. Under their direction the staff collaborates with service managers in organizational analyses and special projects to increase the efficiency and effectiveness of campus support services. The planning staff also supports the administrative review process through which all administrative and support departments are evaluated on a five-year cycle following procedures similar to academic department reviews. (See Chapter 6 for a description of this process.)

7. *Conduct special planning studies, as directed by the president.* While the staff's activities focus on supporting and coordinating the planning efforts of re-

sponsible administrators, from time to time they perform analyses to support specific planning projects.

Priorities Committee Questions

As indicated earlier, departmental goals and objectives are used by the priorities committee to advise the president on budget reallocations, areas for cost reductions, or areas for increased funding. To accomplish this review, the committee convenes meetings with each vice president to discuss their programmatic priorities and budget issues. The VPs are asked to address the following questions. The committee also welcomes written responses or other written material that would help committee members to prepare for the meeting.

1. What are the principal projects and activities through which you are currently addressing university goals and objectives?
2. What does each of the objectives that is most pertinent to your area mean to you? How do you prioritize these objectives? Should any be changed or reformulated?
3. What are your highest priorities? What procedures do you use to establish and review priorities for your unit?
4. What are your most serious problems?
5. What programmatic initiatives are you currently undertaking?
6. What high-priority initiatives are you constrained from undertaking by budget limitations?

LINKING OVERALL GOALS AND OBJECTIVES TO DEPARTMENTAL INITIATIVES

Goals are general statements about intended accomplishments. *Objectives* are more specific statements that explain how the goal will be accomplished.[2] The planning staff developed a draft of overall university goals and objectives and reviewed them in extensive discussions with the president, provost, and vice presidents. After reaching agreement, the provost and VPs developed their department plans. The planning staff then prepared a document that integrated the overall goals and objectives with the departments' initiatives.

This is demonstrated in an excerpt from the draft. Each section of the document begins with a statement of the goal and the objectives associated with it. Departmental contributions are then described. The document is meant to show university administrators and faculty how senior management views the year's planning horizon in relation to the university's goals and objectives. The departmental directions statements do not include all activities in the university that pertain to the goals and objectives. Rather, they highlight the areas of principal concern that may be viewed as priorities or areas for special attention. This is meant as a working document that will be revised annually as goals, objectives, and departmental initiatives change.

Goal I. Undergraduate Education

The university will offer diverse student body access to undergraduate education that is recognized for excellence within and outside the state.

University Objectives for Goal I Addressed by These Initiatives

- Increase the undergraduate student body by 2,000 students.
- Develop programs—including summer sessions, short courses, and evening programs—that take advantage of existing resources to supplement traditional degree programs.
- Improve recruitment of high-achieving, highly motivated undergraduates from a broad geographic area and expand programs for these students.
- Continue to upgrade administrative services for students, especially in the areas of financial aid, student records services, and job placement.
- Upgrade the quality and breadth of programs that promote students' personal development and academic success, especially academic advising and student health and wellness programs.

Department Direction Statements

Academic Programs. Expanding evening school enrollment will be the first priority. Planning for an expanded summer session and further increases in undergraduate enrollment will follow. Enrollment expansion will also be supported by the creation of a transfer student office, strengthened linkages between the admissions process and academic planning, and implementation of recommendations for attracting high-achieving undergraduates that will be developed by a consulting firm.

Health Sciences Center. In the School of Nursing, programs allowing students to complete baccalaureate and master's degree requirements in new ways—like the one-year baccalaureate program already begun—can increase the school's response to the nursing shortage.

Student Services. Improvements in the financial aid office will include facilities rehabilitation, re-funding a counselor position, and an increased mailing budget. Implementing a system that permits students to register from a Touch-Tone telephone will greatly simplify the registration process.

Program expansion will fill major service gaps by establishing the long-discussed commuter service center, reopening the student job placement service—eliminated in response to budget cuts—and restoring support for the learning disabled program. A strategic marketing plan will be developed during the year to increase the enrollment of high-achieving students.

University Affairs. A public relations initiative will implement the strategic marketing plan for high-achieving students. Alumni affairs staff will increase alumni support for the university and their involvement in university issues and activities.

Goal II. Campus Life

The university campus will be a community that supports and stimulates personal growth as well as academic achievement.

University Objectives for Goal II Addressed by These Initiatives

- Develop the intercollegiate athletics program.
- Construct and rehabilitate student facilities that expand opportunities for recreation, social interaction and access to essential student services.
- Insure that the campus is safe for students, faculty, and staff.

Department Direction Statements

Academic Programs. Planning to enter collegiate athletics Division I will continue, but success will depend on a vigorous effort to develop external support.

Student Affairs. Facilities rehabilitation and construction will improve the quality of campus life and support other student services initiatives. The first phase of construction of the new student activities center—the highest priority in the university's most recent facilities master plan written—will be completed in two years. Obtaining funding for the second phase will be a high priority in the next three years. The residence hall revitalization program will also improve the quality of student life at the university.

Campus Services. A safe, secure campus environment is essential to the university's ability to attract and retain students, faculty, and staff and to protect its facilities and other assets. In the next three years, public safety initiatives will focus on safety in the residence halls, including a student affairs' program to supervise student security.

New regulatory requirements and campus growth are increasing the demand for environmental health and safety programs. In response, the university is continuing to expand its services, but reduced funding has compromised the campus's ability to comply with environmental health and safety legislation. Environmental health and safety staff will also contribute to the development and implementation of a comprehensive plan for managing scarce resources including energy, water, and disposal capacity.

Goal III. Regional Economic Development

The university will be recognized as an essential contributor to maintaining and strengthening economic development in the state and local region.

University Objectives for Goal III Addressed by These Initiatives

- Continue to develop academic programs—with educational, research and public service components—in areas of regional importance.
- Develop university-related high-technology enterprises.

Department Direction Statements

Academic Programs. In general, the provost's office aims to satisfy regional and national demands for highly skilled manpower. The university's regional development task force will prepare a refined institutional economic development agenda. The university's regional role in education, research, and cultural and economic development will also be a principal focus of the university's accreditation self-study.

President's Office. The business incubator building will open this fall. Efforts to coordinate innovative financing for a conference center on campus are progressing well.

Goal IV. Management and Human Resources

The university will improve the efficiency and effectiveness of its academic programs, administrative functions, and support services.

University Objectives for Goal IV Addressed by These Initiatives

- Use a comprehensive, integrated process of strategic planning, budgeting, and evaluation to allocate resources and guide program development.
- Create integrated management structures and systems that improve communication and interaction between campus units.
- Develop strategies for functional reorganization to increase efficiency.
- Modernize administrative systems to take advantage of the efficiencies of contemporary information technology.
- Expand staff development and training efforts.

Department Direction Statements

Information Services. A special university steering committee will prepare a comprehensive five-year plan to guide the development of computing and electronic communications to support research, instruction, and administration. Developed from a broad-based campus needs assessment recently compiled by the planning staff, the plan will outline the investment in equipment, software, support personnel, and staff development required to take full advantage of current and anticipated information technology. It will describe an effort to significantly improve instructional computing, a cost-effective means of meeting the demand for research computing, and a plan for administrative systems that enhance institutional management.

Implementation of this plan will begin one year from now to the extent that funding permits. The plan will build on the university's already substantial investment in computing and communications hardware while emphasizing the support services needed to maximize the effectiveness of that investment.

Student Affairs. Implementing a system that permits students to register from a Touch-Tone telephone will greatly simplify the registration process.

Finance and Management. During the next three years, the university will change the way it conducts business by decentralizing transaction authority, strengthening financial management including the budget and planning process, and extending the market economy (system of service contracts specifying inter-departmental cross-charges) to institutional services. These changes will include streamlined human resources procedures, increased staff development efforts, a new materials management system, the continued development of the all-funds budgeting and accounting process, strategic planning, and institutionalization of provider/client relationships between institutional services and campus components that are not state funded. These efforts will rely heavily on the changes in information services described above.

Human Resources. Personnel management will be substantially strengthened by the conversion to a new human resources information system scheduled for completion next year. Systems development will facilitate personnel transactions and the management of personnel budgets.

Staff development, a new institutional priority, is essential to changing the way business is conducted in the university. The human resources department will begin to implement the master plan for training developed by the president's steering committee on employee training in conjunction with the university's management school.

Financial Management. The effective management of scarce resources from diverse sources and fiscal control of a more decentralized organization will require the development of improved financial systems. The university will continue to develop audit procedures and accounting systems to support good management and maintain accountability. The performance management program will become increasingly important as bureaucratic controls on routine transactions are replaced by retrospective financial audits and the assessment of programmatic outcomes. An integrated accounting system will be developed, which will include data from all university funds and automatic links to the new personnel information system and the materials management system.

Budget Management. This coming year, the university will establish a more structured budget-development process that places greater emphasis on the programmatic impact of budget allocations. This process will insure that university goals and objectives are addressed in the budget and continue the development of responsibility center goals, objectives, and performance indicators to increase accountability and provide the basis for total quality management.

Creation of a revenue budget and continued improvement of the capital budget process will also enhance the budget process. A separate revenue budget will improve the management of the increasing proportion of campus resources that come from sources other than the state budget.

All-Funds Management. As the proportion of its budget attributable to state appropriations continues to decline, the university will develop financial systems that support the management of its diverse revenue sources, including fees for noncredit courses and other university services, research grants (direct and indirect costs), revenue from the medical clinical practice, and funding channeled through associated organizations including the university's nonprofit foundation, and various university-run businesses (some run by the faculty student association, which provides a financial return to the campus).

Campus Services/Finance and Management. In the coming year, the university will implement a new procurement system that integrates purchasing, receiving, and accounts payable. This system will replace redundant paper-based processes designed to provide bureaucratic controls with an automated system that streamlines the procurement process and decentralizes authority for purchasing decisions. Investment in systems development will be required, but engineering studies indicate that the cost of this investment will be more than offset by savings associated with increased efficiency. The procurement system will subsequently be extended to include inventory control and fixed-asset management.

To support the "market economy" transformation effort in campus businesses, the university will develop an oversight program for campus businesses. Program staff will provide technical assistance to campus business enterprises.

Other Goals

Additional goals not included here are listed along with their general description:

Graduate Education. The university's doctoral and professional programs will be recognized as among the best in the world, and the campus will offer master's and certificate programs that promote economic development by supplying the regional labor market with highly skilled personnel.

Research and Scholarship. The university will have a faculty of nationally and internationally recognized scholars, including a substantial number who are the top leaders of their fields.

Regional, Cultural, and Social Development. The university will address the social needs of the state and region, and it will offer cultural and recreational opportunities to community residents.

Institutional Advancement. The university will strengthen its financial resources.

Facilities. The university will improve and maintain campus buildings and property to the standards of other public universities.

SPECIAL INITIATIVES

In addition to department-specific goals, there may be special initiatives that the president or other top officers believe should be promulgated. These may be interdepartmental in nature in that they require the contributions of multiple departments. The initiative is articulated by the officer(s), discussed with other officers and managers, written down, and incorporated into the university-wide objectives and departmental plans. Such an initiative is described here as an example.

University as Leader in Advanced Continuing Education

The goal of this proposed initiative is to maintain and strengthen the university's position as the regional resource for advanced continuing education. This is important given that continuous learning is critical in many professions and disciplines. Technological, economic, and marketplace changes have contributed to the criticality of training and development in many organizations. As a major research and educational institution, the university should be viewed as a prime source of advanced knowledge in the most sophisticated areas.

This initiative includes degree programs through the school of continuing education, short courses for continuing professional education tied to licensing requirements, special conferences, and the use of advanced communication technologies to disseminate information.

- Considerable continuing education already takes place at the university. For instance, just about all the schools in the health sciences center offer programs.
- An inventory of these educational efforts should be part of the university's image. This should be incorporated into various public relations material as appropriate.
- Alternative forms of advanced continuing education beyond degree programs and short courses should be considered. These should include discipline-oriented conferences and technology-based conferences that provide industries with the latest knowledge, perhaps associated with solving technical problems.
- The management and engineering schools seem to be areas ripe for expansion of advanced continuing education in conjunction with the school of continuing education.
- The university might partner with another institution or firm to develop and apply advanced communication technologies as a dissemination mechanism (e.g., computer-based training, distance learning programs through satellite transmission, video production, etc.).

If this initiative is to be pursued, the next steps include:

- Conduct the inventory of programs.
- Review this initiative with the deans for continuing education and the graduate school and the vice president for university affairs who manages publications, public relations, and fund-raising.
- Involve appropriate academic and professional school deans in developing ways to increase offerings in advanced continuing education in areas with most promise (resource availability and market demand).

The viability of this and the other proposed university initiatives will be reviewed at an upcoming meeting of university officers.

DEPARTMENTAL GOAL STATEMENTS

Another way to view goal setting is by department. Such goals may refer to university-wide objectives but also outline special departmental initiatives. The following accomplishes this for the human resource department. The example shows how a department expresses strategic action plans as a framework for more specific tasks for units within the department.

Goals for Human Resource Development

The implementation of a comprehensive, innovative initiative in human resource development promises to strengthen the foundation of the organization by enhancing its most valuable resource: the people who are the university. The university should concentrate on three themes: organizational structures, skill and knowledge development programs, and renewed emphasis on quality.

Redesign and development of organizational structures will complement and augment the valuable human capital represented by the members of the university community. Skill and knowledge development programs will create an environment that promotes efficient and effective matching of employee skills, talents, interests, and knowledge with university needs. Quality in the work environment begins with active participation by the individual. A focus on this goal is consistent with rewarding and recognizing participation both as "student" and "teacher."

The university is pursuing these themes through an innovative effort called the campus training initiative. This initiative is coordinated by a committee appointed by the president. The director of human resources has primary responsibility for training at the university. The unifying goal of this effort is to create a stimulating, valuable, challenging work environment. Among the university's peer institutions, UCLA has documented a similar nexus of programs that emphasize a continuous, "life cycle approach" in human resources development at the university.

Development is for enhancing employees' contributions to the organization to do better in their current assignments and to prepare for anticipated job changes. For some employees, development means preparing for a new job, depending on individual career interests and available opportunities. The major criterion for the adoption of a development program must be its usefulness to improving the quality of work output and meeting the objectives of the university.

Development encompasses all ways of learning, including, but not limited to, classroom instruction. Supervisors should recognize, and be rewarded for, their roles as coach and developer. They provide development opportunities by structuring challenging jobs, offering assignments that broaden skills, and creating special training programs to meet the needs of the work group.

The human resource department has general oversight responsibility for the development of all the university employees. The department has operational responsibility for designing and delivering training and development programs in such areas as supervision, benefits, and new employee orientation. Other departments provide technical training and personal development programs in such areas as computer skills, safety, health care delivery, self-improvement, and avocational interests. The human resource department provides integrated systems that promote performance excellence. These systems tie together objective-setting, performance measurement, training, and evaluation.

The campus training committee, established by the president, advises the human resource department on strategy, priorities, and plans for employee development. With members from all major administrative departments as well as the provostial and health sciences academic areas, the training committee recommends directions for training and may work jointly with the human resources department training director and staff to design programs with university-wide applicability. In addition, the committee encourages department-specific training through a recognition program.

Special training committee initiatives during its first year of operation include a Training Resource Guide and Monthly Training Calendar that communicates training opportunities available from more than 18 departments that offer short-programs and self-paced learning; and an annual "training month" (see Chapter 9 for more details), held in the summer, that offers special programs and highlights the importance of employee development to the continued viability and strength of the institution.

YEAR-END STATUS REPORT

Follow-up is needed to be sure that the goals, objectives, and departmental action plans are not forgotten and to be the foundation for the next annual planning cycle. To accomplish this, planning staff members meet with vice presidents and their staffs to review each department's goals and to write a statement of accomplishment. The report notes goals that were anticipated to be more long-term in nature. Some of these should stay on the goals and objectives document next year. Others should come off because they were completed or because priorities have changed. Still new goals, objectives, and actions will be added.

Here is an example of the results of such an evaluation referring to examples of goals and objectives given earlier in the chapter.

Goal IV. Management and Human Resources

The university will improve the efficiency and effectiveness of its academic programs, administrative functions, and support services.

University Objective

Modernize administrative systems to take advantage of the efficiencies of contemporary information technology.

Department Direction Statements

Information Services. A special university steering committee will prepare a comprehensive five-year plan to guide the development of computing and electronic communications to support research, instruction, and administration.

Status: The provost convened a task force to work on this plan, with subcommittees on academic computing, administrative computing, and data transmission. An extensive report is close to completion and is expected in two months.

Finance and Management. During the next three years, the university will change the way it conducts business by decentralizing transaction authority, strengthening financial management including the budget and planning process, and extending the market economy (system of service contracts specifying inter-departmental cross-charges) to institutional services.

Status: In January, the vice president for finance and management established a standing committee on service agreements (memoranda of understanding) to oversee, expand, and coordinate their development. These analyses will drive budgetary allocations for next year. Also, next year the committee plans to further integrate the development of service agreements into the campus budget process and to develop memorandum of understanding documents that all parties view as meaningful management tools.

Human Resources. Staff development, a new institutional priority, is essential to changing the way business is conducted in the university. The human resources department will begin to implement the master plan for training developed by the president's steering committee on employee training in conjunction with the university's management school.

Status: A new training and development manager was hired. She began reviewing current supervisory training programs and developing a new program to begin next winter. Also, during the past year, the human resources department initiated a new orientation program for new employees, an administrative training series, and a program on client relationships and customer satisfaction. The provost convened a retreat for academic department chairs to initiate an ongoing training program in academic management and leadership.

CONCLUSION

This chapter outlined various planning processes. It emphasized the need to link setting broad objectives to departmental action plans and university budgets. A distinction was made between *goals*, which are general statements about intended accomplishments, and *objectives*, which are more specific statements that explain how the goals will be accomplished. The university's planning staff works with the president, provost, and vice presidents to formulate overall university goals and objectives. After several iterations the goals are formalized. Then departments add action plans related to applicable objectives. In addition, there may be special initiatives that the president or other top officers believe should be promulgated. In this sense, planning is both a "top down" and "bottom up" process. The plans highlight how different units contribute to the same goal, thereby helping to accomplish elements of the university's mission. Examples are given of general university objectives, departmental contributions to those objectives, and special departmental initiatives. Annual reviews are necessary to determine the degree to which goals and objectives were accomplished. This sets the stage for next year's planning process. The chapter indicated that (1) planning needs to have a reasonable future time horizon (e.g., annual updates to a three-year plan), (2) university-wide planning drives strategically oriented department initiatives, (3) departments develop their own special initiatives to meet their specific functional objectives,

(4) planning can be an involving process that builds commitment and teamwork, and (5) having planning staff members who are representatives of departments rather than permanent central staff reduces the likelihood that planning will be a mere bureaucratic exercise.

The next chapter extends this discussion by describing planning processes for three major areas: finance, enrollment, and facilities. The key word here is *process*, in that each of these areas cuts across several major departments and requires deliberate process management. Planning requires process leadership, clear ties to existing and anticipated needs and conditions, and cooperation from multiple departments.

NOTES

1. The section entitled "A Participative, Finance-Driven University Planning Process" was written by Emily Thomas.

2. The section entitled "Linking Overall Goals and Objectives to Departmental Initiatives" was written by Tammy Feldman.

5

Strategic Mechanisms: Financial, Enrollment, and Capital Facilities Planning Processes

The previous chapter referred to three major processes that tie into the overall university planning process: financial planning, enrollment planning, and capital facilities planning. Each scenario in this chapter outlines an example of a specific process. However, they have some common features. They demonstrate the importance of a process manager or team leader who is responsible for the overall process and involves administrators from relevant departments in a coordinated team effort. Another common feature is a calendar of major events or hurdles subject to fiscal and academic-year constraints. Each planning process is central to campus operations and ties to the process of setting overall goals and objectives for the university, as described in Chapter 4. Another feature of all three planning processes is consultation with relevant departments and community groups as information becomes available and decisions unfold. Further, plans and decisions are made and revised over time as information becomes available, uncertainties are resolved, and input from affected parties (departments and advisory groups) is received. We begin with financial planning.

THE FINANCIAL PLANNING PROCESS

The financial planning process supports the overall strategic planning process and creates trust within the institution ("Communicating Financial Data," 1993).[1] In this scenario, the university budget consists of two parts: the three-year financial plan and the university annual operating budget. The three-year plan is updated twice per year in early February (Phase 1 decisions) and in June (Phase 2 decisions). The operating budget is established in June when the Phase 2 decisions are made. Both plans include all major sources of revenue and objects of expenditure (the all-funds approach) but the three-year financial plan only gives summaries by fund at the vice presidential level for the current year and estimates for two future years. The operating budget is published in a "budget book" that contains data for every university account. In practice, while the significant Phase 2 decisions are published in a memorandum from the president in May or June, the full financial plan is not published until several months later to allow time for vice presidents to distribute the authorized funds to their accounts.

The budget process starts during the fall semester in preparation for the Phase 1 decisions (mid-January). In Phase 1, the president adjusts the three-year financial plan, based on recommendations from the priorities committee and the officers. The three-year plan numbers are deliberately conservative so that managers can count on them as budget floors. These are the numbers that should be used for long-range planning in each vice presidential area.

The numbers in the three-year plan that refer to the forthcoming fiscal year, also called "Phase 1 allocations," provide the basis for detailed budget planning for the forthcoming year. (The officer group is called the "cabinet.")

Priorities Committee

Additional revenues (or deficits) that result from the difference between the Phase 1 allocations and a better estimate of the availability of funds are allocated in Phase 2 of the budget process. Phase 2 also distributes miscellaneous revenues that cannot be accurately predicted until near the end of the fiscal year.

During the winter, vice presidents and deans begin to develop departmental budgets based on the Phase 1 allocations. In the process, they identify budget problems and determine the extent to which they will be able to undertake new initiatives with their Phase 1 allocations. On the basis of this analysis, they prepare requests for Phase 2 funding that document specific programmatic needs. The priorities committee reviews these requests and meets with the administrators who use them as the basis for making Phase 2 recommendations to the president. The priorities committee is appointed by the president and includes representatives from administrative and academic departments. The committee is chaired by the provost and has staff support by the vice president for finance and management.

Phase 1 Decisions

The university budget office identifies items to be considered in preparing the Phase 1 allocations in consultation with the department managers responsible for finances, the cabinet, and the priorities committee. Topics include major budget assumptions, open financial and policy issues, and programmatic initiatives to be considered for funding in Phase 1. The budget office then issues a preliminary report on anticipated Phase 2 funds. Although the funds that will be available in Phase 2 cannot yet be accurately predicted, a preliminary projection is issued in February.

The president allocates the projected budget to vice presidents guided by recommendations from the priorities committee and the cabinet. These allocations incorporate the five kinds of decisions described below. The recommendations of the priorities committee and the president's response to the committee are published with these allocations.

To establish the Phase 1 allocations, the president must make five kinds of decisions, guided by recommendations from the cabinet and the priorities committee:

- What basis will be used to distribute a budget cut or increase across vice presidential areas?
- What revenues from other funding sources—such as indirect costs recovered from funded research—should be incorporated in the Phase 1 allocation decisions?
- Should a portion of expected funds be reserved for distribution in Phase 2?
- What if any units should be held harmless from a cut?
- What if any major initiatives or problems should be explicitly addressed in Phase 1 and how should they be funded? Specific initiatives are more likely to receive attention in Phase 2, but a few urgent problems and major strategic issues may be addressed in Phase 1.

Phase 2 Decisions

In Phase 2 of the budget process the budget office issues five documents:

1. Briefing book on Phase 2 requests. Vice presidents submit requests for Phase 2 funding in a uniform format. These requests, called exceptional request narratives, document specific problems and initiatives. They are distributed to the priorities committee, the cabinet, and the president.
2. Report on available funds. The budget office prepares a final report on the funds available for distribution in Phase 2 from all sources.
3. Phase 2 allocations. The president makes Phase 2 allocations guided by recommendations from the priorities committee and the cabinet. The recommendations of the priorities committee and the president's response to the committee are published with these allocations.
4. Operating budget. The operating budget gives account-level detail for the current budget year.
5. Three-year plan. The updated three-year financial plan is issued in conjunction with a three-year program plan (the narrative portion of the financial plan).

Phase 2 of the budget process includes four kinds of decisions:

- What budget problems should be addressed?
- What new initiatives should be funded?
- What pools and contingency funds should be retained or established?

- How should the initiatives with ongoing costs that were funded in Phase 2 of the previous year's budget be treated in future years? Should they be (1) included as Phase 2 allocations at the previously budgeted level, (2) included as Phase 2 allocations at an adjusted level, or (3) folded into the base budget?

Funds are allocated in Phase 2 in three ways: for specific purposes, in special-purpose pools, or as unrestricted support for selected programs.

Funding is provided for specific problems and initiatives, on a one-time or ongoing basis, based on projections of their cost. For example, one year money was allocated to pay for hepatitis vaccinations for at-risk employees required by federal regulations.

Funding is set aside in pools to address broad campus priorities through initiatives developed during the course of the fiscal year following spending plans developed by the responsible administrators. For example, one year pools were established to fund early retirements, space rehabilitation, and administrative initiatives.

Budget Calendar

Phase 1

December	Vice presidents submit Phase 1 decision items for cabinet discussion.
	Cabinet and departmental finance managers initiate discussion of Phase 1 budget.
January	Cabinet completes review of Phase 1 decision items and assumptions.
	Priorities committee begins discussion of Phase 1 issues.
	Vice president for finance and management issues final Phase 1 revenue estimate.
February	Priorities committee completes Phase 1 recommendations.
	Cabinet discusses priorities committee Phase 1 recommendations.
March	President announces Phase 1 budget decisions.
	Budget office issues Phase 1 allocations.
	Standing committee on interdepartmental service agreements for cross-charges issues Phase 1 report including expected funding levels for completed service agreements and status report on work in progress.
	Budget office issues three-year financial plan update.

Phase 2

March–April	Priorities committee meets with vice presidents and other senior administrators to discuss priorities and budget issues.
	Provost and vice presidents submit Phase 1 account-level all-funds budget proposals.
April	Vice presidents submit Phase 2 decision items.

	Cabinet discusses Phase 2 decision items for submission to the priorities committee.
	Budget Office issues comparison by major responsibility center of proposed Phase 1 budget and prior-year allocations.
May	Vice president for finance and management issues report on funds available for distribution in Phase 2.
	Priorities committee begins review of Phase 2 requests.
	Standing committee on service agreements issues Phase 2 report including final budget levels.
	Priorities committee completes Phase 2 recommendations.
	Cabinet discusses Phase 2 recommendations.
June	President issues Phase 2 decisions.
	Budget Office issues final allocations incorporating Phase 2 decisions.
	Vice presidents provide the budget office with distribution of Phase 2 allocations and adjustments to Phase 1 account-level budgets.
August	Budget Office issues final budget for the coming academic year and issues updated three-year financial plan.
	President issues updated three-year program plan.
	Provost and vice president of the health sciences center issue updated long-range academic plan.
September	Priorities committee is briefed on final academic year budget, academic plan, and three-year plan (financial and programmatic).
	Priorities committee discusses priority issues for possible inclusion in the next academic year budget; vice presidents describe current efforts to address university goals and objectives and proposed future initiatives.
October	The university formulates initial budget request for the next academic year.
November	Call to vice presidents for budget decision items for next year's budget.

Summary

This is a consultative planning process led by top university officers and staffed by the university planning coordinator. Consultation with the campus priorities committee and cabinet of officers, including the president and provost, occurs in tandem throughout the planning cycle. All departmental vice presidents have a chance to submit requests for special funding. The mechanism provides a way to evaluate priorities and reallocate resources to meet changing needs. Moreover, it is linked to information about incoming resources and requirements. Thus, two other planning processes become important comechanisms for meaningful financial planning: enrollment and facilities planning. Enrollment planning is the business of educating students—the core of any university's mission. This is discussed next.

ENROLLMENT PROCESS

The university enrollment planning process described here includes three activities: (1) the development of enrollment and tuition revenue projections; (2) planning for enrollment-related initiatives; and (3) monitoring and assessment.[2] As indicated, enrollment planning is closely related to the budget process in order to insure that the campus budget accurately anticipates tuition revenue, and that funding requests for enrollment-related initiatives are developed in a timely fashion.

The enrollment planning process is coordinated by the enrollment executive committee (EEC). The EEC reports its conclusions and recommendations to the university's president. The president distributes these reports to the cabinet, the priorities committee, and the executive committee of the university senate.

Components and Calendar

The timing and content of the reports of the enrollment executive committee and other enrollment-related documents are outlined below. A description of each component of the process follows.

September   Implementation Plan for current-year enrollment initiatives.

October   Preliminary Enrollment/Tuition Projection for subsequent fiscal year.

Enrollment Assessment Report (prior year).

> Part 1: Undergraduate Students (undergraduate admissions).

> Part 2: Special initiatives to bolster the undergraduate program.

> Part 3: Graduate Students (vice provost for graduate studies; dean, school of continuing education).

> Part 4: Health Sciences Center (vice president for health sciences; includes departments of medicine, dentistry, nursing, social welfare, and health technology and management).

November   Enrollment initiatives plan for subsequent fiscal year.

December   Phase 1 budget request for enrollment-related initiatives (if any).

February   Phase 1 budget enrollment/tuition projection.

April   Phase 2 budget request for enrollment-related initiatives (if any).

May   Phase 2 budget enrollment/tuition projection.

Enrollment/Tuition Projections

Preliminary enrollment/tuition projection: The enrollment executive committee prepares a preliminary enrollment projection for the coming academic year in late September, as soon as snapshot enrollment data for the fall semester are available. The tuition revenue projection derived from this enrollment projection is incorporated in the revenue estimates used for Phase 1 budget planning.

Phase 1 budget enrollment/tuition projection: The EEC prepares a Phase 1 budget enrollment projection in mid-February, as soon as snapshot enrollment data for the spring semester are available. This projection also incorporates early data on application and admission rates. The tuition revenue projection derived from this enrollment projection is incorporated in the Phase 1 budget.

Phase 2 budget enrollment/tuition projection: The EEC prepares a Phase 2 enrollment projection in late May as a basis for the Phase 2 budget. This projection permits adjustment of the final campus budget for tuition-revenue estimates that are significantly more accurate than those available in Phase 1 estimates.

Enrollment Initiatives

Implementation plan (current year): At the beginning of each academic year, the EEC finalizes a campuswide implementation plan for enrollment-related initiatives during the current fiscal year. This plan incorporates and integrates plans from the dean of admissions, enrollment planning and management, the vice president for student affairs, the vice provost for undergraduate studies, the vice provost for graduate studies, the dean of the School of Continuing Education, and the vice president for health sciences. This plan includes specially funded projects geared to enhancing the undergraduate experience.

Enrollment initiatives plan (subsequent year): During the fall, the EEC prepares a proposal for enrollment-related initiatives to be funded during the coming fiscal year with input from all relevant offices (as indicated above). As chair of the EEC, the provost submits the enrollment initiatives plan to the president for approval. Following cabinet discussion, the final version of this plan is distributed to the priorities committee and the senate executive committee.

The enrollment initiatives plan forms the basis for a Phase 1 budget request if funding is needed for special undergraduate projects. The EEC may generate—through an appropriate vice president—a request for additional funding in Phase 2 of the budget process if such a request is justified by specific circumstances unforeseen in Phase 1.

Monitoring and Assessment

Enrollment assessment process: At the beginning of each academic year, the administrators responsible for each of the university's student cohorts assess and report on the results of the previous year. These assessments are based on the quantitative analysis of application, admission, enrollment, and retention rates. They also include evaluations of enrollment-related programmatic initiatives.

Ongoing monitoring: From January through August, the administrators responsible for each of the university's student cohorts receive weekly target reports on fall applications, admissions, acceptances, and deposits. A similar process occurs for tracking spring enrollments. The Office of Institutional Studies produces campuswide enrollment projections on a monthly basis from mid-February through mid-August. These reports provide the president, the EEC, and other campus constituencies up-to-date summaries of projected fall application, acceptance, and enrollment rates, and their fiscal implications. These reports include revenue projections by the budget office.

Summary

Enrollments are a vital source of university revenue even in a state university. This consultative planning process establishes tuition revenue projections, implements ways to enhance enrollment for targeted groups of students, and tracks the results. It treats enrollment as a process combining multiple functions and crossing several departments. Also, it monitors events closely and creates initiatives to suit evolving needs. In this case, the provost assumed responsibility for process leadership and involved as many relevant individuals as necessary organized into several workable structures.

FACILITIES PLANNING PROCESS

The university has an integrated facilities planning process that includes long-range facilities planning, preparation of an annual capital plan and budget request, facilities management and rehabilitation, and space allocation.[3] The facilities planning process is designed to insure that the university takes maximum advantage of all funding sources to support university priorities by involving the appropriate university constituencies in facilities matters.

There are nine specific tasks included in the facilities planning process, and each task has several groups responsible for carrying out the work.

1. Coordination of the Facilities Planning Process

The facilities planning council (chaired by the assistant vice president, facilities operations) coordinates the university's facilities planning process and makes policy recommendations. Under the leadership of facilities operations, the council includes a representative from each vice president, the provost, and the president (seven members in all). The council monitors the identification, prioritization, and accomplishment of all facilities projects. It identifies the facilities areas and issues most critical to the fulfillment of the university's missions and proposes a process for addressing each one that ensures a coordinated approach. The council also ensures that special programmatic needs and technical requirements are met.

The facilities planning council coordinates and draws on the work of the other committees and teams responsible for long-range facilities planning, preparation of the capital budget request, and setting priorities for facilities rehabilitation and remodeling. Specifically, the council:

1. Seeks the advice of the campus space advisory committee in matters pertaining to programmatic needs of the university for space, both short- and long-range need/availability.
2. Coordinates the planning effort accomplished under the direction of the capital budget request team.
3. Assesses the ongoing rehabilitation and remodeling of facilities tracked by the facilities planning council, including the potential impact on short- and long-term planning.
4. Assures integration of approved projects from the campus master plan into the planning process through the activities of the master plan implementation team.
5. Integrates into a university-wide plan for maintenance and rehabilitation the recommendations of the academic facilities committee and the research facilities user group.
6. Causes others to be charged with the task of addressing specific facilities planning concerns as they may arise.
7. Reviews the work of the groups identified and prepares recommendations for the president's cabinet regarding facilities priorities and investment, which will give positive support to the research, teaching and service missions of the institution.

2. Long-range Facilities Planning

The facilities master plan committee (chaired by the campus architect) develops long-term plans addressing major capital and facilities issues. The committee's responsibilities include implementing the campus facilities master plan and updating that plan to address changing needs and opportunities.

3. Preparation of the Capital Budget

The university's capital budget request team (chaired by the director of facilities engineering) develops the capital budget plan. Capital budget planning is a *continuous* activity. The director of facilities engineering maintains a continuously updated inventory of planned construction and rehabilitation projects. Campus plans are developed from the capital projects list twice a year.

In August, the capital budget request team prepares a three-year capital budget plan for the current fiscal year. Following the president's approval, this plan becomes part of the university three-year plan, which also includes the three-year financial plan and the three-year program plan. In January, the capital budget request team reviews the three-year capital plan and updates the third year for changing priorities. In February, the plan is reviewed by the cabinet and the president, who submits the plan to the university's trustees.

4. Setting Priorities for Classroom Conditions and Space Needs

The academic facilities committee (chaired by an associate provost) reviews classroom conditions and space needs. Faculty and student concerns about classroom accessibility, maintenance, and teaching requirements are addressed. This includes accommodating changes in teaching methods, such as planning for the incorporation of new instructional technologies into the curriculum.

5. Setting Priorities for Research-Related Rehabilitation Projects

The research facilities users group (convened by the deputy to the president) addresses researchers' concerns about maintenance, rehabilitation projects, and other facilities issues through enhanced communication between principal investigators and facilities personnel. This group includes members of the office of research administration, campus principal investigators (representatives from the provost's research advisory group), and the facilities operations department.

6. Setting Priorities for the Design and Construction of Rehabilitation and Remodeling Projects

The provost establishes priorities for design projects in order to insure that scheduling decisions within facilities engineering reflect programmatic priorities. Projects are scheduled for construction by the physical plant managers. The physical plant department schedules campus projects.

7. Space Reallocation Decisions (between vice presidents)

The campus space advisory committee (chaired by an associate provost) deals with these needs, once the provost reallocates space among the vice presidents. In general, space needs are expected to be met by reassignments within vice presidential areas, and space reallocation is considered only for projects with a very high institutional priority. Requests for additional space must be accompanied by a thorough analysis and justification of existing usage. The provost's reallocation decisions are guided by this broad-based campus space advisory committee that maintains awareness of space utilization within all vice presidential areas and negotiates optimal space arrangements. The committee includes the assistant vice provost for education resources and services, the assistant to the provost, the assistant vice president for facilities operations, the director of facilities engineering, the assistant facilities program coordinator for the School of Medicine, and representatives of the vice president for finance and management, the vice president for health sciences, and the departments of student affairs and university affairs.

8. Space Management

Vice presidents are responsible for managing the space assigned to them. The office of institutional studies maintains official records of space allocation and function.

9. Management of Rehabilitation and Remodeling Projects

The facilities planning council (chaired by the assistant vice president, facilities operations) insures logical prioritization in accordance with the provost's programmatic needs, the university mission, and the campus facilities master plan. The purpose of the rehabilitation/remodeling planning process is to insure a proper, consistent, and timely course of action and direction in the administration and execution of campus remodeling and rehabilitation projects. All rehabilitation and remodeling must be accomplished in accordance with university guidelines. The vice president for campus services has primary responsibility for monitoring such compliance.

The specific charge of the facilities planning council is as follows:

- Review all rehabilitation (alteration) and remodeling (repair) prior to any accomplishment of work, insuring compliance with the planning process.
- Coordinate the activities of the university community in the rehabilitation and remodeling of space. (Facility planning by analysis of space layout.)
- Insure that a proper funding source is available prior to committing the university to any course of action.
- Monitor the compatibility of work with the approved facilities master plan.
- Act as a complementary and parallel committee to the campus space advisory committee, insuring that work is done subject to formal assignment of space to the requesting party.
- Monitor completion of work for compliance with university regulations.
- Detail operating guidelines that will insure the process and success of the committee charge.

Funding Sources for Rehabilitation Projects

Most rehabilitation and repair projects must be funded by the requesting department. In addition, the campus budget includes two funding pools to finance projects of campuswide priority: (1) *Program-Related Rehabilitation Pool*, which was established to fund rehabilitation projects and moving expenses associated with inter-vice presidential space reallocations and other programmatic needs. The pool is managed by the vice president for campus services, and allocations of funds from it are made by the provost or designee on the recommendation of the campus space advisory committee. (2) *Infrastructure Rehabilitation Pool*, which was established to fund rehabilitation projects related to the condition of the campus physical plant. The pool is managed by the vice president for campus services, who allocates funds from it on the recommendation of facilities operations.

Integrating Academic Planning and Setting Deferred Maintenance Priorities

Other universities are coming up with good, commonsense approaches to answer the questions that need to be answered and to maintain an institution-wide perspective when making the necessary decisions. There are parallels between this and some of the participatory approaches to facilities-related issues we describe in this book—for instance, the Research Facilities Users Group. Berkeley has made impressive progress toward rationalizing and focusing attention on a very difficult and complex process.

Similar to other campuses, Berkeley does not fully fund regular maintenance (to prevent additional projects from being added to the deferred maintenance inventory). This results in a constant game of "catch-up." This points out the circular nature of this problem: If you fix something and cannot afford to maintain it, you will be fixing it again in several years. With their current resources and operations, it is not likely that they will get ahead of the problem, but a strategic approach to using existing resources may help them keep their head above water.

In a recent conference presentation, Eric Broque, assistant provost, and Peter Lin, associate director of facilities at the University of California at Berkeley described how they created the university's Deferred Maintenance Policy Board (DMPB) (Broque & Lin, 1994). The purpose of this group is to provide rational, structured guidance to the campus in the prioritization of deferred maintenance projects with consideration to academic program directions and needs. While all universities face deferred maintenance problems and campus administrators are aware that these issues require their attention, these problems are generally uninteresting to all involved and traditionally there has been little productive discussion to promote academic program managers' awareness of these issues. As a result, maintenance activities have not necessarily coincided with program priorities and directions, program administrators have not been engaged in a productive dialogue on deferred maintenance issues, campus management has little confidence in the ability of facilities personnel to solve these problems effectively, and little has been done to understand and begin to resolve the problem. Berkeley has structured the DMPB in a way that engages not only facilities personnel, but academic program managers as well in a process of understanding, prioritizing, planning, and acting upon deferred maintenance.

UC Berkeley is the oldest of the nine UC campuses. A preeminent public research university, it has 29,000 students (including 8,000 graduate students), 1,500 faculty, 19 colleges and divisions, and annual expenditures of $800 million (40% from the State of California). The school has approximately 12 million square feet of space (excluding auxiliaries). Nearly 1,000 projects were identified in its current deferred maintenance inventory. In 1986–87 its deferred maintenance backlog was $46 million. In 1993–94 it was $136 million. In 1986–87, Berkeley received $5 million from the state for deferred maintenance. In 1993–94 it received $3.2 million.

The development process for the DMPB consisted of four steps:

1. Create the oversight committee (DMPB) for the process.
2. Identify a complete inventory of deferred maintenance projects requiring action, along with the cost to "replace in kind to current code." This required assignment of facilities personnel, reporting to the DMPB to conduct surveys of all campus buildings.

3. Attract funding to the program. This required that the process attract the interest and elicit the confidence of the parties in a position to provide the necessary financial support.

4. Develop an evaluation process that allows intelligent choices to be made in the use of resources.

The need for this process evolved out of a project that occurred several years ago that required extensive coordination between facilities and academic program management in order to accomplish vital maintenance work while allowing academic units to continue functioning. This project was used as an experiment in collaborative problem solving. The DMPB resulted from this experiment. 1993/94 was Berkeley's first year through the cycle.

There are three important elements in this process: the structure of the Deferred Maintenance Policy Board, the evaluation criteria, and the reporting mechanism. Important attributes of each include the following: The board needs to ensure a balance between service providers and program administrators who can address policy issues, provide a broad institutional perspective, and prioritize backlog. The board consists of nine individuals representing academic program administrators (the library; the schools of arts and sciences, professional schools, and research; and undergraduate affairs), facilities staff (service providers from space management/capital programs planning, design and construction, environmental health/safety, and physical plant), and a staff of two facilities engineers who conduct audits to identify and evaluate deferred maintenance problems using criteria developed by the DMPB. The DMPB is empowered to make decisions concerning deferred maintenance funding. All members need to be knowledgeable and/or willing to learn about facilities issues. Discussion occurs at the policy level, with details introduced only where necessary. This keeps the discussion at a useful level. Problems can be viewed in a broad context. DMPB members visit and view potential project sites and see firsthand the effect on program operations, campus aesthetics, safety, and so on.

The evaluation matrix outlines explicit criteria and systematic evaluation methods. A comprehensive inventory is developed, and evolving university directions are considered. Each of six criteria are rated on a scale of 1 to 10 by the DMPB staff and then the multipliers are applied to the rating for each criterion. Berkeley's method makes health and safety concerns and program impact the most important determinants of a project's ranking. The following are the six criteria and their weights: Health and Safety (3.0), Programmatic Impact—Teaching/Research/Public Service (2.0), Building Damage (fundamental damage if not fixed) (1.5), Difficulty and Expense of Maintenance (1.5), Opportunity and Coordination (1.0), and Visual Impact (1.0). The DMPB members view these criteria as a "first cut" in managing the problem, not a formula for making decisions. The criteria and weights help the group structure discussion of the projects in the inventory. The idea is to distinguish between "order of magnitude" differences in severity and need. Actual decisions require sound judgment from a broad institutional perspective. This is what the DMPB members contribute to the process.

The DMPB generates two reports for the campus and the UC system president: (1) an annual Deferred Maintenance Backlog Report listing projects identified in the DMPB inventory of deferred maintenance projects, and (2) an annual Funded Projects Report listing projects funded through the DMPB, their current status and total costs.

The process has the benefits of improving communication, empowering decision making, coordinating deferred maintenance activities with the academic program plan, and withstanding challenges, "end runs," and willful attempts to derail facilities or bypass the process. The explicit criteria focus the discussion on policies and programs rather than the merits of a particular facility. Also, the process engages broad constituencies in the university and attracts interest in deferred maintenance projects. Next steps and challenges include (1) ensuring that the classification scheme incorporates the chancellor's priorities (e.g., classrooms), (2) refining the rating methodology by defining the individual rankings (for instance, clarifying what a 6 means in terms of programmatic impact and how it differs from an 8), (3) fine-tuning the weights where necessary, and (4) using the process as a budget advocacy tool at the campus/system levels.

Summary

These processes show the need for multiple assessments and the involvement of multiple constituencies to plan for the operations and maintenance of complex physical facilities. Different planning groups, some with the same people, carry out designated tasks, including assessment of academic needs, space reallocations, funding requests for building repair and rehabilitation, and formulation of a campus facilities master plan taking into account long-term needs and desires. The overall process is essentially the coordination of all these committees and task forces—a joint responsibility of the university planning coordinator and the facilities executives (for example, the campus architect and the associate vice president for facilities operations) under the vice president for campus services. While the process involves ample consultation, it is not as cumbersome as it may appear. The committee structure is intended to separate aspects of a complex process and puts the component tasks on a reasonable calendar. The process also refers to opportunities for facilities users to provide input and be an early warning system to head off problems before they become catastrophes.

With this in mind, the next section offers an example of a call for assessment of the conditions of university research facilities; the adequacy of current funding for, and management of, maintenance and repair; and the development of a funding strategy to close the gap between existing and needed resources. This demonstrates how facilities managers, research managers, and principal investigators can work together to recognize the need for information and forward thinking. Also, it shows the broad scope required for a thorough facilities assessment—one that could be expanded to include all campus facilities, including classroom space, residence halls, recreation facilities, health care operations, and fine and performing arts facilities as relevant to the particular campus.

RESEARCH USERS GROUP FACILITIES NEEDS ANALYSIS: REQUEST FOR CONSULTANT'S PROPOSAL

The following is a proposed set of requirements for a study of the conditions, needs, and operations of the university's research facilities.[4] The university seeks proposals from qualified consulting firms for a facilities needs assessment focused on its research mission. This study is intended to help the university to identify, assess, and respond to current and future research facilities needs. It will involve a review and evaluation of the university's deployment of existing and future facilities resources (financial and space) for research purposes, and assistance in planning for the strategic development of new facilities and rehabilitation of existing facilities, in the context of the existing campus facilities master plan and the anticipated growth in research activity. Consulting firms responding to the university's forthcoming request for proposals should be experienced with research universities nationwide. The consultant will work closely with both academic and facilities personnel to meet the objectives of the study.

Method of Award

Evaluation of proposals will be made by the research facilities users group based on cost to provide services and demonstrated experience in higher education. Each contractor must provide an all-inclusive cost to provide the services specified in the proposal. Each contractor must have extensive experience in higher education and show a record of providing similar services to at least two comparably sized research-intensive institutions. Each contractor's experience will be evaluated, references will be verified, and the results will form part of the basis for award of the contract. A site visit is required in order to be considered for this work.

Background

The university has three primary missions: education, research, and health care. It also has secondary missions, including regional economic and cultural development and providing for the needs of its residential and commuter students. The university pursues these missions in over 100 academic, research, clinical, and residential buildings (over 9.5 million gross square feet) on its 1,100-acre campus. The university has been successful in developing a worldwide reputation as a leading research university. Support for organized research and sponsored programs at the university totals about $100 million annually, reflecting the university's commitment to scholarly research and its pivotal role in revitalizing the regional economy. About 80 percent of the total dollar volume of all research at the university came from federal sources such as the National Institute of Health and the National Institute of Mental Health, and the National Science Foundation.

As its research volume continues to increase, the university recognizes the need to understand and evaluate its deployment of existing and future facilities resources (financial and space) for research purposes and to plan for the strategic development of new facilities, in the context of the existing campus master plan and the anticipated growth in research activity.

The research facilities users group (the users group) believes that the university's continued development in its research and teaching missions is dependent on the ability to structure a capital planning process that is responsive to the needs of its aging and growing infrastructure. Informed decisions will need to be made concerning future investments in the operation, maintenance, and rehabilitation of existing facilities. These decisions will require a thorough understanding of facilities issues and needs and how well existing facilities resources are deployed to address them. The users group proposes retaining an external consultant, experienced with research universities nationwide, to help the university identify, assess, and respond to these needs. The consultant will work closely with both academic and facilities personnel to meet the objectives of the study. This assessment should be viewed as a tool to assist management in making informed decisions.

Services Requested

A review of research space allocation in representative campus research facilities identified by the users group to determine suitability, amount allocated, and additional space need is desired by the campus to establish benchmarks for planning purposes in the following areas:

1. Allocation/placement model for space with research facilities.
   a. Work with campus academic, space, and engineering operations to collect specific data consisting of space assignments and allocation for departments identified by the campus to participate in the study.
   b. Use the data collected above to analyze how existing space assignments compare from space type and individual research allocation perspective and organize the information.
   c. Assess the efficiency of the current placement and allocation of research space based on the data collected above.
2. Justification of project programs for research facilities identified on the campus facilities master plan.
   a. Develop a series of lab space standards describing how space should be assigned. Work with campus academic and facilities personnel to review various space allocation options and obtain concurrence regarding standards that should be used in projecting and allocating future space requirements.
   b. Based on growth space projections, analyze the current and future research space allocations on the campus, the relationships between research programs, and the impact

on the establishment of space allocations adjacencies in campus facilities. Prepare plan and blocking diagrams of all campus facilities as required.

3. Allocation of resources for the maintenance and operation of research facilities.
   a. Review the university's existing facilities conditions to identify major facility deficiencies and structural defects and to assess the condition of the identifiable buildings and systems that comprise the university's facilities/infrastructure.
   b. Identify the major infrastructure issues facing the university and their relative severity based upon the above review.
   c. Recommend a plan of action (including resource requirements) to restore and maintain the university's facilities in good operating condition.
   d. Provide a basic model to determine the impact of research facilities allocation on operational costs and modeling of future capital project requests within the capital planning process.

4. Assessment of efficiency of existing facilities operations and maintenance services. The study will produce a listing of maintenance and operations costs of representative research spaces, inclusive of operations and maintenance analysis of utility systems, distribution and tunnel network as necessary, and provisions for emergency power.
   a. Identification of the resources (people, materials, and dollars) that the university currently allocates in support of facilities operations and maintenance and the services currently provided with those resources.
   b. Comparison of the university's spending levels, patterns of spending, service, and space mix with generally recognized national benchmarks for similar institutions. The contract study will be conducted in accordance with the applicable NACUBO (National Association of College and University Business Officers) standard system of accounts and will address all relevant maintenance and operations costs including, but not limited to, all utility systems, distribution and tunnel network as necessary, and provisions for emergency power.
   c. Recommendations for future levels of funding and mix of services for facilities operations and maintenance, based on the current condition of the university's facilities and various levels of implementation of the restoration plan. The consultant(s) shall prepare a comprehensive report incorporating their recommendations for the identified tasks.

Project Scope

The representative research facilities (identified by the research facilities users group) to be included in the assessment, along with their gross square footage are:

Facility	Square Feet	Year Constructed
Health Sciences Center-Basic Sciences Tower	147,134	1973
Health Sciences Center-Clinical Sciences Tower	952,100	1973
Life Sciences Building	342,613	1970
Physics Building	307,956	1971

Heavy Engineering Building	54,274	1967
Light Engineering Building	85,851	1966
Graduate Chemistry Building	317,524	1973
Total	2,207,452	

Requirements for Bid

All bidders must provide the following information:

1. Description of the consulting organization, including staff experience and areas of expertise relevant to the services requested.
2. A reference list of major higher education institutions who have used or are currently using the bidder's services. List names, addresses, and telephone numbers of individuals or departments that can be contacted for reference purposes.
3. A narrative description of how each of the objectives outlined in services requested above will be accomplished, including a work/time plan for each.

Cost

Bids ranged from the low $100,000s to more than $400,000. Bidders were encouraged to divide the project into subcomponents so that a decision could be made on whether to fund the entire study or one or more pieces of it.

Summary

Facilities planning requires comprehensive information to understand immediate and long-term needs. Such an assessment is not cheap. But in comparison to the total worth of the infrastructure, it can be money well spent. The above request for proposal can be used as a model for designing similar assessments or, for less money, smaller components of the larger assessment. Indeed, the proposals that were submitted broke the project into its elements with separate budgets for each. This allowed choosing priority elements based on immediate needs and changes in funds available.

The next section describes an actual capital facilities plan based on an understanding of the current state of campus facilities and academic program initiatives. The plans for each major facility are tied to a campus facilities master plan, showing changes in the original plan based on resource availability and changes in strategic programmatic objectives. The plan was developed in a team effort by the campus facilities planning council.

CAPITAL FACILITIES PLAN

This document identifies the principal components of the university's capital facilities agenda for major construction and reconstruction projects.[5] This agenda is placed in context through a description of its relationship to the most recent campus facilities master plan developed with input from an independent architectural firm. Most of the rehabilitation and repair projects for which the university needs routine funding are not addressed here. The few rehabilitation and repair projects included in this document are directly related to programmatic initiatives.

The campus was originally conceived as a low-rise college campus for training educators in sciences and technology, with buildings that used a mixture of modern and Federalist architectural vocabulary. During this period, the humanities building, the library, several classroom and laboratory buildings, two residence hall quads, and an infirmary were constructed. An early plan set the framework for new construction to support the expanded role for the campus as a major research university center, and established the limits for additional property acquisition. It conceived of the campus as a densely built, urban-like environment of low-rise structures. Spatially, it emphasized informally linked plazas centered on key buildings, such as the library and lecture center. These plazas would be connected by corridors formed by background buildings such as the older academic buildings.

Due to the accelerated growth of the campus, the spatial scheme was completed around a central mall with poor connections to the planned fingers of the core campus. The peripheral quads and spaces have poor service access, inadequate parking access, and spaces without clear definition of boundaries or gates.

The facilities master plan was prepared to organize growth of academic and research programs, and complete development of the physical environment of the campus. Major goals included:

- Redefining the physical image of the campus and the quality of its environment so that it reflects and supports the missions of the campus.
- Creating a more distinctive environment that defines the academic core of the west campus and improves the physical sense of community on the campus.
- Establishing patterns for landscaping, landmarks, and site amenities that support the preceding goal.
- Assessing existing campus service routes and patterns, service access to building, and the facilities support for various campus services components.

This master plan identified about 50 construction projects to move the university toward these goals over a ten-year period. Some of the projects have been completed or started (e.g., a graduate student housing complex, a high-technology business incubator facility, and expanded garage-parking facilities). Also the campus has begun three additional major building projects (a new student activity center, a life sciences center, and a cogeneration facility) and a road reconstruction project.

The master plan included two projects that have been dropped from the university's current capital plan: an addition to the computing center and facilities for a new physics institute. Since the university is moving toward distributed computing, the expansion of the computing center was deemed unnecessary. Federal funds for the institute were not forthcoming.

Current Capital Plan

The university's capital planning agenda currently includes 40 projects, organized into eight categories: (1) facilities to support expansion of academic programs, (2) major building and renovation projects, (3) academic infrastructure (rehabs of existing classroom, office, and research space), (4) student services projects, (5) athletics projects, (6) support service projects, (7) facilities infrastructure and site projects, and (8) other projects and planning issues. The following are several examples of projects. Their description provides a flavor of the depth of planning needed at this point.

Facilities to Support Expansion of Academic Programs

Life Sciences Addition. The master plan identified the life sciences research facility as the university's second highest priority after the student activities center now under construction. The life sciences addition will consolidate all undergraduate biology laboratory instruction in one building and provide space for the expansion of biomedical research. The campus facilities master plan recommended the addition of new space for teaching and research in the life sciences. A space and program study by outside architects and planners recommended an addition of about 30,000 square feet for teaching and about 120,000 square feet for research. The project has been reduced to about 27,000 square feet for teaching and about 60,000 for research. Site work associated with the construction of this building will improve traffic flow on the campus. The new complex was allocated $40 million for construction. A steering committee involving the relevant deans, representatives of the office of the provost, and the campus architect has programmed the new space and is working with faculty groups in the final design process during the coming academic year with groundbreaking expected early the following year.

Major Building and Renovation Projects

Humanities Building Rehabilitation. The master plan included a project to renovate the library building for library facilities and humanities. The goal now is to renovate the existing humanities building to provide a focal point for humanities programs. The humanities building is 33 years old and needs to have all major building systems replaced so that a facility that meets contemporary standards for environmental conditioning and power requirements is available to support instructional and administrative activities. An addition may be required to permit consolidation of all humanities programs in one location. Approximately 70 percent of the building is currently used for academic purposes. The rest is used for administrative purposes and a cafeteria. These uses and alternative locations for these functions will be evaluated by the Campus Space Advisory Committee and other groups. A task force has been appointed by the dean of humanities and fine arts to determine beneficial adjacencies between humanities programs and the options available to provide functional space for the humanities programs. This group will make a report to the dean before the end of the current academic year.

Academic Infrastructure (rehabs of existing classroom, office, and research space)

The projects in this category affect a variety of buildings. The needs they identify must be taken into account in all construction and major reconstruction projects.

Classroom Facilities. The master plan included two classroom projects: building a general classroom facility and general classroom renovation. The university must have an adequate supply of classrooms of appropriate sizes, with facilities for current and emerging instructional technology. Developmental priorities include:

- Create classroom facilities in the sizes and with the facilities needed to meet instructional demand. The supply of large classrooms—in the 75–100 range and above—is particularly inadequate.
- Establish ongoing maintenance and rehabilitation programs to maintain facilities in a functional condition.
- Develop a plan to integrate current and emerging instructional technology into classroom areas.

The registrar has prepared a preliminary need statement for classroom demand. The Academic Facilities Committee will develop a strategic plan to propose solutions for facility deficiencies. Planning will be coupled with the plans for enrollment expansion.

Several lecture halls and smaller classrooms have been renovated during the last two years, and this program will continue contingent on available funding. The installation and use of an automated classroom scheduling computer system this year will provide the opportunity to prepare a systematic inventory of facilities conditions because a detailed inventory of classroom features and amenities is required to make the system operational. A task force to inventory and assess the requirements for campus instructional technology has been appointed by the provost.

Data Network. The need for data communications was not addressed in the most recent campus facilities master plan. Currently, the campus division of computing and communications plans to standardize and expand the campus data network to provide network services to those areas that currently do not have access and to modernize those buildings that have outdated network equipment. This project is essential to providing network services to the residence halls and to other academic and administrative buildings throughout the campus. A pervasive network is an essential component of the client/server environment. This project involves 18 academic buildings and 33 dormitories. A combination of fiber optic and coaxial cable is needed to provide a building connection to the campus backbone. Preliminary cost estimates were completed several months ago. No further progress is possible without funding. The project could be incorporated into the proposed upgrade of the campus telephone system. In general, the data network project requires capital funds over a multiyear period. The initial fiber infrastructure expansion cost is $120,500 and includes wiring of one dormitory building. Additional buildings will range in cost from $15,000 to $65,000, depending on the model chosen for implementation. The cheaper model has a provision for a community computing site rather than individual room connectivity.

Summary

This plan covers facilities to support expansion of academic programs, major building and renovation projects, and academic infrastructure. Programmatic and administrative needs are merged with an evaluation of the conditions of facilities and strategic, long-term goals for the campus. This plan, combined with the assessment methodology and the facilities planning process presented earlier, forms a complete view of facilities operations plans. Of course, this process is related to enrollments and finances, which all come together under the overall set of university goals and objectives. Some other processes may be involved as well.

OTHER PLANNING PROCESSES

The concept of process planning can be extended to other key processes that cut across departmental lines. This requires someone assuming the role of process leader, recognizing the departmental interfaces, getting the right people together, and facilitating group discussion and cooperation. Another example might be a scholarship fund-raising process, perhaps tied into the enrollment process and geared to projecting funding needs and raising the funds.

Yet another process would be marketing and communications. There would be a process for overseeing and guiding marketing objectives and methods, such as communicating the university image, helping divisions collect information on constituent expectations, designing and distributing coherent and consistent messages through multiple media, and such. This would be a university-wide process that integrates current efforts of key departments (e.g., admissions, the center for performing arts, the school for continuing education, the division of athletics, the medical center, and the business and engineering schools). The logical process leader would be the campus head of media relations and communications. The goal would be to maximize leverage of existing resources rather than create central control over departmental initiatives and resources. This is a fine line that requires sensitivity to departmental needs and the ability to communicate university objectives and enlist team support. The marketing/communications planning process would have dates throughout the year of regular occurring events that can benefit from interdepartmental coordination, such as regular annual mailings of certain programmatic brochures. The marketing planning process would join the financial, enrollment, and capital planning processes as components of the overall university-wide planning process that was described in Chapter 4.

CONCLUSION

This chapter described financial, enrollment, and capital facilities planning. They have common features and are reciprocally related. Each ties into the other, and indeed each involves some of the same departments and managers. They demonstrate process management, team efforts, and specified events at specified times. Together, the processes support overall university goals and objectives. Consultation and opportunities for user input, expert judgment, and shared decision making are hallmarks of all three processes. They provide a means of setting priorities, evaluating success, and making corrections and refinements as the plans are implemented and new plans are formulated. They deal with elements that are vital to the university's operations and success.

The next part of the book moves from planning to using plans to achieve performance excellence. It describes interventions for organizational change. Chapter 6 begins Part III with a description of performance management functions that evaluate organizational conditions and facilitate change to more efficient, customer-oriented policies, programs, and operations.

NOTES

1. The section entitled "The Financial Planning Process" was written by Emily Thomas.
2. The section entitled "Enrollment Process" was written by Emily Thomas.
3. The section entitled "Facilities Planning Process" was written by Emily Thomas.
4. The section entitled "Research Users Group Facilities Needs Analysis: Request for Consultant's Proposal" was written by Douglas Panico.
5. The section entitled "Capital Facilities Plan" was written by Emily Thomas.

PART III

ACHIEVING PERFORMANCE EXCELLENCE: INTERVENTIONS FOR CHANGE

6

Promoting Organization Effectiveness: Performance Management, Internal Audit, and the Administrative Review Process

So far, we have shown how organizational change and effectiveness can be accomplished through positions (e.g., the university president and deputy to the president), staff functions (e.g., human resources), and processes (e.g., financial, enrollment, and facilities planning). Many institutions have functions that are specifically responsible for reviewing administrative operations and facilitating achievement, quality, and continuous improvement—that is, managing for excellence. This chapter reviews internal audit and performance management functions. It shows how these functions can provide constructive input and consultation to develop more effective work structures. The administrative review process, one that parallels traditional academic department reviews, is described. A proposal is made for integrating these functions under an organizational effectiveness unit. The chapter demonstrates that control functions don't have to be rigid guards of bureaucratic regulations but can be promoters of organizational analysis and continuous learning.

MANAGING FOR EXCELLENCE

The university's performance management program provides a coordinated approach to strategic planning, general policy-making activities, risk assessment, program review, management reporting, and other management initiatives designed to improve performance and increase accountability of campus programs.[1] The overall goal of the performance management program is to maintain an integrated approach to managing these activities as part of the day-to-day operations of the university. This approach reflects the university administration's management vision of effective internal control and information flow. This coordinated approach to supporting performance excellence involves four campus functions.

1. The Internal Audit Department

The university's internal audit department conducts an ongoing program of audits of university activities to monitor, test, and report on the university's internal controls. The strategic model for internal audit activity is built on a five-year audit plan, continued development of audit risk assessment, and enhancement of audit planning methodologies. The effectiveness of the internal audit program is enhanced by the coordinating efforts of the performance management office.

2. Performance Management Office

A portfolio of management initiatives contributing to university's management effectiveness is carried out by the performance management office. The office is under the direction of a full-time performance management administrator (a former internal auditor) who reports to the deputy to the president. Performance management is meant to be a coordinative and analytic function providing management consultation support and program development services to the university community.

Specific responsibilities and projects include:

a. Performance Management Program
   Coordination of Management Initiatives
   Vulnerability/Risk Assessment
   Education and Training
   Reporting and Compliance Staff Role
b. Management Reporting
   Key Indicators
   Department Profiles (academic and administrative)
c. Coordination of Administrative Review
   Efficiency Initiatives
   Upward Feedback
d. Training and Development
e. Management/Policy Analysis

3. Development of Accountability Mechanisms and Operational Budgeting

Ongoing initiatives to rationalize budget processes and improve program accountability are encompassed by a university initiative to generate an internal market economy—that is, a system of charge-backs for services based on competitive market rates. Currently, the key component of this initiative is the memoranda of understanding project, which focuses on developing transfer pricing contracts (service agreements) for administrative services between various campus units and constituencies. The process of designing these contracts identifies services provided, acceptable levels of service quality, costs, and enforcement mechanisms for delivery. The agreements are based on management engineering studies that identify the potential for improvements to work processes, including automation, and related reductions in cost.

4. The Planning/Budget Process

Under the direction of the university's planning coordinator, the university has developed and continues to pursue an ambitious portfolio of planning and budget initiatives. The strategic model for the planning and budget process is the development of explicit resource allocation decisions (a three-year financial plan), which are consistent with the university's short- and long-range plans as embodied in the three-year operating plan, university initiatives, the university academic plan, and university goals and objectives (see Chapters 4 and 5 for outlines of these processes and plans). To promote accountability, the university is moving toward programmatic budgeting and consistent tracking of revenue flows, both based on an integrated, all-funds approach.

Summary

This section suggests that managing for excellence can be supported through a series of functions and processes that work together. Some organizations view these as control mechanisms for ensuring the status quo and adherence to regulations. The view taken here is that these functions can be sources of support for organizational analysis, self-reflection, and directions for change.

This is not to say that there is no need for internal controls and independent audits. Indeed the internal control function can be a valuable source of ideas to avoid waste and improve efficient use of resources. Internal audit units need an organizational charter to ensure their access to records and personnel in any department. But this can be more than a watchdog function in the guidance and recommendations that result from the audits. The following sample internal control charter recognizes the need for independent review through availability of information. However, this comes with the informed consent of university officers.

INTERNAL AUDIT CHARTER

Internal auditing is a staff function that serves university management by *reviewing and appraising the activities of the institution, the integrity of its records, and the general effectiveness of its operations.*[2] The objective of internal auditing is to assist members of the organization in the effective discharge of their responsibilities (Price Waterhouse, 1993). To this end, internal auditing furnishes them with analyses, appraisals, recommendations, counsel, and information concerning activities under review.

The general objectives of internal auditing are:

1. Determining that the overall system of internal control and the specific controls in each activity under audit are adequate, effective, and functioning.
2. Insuring that institutional policies and procedures, state and federal laws, contractual obligations, and good business practices are followed.
3. Verifying the existence of assets shown on the books of accounts and ensuring maintenance of proper safeguards for their protection.
4. Determining the reliability and adequacy of the accounting and reporting systems and procedures.

Reporting Relationship

At this university, the office of internal audit is directly responsible to the campus president. The office is headed by the director of internal audit, who reports to the president through the deputy to the president, who is designated the campus internal control officer. This reporting relationship ensures the office's independence, promotes comprehensive audit coverage, and assures adequate consideration of audit recommendations.

Official reports prepared by internal auditors are issued to the campus president and to the vice president responsible for the audited area.

Authority and Responsibility

The office of internal audit has unlimited access to all facilities, personnel, and records maintained, either electronically or manually, by all units of the university center and its affiliated organizations, with stringent accountabilities of safekeeping and confidentiality. While approval is not required, notice normally is given to the affected vice president before such access, except in cases where the nature and sensitivity of the inquiry dictate otherwise.

Independence

Internal audit is a staff function and is independent of the areas audited. It does not participate in the direct operation of any activity other than internal auditing at this campus. The independence and objectivity of the internal auditing function must be maintained at all times.

Scope of Audits

Internal audits or reviews are not limited in scope by campus management. Audit responsibilities extend to all campus-managed entities, all areas of operations, and include all systems (manual and electronic, in use or under development) that support the activities at this campus.

Standards

In the performance of its responsibilities, the office of internal audit adheres to the Standards for the Professional Practice of Internal Auditing published by the Institute of Internal Auditors, Inc.

Summary

Internal audit can be more than an internal accounting staff performing routine audits. Auditors do more than keep managers on their toes and deal with problem situations, such as possible security breaks or financial improprieties. Internal auditors can be organizational consultants able to recognize financial, organizational, methodological, and personnel interfaces that influence a unit's effectiveness and efficiency. This chapter says more about the internal audit function later in a proposal for an organizational effectiveness unit. Next, consider a related but more general program and function called "performance management." This refers to helping departments achieve performance excellence through management reports, administrative reviews, and facilitation of interdepartmental agreements.

PERFORMANCE MANAGEMENT PROGRAM

The performance management program is designed to coordinate and integrate ongoing management initiatives into a cohesive program for enhancement of management performance and accountability.[3] The program also incorporates risk assessment, education and training, and reporting needs for university control.

Management Reporting

Management reporting is an ongoing performance management initiative coordinated by the performance management office to identify, catalogue, analyze, evaluate, and enhance management information and reporting at the university. The current focus of this project is on management reports reaching the highest levels of the university. This initiative also includes development and preparation of quarterly key indicator reports for university management and coordination of the annual update of the department profiles (with information about the mission, structure, number and types of people, and departmental outputs—such as inquiries processed, number of students admitted, campus tours conducted, performances, checks cut, etc.—as appropriate to the function).

Administrative Reviews

The administrative review process (described later in this chapter) provides regular, objective reviews and evaluations of campus administrative/service units.

Under the direction of the president and the performance management advisory committee, the performance management director coordinates and serves in a staff role in the administrative review process.

Training and Development

There is a continuing program to provide training, as well as professional and personal development opportunities, to university employees. An annual "Summer Is Training" program of scheduled activities is coordinated through this program (see Chapter 9). The performance management office provides staff support, using graduate business school students serving management internships.

Management Development

This initiative uses management development tools to build a more cohesive management structure through programs such as team-building retreats and upward feedback surveys (see Chapter 9 for a description of training programs and Chapter 10 for review of employee survey feedback methods).

Accountability Mechanisms

Service agreements (memoranda of understanding): The MOU process is a program designed to rationalize budgeting and promote accountability for campus administrative/support services. This program first identifies current services and related costs. Then management engineering studies are conducted to identify opportunities for efficiency enhancement and cost reduction. Next, the costs and benefits of alternative approaches to the provision of these services are considered. Ultimately, service agreements are written to indicate the type and amount of services to be provided by one department to another. The director of performance management serves as staff to the campus MOU committee, chaired by the associate vice president of finance. The committee oversees and facilitates the MOU process, ensuring that service and client departments come together and reach reasonable and timely agreements. Service contracts are revised and renewed annually. (This process is described in more detail later in this chapter and in Chapter 7.)

Planning and Budget Processes

The director of performance management assists the university planning coordinator to produce several key documents annually. The elements of the planning and budgeting processes have been described in Chapters 4 and 5. They include the following:

Mission and vision statements: Statements of the university's mission and the president's vision for the institution. These are prepared by the president and communicated to the campus community. They are reviewed annually and revised as deemed necessary by the president.

Goals and objectives: A set of 11 university-wide goals and specific objectives developed by the president, provost, and vice presidents in consultation with appropriate university bodies and communicated widely. It is revised annually.

Academic plan: A one-year plan for the development of the university's academic enterprise.

University initiatives: A set of key initiatives, linked to the goals and objectives, that are identified and developed by the president, provost, and vice president as requiring university-wide attention. They are revised as needed throughout the year.

Three-year plan: A key management document that summarizes university financial and operational plans for the upcoming three years. The three-year plan includes a three-year financial plan and a statement of university directions and initiatives.

Three-year financial plan: A numerical representation of the projected provostial and vice presidential all-funds budget allocations for the upcoming three-year period. This is revised twice a year by the university's budget office to reflect budget allocation decisions made during Phase 1 and Phase 2 of the university budget process. (See the description of the financial planning process in Chapter 5.)

Directions and initiatives: A narrative description of provostial and vice presidential plans for the upcoming three-year period. Revised annually.

Project listing: A tracking and feedback mechanism for the provostial and vice presidential projects identified in the three-year plan.

Annual university operating budget: A comprehensive annual university budget, in book form, summarizing the account-level allocations, from all funding sources, to each unit in the university. This is produced by the office of finance and management.

Department profiles: A reporting mechanism designed to provide a brief snapshot of academic and administrative department activities (historical and planned). These documents provide a synopsis of the resources (financial, personnel, space) allocated to each department along with measures of departmental accomplishments (services provided) within those resources. They are revised annually.

Summary

The performance management function coordinates activities that prompt increased department effectiveness. The function helps to produce management reports that are key indicators of university effectiveness and that serve as feedback to officers to track achievements. In large part, this requires simply collating, refining, and integrating regular reports produced elsewhere. Other performance management functions—not necessarily under the direction of the performance management department—support management development, employee training, and the negotiation of service agreements between departments. A function coordinated by the director of performance management is the administrative review process. This is described next.

ADMINISTRATIVE REVIEW PROCESS

The administrative review program described here is a key component in the general university strategy to foster excellence in management.[4] The philosophy motivating the administrative review process is one of using self-study and input from external constituencies to generate new ideas for increased efficiency and management effectiveness for the unit under review. While not intended to replace continuous self-examination involving customers of units and training/development programs, this review process encourages a continuous evaluation of customer satisfaction, quality orientation, and professional development within administrative units. The university's goal is to review each administrative/service unit every five years. In general these reviews should answer the following questions:

1. What are the missions of the unit?
2. What are the unit's goals for the next three–five years?
3. How do these goals fit into the overall strategic plan for the unit's area; for the entire university?
4. What is the unit's record of accomplishments against its objectives?

The *objectives* of these reviews are to:

1. Determine objectively if a unit is operating efficiently and is providing essential services to the university.
2. Assess leadership effectiveness.
3. Provide a formal way for users of a unit's services to have input into the objectives and operation of the unit.
4. Provide a constructive mechanism by which all members of the unit can participate in determining its objectives and operation.

Important principles of the review process are that it should be a constructive process that produces positive suggestions and a relatively simple process, lest it become too time-consuming to continue.

Review Process

I. Coordinator

The administrative review process is administered by the director of performance management, a position that reports to the deputy to the president. The duties of review coordinator occupy about a fourth of the director's time. The coordinator works with and makes reports to the performance management advisory committee, a steering committee convened by the president and representing various administrative areas of the campus community. Two positions on the performance management advisory committee are filled by members of the administrative review committee of the university senate.

II. Definition and Determination of Units for Review

The president, provost, and vice presidents prepare a priority list and make a preliminary determination of the type of review required for each unit. The administrative review committee of the university senate has a consultative role in the process of determining the units to be reviewed. The coordinator solicits this committee's input during semiannual meetings devoted to the topic of the administrative review process. On the basis of this input, the coordinator and the performance management advisory committee develops an annual administrative review schedule. The precise charge for a particular review committee is prepared by the coordinator and takes into account the issues raised in a self-study document prepared by the unit prior to the review.

III. Self-Study Process

Each unit director works with the program coordinator and all professional staff in the unit to prepare a self-study. Although the framework should be flexible enough to adapt to each unit, the self-study should address the following questions:

1. What are the objectives of the unit? What changes in these objectives would the unit like to make?

2. What internal and external criteria or benchmarks are used to determine if the objectives are being met?

3. How do these benchmarks compare to comparable units in other institutions (university hospitals, corporations, universities)?

4. Who are the major users of the unit's services?

5. What initiatives or programs does the unit support (a) to ensure customer satisfaction and quality orientation in providing services? (b) to promote effective team building/teamwork? and (c) enhance professionalism and training for the administrative staff?

6. How much money and what funding sources support the unit?

7. What kinds of staff does the unit have? List the number of each type of position (e.g. secretarial grade, staff grade).

8. Who are the members of the senior staff of the unit?

9. In what university-wide processes does the unit play a part? What are the key interface points with other campus departments? How well are these interfaces functioning?

10. What past accomplishments and efforts have there been to enhance the operation of the unit and its linkages with other units and processes?

11. What support does the unit require from the university to make additional improvements?

12. What focus/charge does the unit propose for the review committee?

Department Productivity Inventory. A survey approach to aid self-study is an effectiveness rating form to be completed by the department managers. Kaiser (1992) suggested the components for such a form in facilities management. For each item in the survey, the department manager is asked to indicate the extent to which it is in use (on a 0 to 3 scale) and implemented (again on a 0 to 3 scale). Categories and items rated include (1) *organization* (policies/rules, functions, staffing, supervision), (2) *workload identification* (facilities inventory, facilities condition inspection, work request procedure, equipment inventory, preventive maintenance, service work, routine recurring work, and work requirements documentation), (3) *work planning* (priority criteria, work approvals, work-order preparation, budget requirements, backlogged deferred maintenance and repair, budget execution plan, and backlogged funded work), (4) *work accomplishments* (shop scheduling and planning procedure, craft and material availability, training program, shop spaces, tools and equipment, storeroom operation, transportation, shop supervision, and use of contracts), and (5) *appraisal* (management information systems, performance measurement, productivity measurement, variance reviews, facility history records, equipment history records, and trend data). Kaiser (1992) recommends that the form be revised to reflect the systems and language used by the institution. The results become part of the self-study document.

The self-study document is submitted to the appropriate vice president in charge of the unit for review and comment. After his or her approval, it is sent to the coordinator, at least four weeks before the scheduled review. Working with the performance management advisory committee, the coordinator prepares a charge for the review committee that addresses the issues raised by the unit's self-study process.

IV. The Review

The coordinator, in consultation with the appropriate vice president and unit director, generates a list of potential reviewers. Depending on the unit and the depth of the review, the list could include users of the unit's services, staff from related units, staff from specialized units such as hospital management, and others from within the university. On certain occasions, an in-depth review may be called for, involving reviewers who would be brought from outside the university (from industry or from peer institutions) to supplement a smaller internal review team. In most cases, external reviews are reserved for major responsibility centers and/or top-level management areas.

The review team of five–six people is selected from the list by the president after discussions with the vice president. If the review team consists of both external and internal reviewers, external reviewers comprise approximately half (two–three members) of the team. For each review, a member of the performance management advisory committee serves as liaison and advisor to the review team. The liaison does not have a reporting relationship within the same vice presidential area as the unit under review. The coordinator provides staff support to the review team.

While the nature of the review is open enough to reflect the differences across administrative units, several required elements are to be included in the review:

1. The review team reads the self-study and designs their review to incorporate/address issues raised in the self-study.
2. The review team visits the unit and talks with the staff. Assessment of leadership/management effectiveness is one of the key goals of this aspect of the review process.
3. The review team meets with a focus group of users of the service to verify and expand on material provided in the self-study. Customer satisfaction and quality orientation are important issues for the review team.

Additional assessment and documentation tools that may be used during the review process include, but are not limited to, flowcharts, observation, examination of processes and levels of automation, surveys, review of relevant documents, and interviews/benchmarking with similar departments in other organizations. The level of detail required will generally be a function of the type of review and the unit being reviewed.

4. The review team maintains frequent communication with the unit manager throughout the review to inform the manager of their progress and conclusions/recommendations as they develop.
5. The review team briefs the vice president on the results of the review as the review phase of the process is completed.

At the end of the review phase, the review team gives an oral report to the president, the relevant vice president, and the review process coordinator. The review team prepares a written report that is sent to the president. The latter gives a copy to the vice president, the manager of the reviewed unit, and the process coordinator.

The vice president, after discussions with the unit, prepares a response for the president that should address any recommended changes and should provide a timetable for their implementation, if appropriate. The vice president's response is also sent to the coordinator. The coordinator, working with the performance management advisory committee, maintains contact with the reviewed unit and ensures that in one year's time a progress report is submitted to the president and the coordinator on the implementation of the recommendations.

The review and the response (and, the following year, the progress report) are to be forwarded to the president's university priorities committee and the administrative review committee of the university senate.

Excerpts from a Review

The following is an excerpt from the review team report (done early in 1994) on the administrative review of a student services office. The members of the internal review team were the university controller, the vice provost for undergraduate studies, a professor from the English department, the assistant dean for enrollment management, and the director of performance management (who coordinated the review process). During the two-day review, the internal review team met with the director and assistant director and the professional and clerical employees of the area and worked with an outside reviewer who was dean of student services at another university. The outside reviewer was selected by the associate vice president responsible for the area. The consultant submitted a separate report (not provided here). This report is a chance for the review team to comment on the recommendations in the consultant's report and provide an organizational perspective to them.

A. Review Team Response to Consultant's Recommendations

1. *Student information system*: The review team agrees that the student services office should be an active participant in the improvement and/or development of the student information system. Responsibility for initiating and supporting this broad-based development project lies with senior campus management.

2. *Communications links to students*: The review team agrees that the university should study the communications links to its students and believes that the director should take an active role in this process, but also feels that communications with students cross organizational lines and could be improved through increased coordination among offices.

3. *Office automation*: The review team agrees that the director should develop a plan to further automate the office to improve efficiency and customer service.

Other recommendations dealt with professional development, office management, software implementation, and evening student services.

B. Review Team Recommendations

1. The director should take a more active role in the management and operations of the office. This includes, but is not limited to, active participation in: major systems projects that directly affect the office and its interfaces with students, university initiatives that are related to the officer's role, day-to-day management of office activities, planning and executing professional development initiatives, and attending staff meetings.

2. The director should work closely with his staff to provide meaningful opportunities for professional development and contact with colleagues in the field. The director should work with the associate vice president to secure financing (and other necessary support) for the resulting staff development plan. Existing university resources (e.g., the employee training and development office in the human resources department) should be consulted where necessary for technical support.

3. The director should work with the associate vice president to prepare a development plan to help support his role as manager of a vital, technology-sensitive university function.

C. Recommendations to the Associate Vice President

1. The associate VP should continue to encourage the director to become more active in the management and operations of the office and to develop skills that enable him to do so. The associate VP should work with the director to prepare and pursue a professional development plan that builds upon areas of strength, while addressing areas requiring improvement.

D. Recommendations and Comments to the Vice President

1. The vice president should continue to pursue the financial support necessary to implement the specialized software needed to improve efficiency in the office.

E. Recommendations and Comments to Senior Campus Management

1. The university should develop a coordinated plan to improve its student information systems. The review team believes that improvement/replacement of the student information system is an essential step to improve customer service (and the university's competitiveness with peer institutions) and enhance the management information available to support university operations, planning, budgeting, and assessment. (During the review, the discussion of information systems was necessarily broad in scope and centered around the lack of sophistication and poor integration of the key university systems that support student services—registrar, admissions, financial aid, student accounting and bursar).

2. The university should study and improve its communications links with students. The review team recommends that the president charge a task force (an existing group, if possible) to review and make recommendations to improve the quality and efficiency of the university's communications with students. This includes improving the informational content of the main vehicle for communicating the registration process to students (the class schedule), improving the coordination of informational mailings to students across student service areas (e.g., admissions, bursar, financial aid, registrar, student accounts, the school of continuing education, the graduate school, and the undergraduate school), and planning for new modes of communicating vital information to students (e.g., enhanced uses of the voice and other technologies).

The review team believes that the results of these efforts should present the students with a more organized, user-friendly impression of the university, improve service quality, and allow for improved efficiencies in the use of postage, paper, and personnel, providing some budget relief to the affected areas.

3. The university should continue to develop a management culture that is responsive to the need to invest in its employees. This is essential if the university is to make its written policy on employee training and development generally recognized management practice.

Summary

The concept of departmental reviews is traditional for academic departments. Usually they occur every five years, and they often tie in to the accreditation processes run by academic/professional associations. So the idea is certainly not foreign to the university setting. The concept of an administrative review extends the academic review process to administrative departments. Of course, administrative departments need to be dynamic in responding to changing institutional needs and advancing administrative technologies. They can't stand still waiting for a once-in-five-year review. Academic departments don't stand still either. Administrative reviews provide an opportunity for self-reflection and feedback from outside observers. While internal audits have the flavor of experts combing through material and examining procedures and decisions, administrative reviews are more participatory processes. The process engages departmental representatives, or perhaps all employees in the department, along with users of the department's products and services and, if relevant, one or more outside experts. Recommendations focus on possible changes in the department for improved efficiency. And recommendations may extend to other departments that should provide more support and resources for the target department. As such, the administrative review recognizes interdepartmental interfaces and may improve overall coordination and work processes.

Internal audit, performance management, and management engineering studies do not occur in isolation. While each has a somewhat different purpose, they all promote managing for excellence. The last section in this chapter is a proposal for integrating the functions to form an organization effectiveness unit. The recommendation resulted from a study of the work process and outputs of each of the units. The goal is not to merge the functions but rather take advantage of their unique contributions while maximizing the use of these resources.

INTEGRATION OF FUNCTIONS: TOWARD AN ORGANIZATION EFFECTIVENESS UNIT

This project was undertaken in response to the recognition that several current administrative processes and programs share the objective of improving quality and efficiency.[5] An examination of how resources are deployed among these activities revealed interrelationships and some overlap. A reconceptualization is proposed that would leverage the sources currently devoted to performance improvement so as to have substantially increased impact. Synergy is possible through creation of an *organizational effectiveness program* (OEP) that would rationally unify performance improvement activities. Because of this synergy, it is anticipated that the program can be implemented without increased resources. However, it is important to note that many of the specific recommendations contained in this proposal are free-standing in that they may be implemented with or without implementing other recommendations of the full OEP concept.

Project Objectives

Taken as a whole, this proposal could form the basis for a *quality initiative* for the university. The objectives of the proposed organizational effectiveness program are in support of the university's academic, research, and health care missions, and the specific goals and initiatives are outlined in the latest three-year plan. These objectives are: enhance quality of operations, increase efficiency and reduce cost of operations, increase orientation toward customer service, improve interdepartmental communication and cooperation, inform the university's strategic planning process, inform the development of objectives by individual departments, and, as a state institution, respond to the state governmental accountability, audit, and internal control policies and laws.

Information Sources

The present proposal is the result of research conducted during the spring semester. A wide range of administrators were interviewed, including administrative vice presidents, their direct reports, and mid-level managers. Key players in each of the programs related to performance improvement were interviewed, as were managers in units that have used the services related to performance improvement. Relevant documentation was examined for each program or activity.

Organizational Effectiveness Program

The creation of an organizational effectiveness program is proposed, which will report to the president. The centerpiece of OEP will be a sequence of four management consulting functions that build on an extended and refined version of the current administrative review process:

1. Selection of departments, programs, or processes for administrative review.
2. Review and diagnosis of organizational performance, process, and structure.
3. Referral and consulting services for client departments.
4. Continuing implementation support and follow-up review.

Client Support Provided by OEP

The current administrative review process is excellent, as far as it goes. Its major limitation is that it is not possible to provide departments with substantial ongoing support as they attempt to implement the recommendations produced by the review process. In contrast, OEP is conceived as a broad-based management consulting process that will move seamlessly between the various phases of diagnosis, prescription, management education, and implementation support.

OEP will provide client support from one of four generic sources: expertise within OEP, expertise elsewhere on campus, expertise external to the university, and referral of issues to top management that cannot be handled in other ways. OEP will have the resources internally to provide the support needed by most administrative clients. Toward this end, OEP will consolidate several functions and responsibilities related to organizational strategy, efficiency, quality, and cooperation. OEP will also include new capabilities not widely available to client departments at present. It is proposed that several existing functions be refined or expanded and moved into OEP as described below.

Major Functions Consolidated Within OEP

In the referral, consulting, and implementation support phases of the process, OEP will have six major functions at its disposal, consolidated within OEP: performance management, university planning, coordination of service agreements (memoranda of understanding), management engineering, management education, and internal audit.

Performance management and internal audit currently report to the deputy to the president. The director of performance management is responsible for the administrative review process, serving as staff to the MOU committee (see Chapter 7), and a number of other activities. Planning is currently conducted by the planning staff under the university's planning coordinator, who reports to the president. The campus does not currently have management engineering services. These services are purchased from the university hospital's department of management engineering. Management education is currently done on a limited basis by the department of human resources and, occasionally, by external consultants hired by departments. The following suggests some proposed changes for these functions to increase their effectiveness and maximize synergy among the various functions.

1. Refinement of the Administrative Review Process

The process can be refined in several ways.

(a) *Self-study*. Early implementations of the administrative review process have shown that the self-study exercise has been only partially effective. In conducting self-studies, managers have tended to omit a crucial element: the comparison of current performance with performance goals, targets, or standards, and critical analysis of any disparities and their causes. The administrative review process should be modified to include training for managers in how to conduct a self-study. Additionally, managers need to understand at the outset of the process that this critical reflection is not optional. Further, the process should require managers to respond explicitly to disparities between the review team's report and the self-study results.

(b) *Value of external consultants*. A clear consensus emerged among those interviewed (including managers who participated in initial implementations of the administrative review process) concerning the usefulness of including at least one reviewer external to the university. It was felt that the review process benefits greatly from (1) reviewers with specific expertise in the substantive functions of the department being reviewed, and (2) reviewers without strong preconceptions concerning the university or the target department. Therefore, it appears that external consultants are generally worth the extra cost and should normally be used in administrative reviews.

(c) *Logistics of site visits.* Most of the information for an administrative review is collected during an approximately two-day site visit by a team that includes administrative reviewers (i.e., OEP staff), other selected individuals from within the university, and one or more external consultants. The following three recommendations are aimed at enhancing the information-gathering effectiveness of the site visit.

First, team members must be present for the entire visit. Such a commitment must be elicited up-front from each person, before he or she is added to the team.

Second, the agenda for the site visit should be determined in three ways: (1) the target department should have input, (2) the review team should have input prior to the site visit, and (3) allowance should be made for the review team to dynamically modify the second day's agenda based on learning from the first day. Determining the agenda in this way has several advantages, including reducing the need for costly or poorly attended follow-up visits.

Third, review team members should be instructed not to share their evaluative or prescriptive conclusions with each other until after the site visit. Each team member should have the opportunity to form his or her independent, individual judgment before being subjected to the possible influence of other team members' strongly held views. Following the site visit, use of a nominal group technique is recommended in which each team member independently prepares a brief outline of his or her conclusions and recommendations. These outlines can then serve as starting points for team discussion and a subsequent team report. This approach significantly reduces the likelihood of illusory consensus or "group think" and ensures that all review team members will be heard.

2. University Planning Process

Strategic planning has been conceived as a participative process that integrates strategic priorities established by the president with plans developed by the administrators and managers. Because of its close contact with specific program plans, the planning staff is obviously well positioned to participate in recommending departments for administrative review and management consultation. However, this will not be the planning staff's only role in OEP. The administrative review process may reveal disparities between the existing program plan and the current focus of a department's activities. The planning staff should collaborate with the administrative review team in identifying and making recommendations concerning such disparities. The department's program plan may need to be revised and the implications, if any, for broader strategic priorities assessed. Alternatively, such disparities may signal a need to refocus or reprioritize a department's activities. In this case, the planning staff should work with the department to ensure that these changes are consistent with the university's strategic priorities.

3. Serving as Staff for the MOU Process (MOU/Service Agreements)

The MOU process has been successful in creating accounting-based solutions for internal transfer pricing problems. Accounting-based agreements are practical transactions in which costs and deliverables are easily quantified and measured. Unfortunately, accounting-based solutions become cumbersome and impractical for many internal transactions of a more qualitative nature. Nonetheless, an important insight has emerged from attempts to implement the MOU process. Perhaps the greatest benefit of the process has been that it results in more clear and open communication among parties who may have had difficulty reaching agreements in the past.

Building upon this realization, an expanded MOU process is proposed around the concept of "getting to yes." The process will be applied to a much wider range of interdepartmental transactions, including transactions that do not permit straightforward accounting solutions. The MOU process will serve to facilitate and mediate interdepartmental negotiation.

Until now, the MOU process has focused explicitly on only the last principle. In order to expand the applicability and increase the effectiveness of the MOU process, MOU facilitators will receive training in the application of the full set of principles, plus supplementary techniques for creating win-win solutions. Individuals thus trained will be well prepared to contribute to improving interdepartmental communication and cooperation, even where purely qualitative issues are at stake.

4. Management Engineering

Currently, the need for engineering efficiency and operations management studies far exceeds the capacity of the department of management engineering. One reason for this high demand is that the management engineers borrowed from the hospital have had several highly visible successes in departments on campus. Both the university hospital and the academic side of the campus want and need this kind of management support in many areas. The campus should form its own management engineering team. The administrative review process, along with other OEP functions, will help to prioritize management engineering projects in a manner consistent with the university's goals and objectives.

5. Management Education

In addition to serving specific departments and programs, OEP will have the capability to offer training in skills critical to management effectiveness. For example, at the request of senior management, training might be provided to managers and other key staff members in skill areas such as quality improvement, customer service, participative management, team building, and negotiation and conflict resolution. Often the need for management education may be revealed by an administrative review. Or initial stages of an MOU process may suggest a need for management training in negotiation and conflict resolution, or an engineering study may suggest a need for training in quality improvement or customer service. Training of this type may be appropriate for managers in administrative, academic, and support services departments.

6. Internal Audit

A striking consensus emerged among those interviewed concerning the need for a broader and more visible role for the internal audit staff. The internal audit office should be refocused in three ways:

First, instead of conducting a small number of exhaustive reviews, the office should conduct a large number of limited audits. The rationale for this recommendation is that extremely detailed audits extend beyond the point of diminishing returns. In contrast, the outcomes of limited audits will be more informative relative to their cost. The information acquired in limited audits can then be used to assess the need for comprehensive audits of certain units or processes. However, comprehensive audits will be considerably rarer than is the current practice, and when comprehensive audits are warranted, they will typically be less detailed than is the current practice. This sort of refocusing of the internal audit function has been undertaken by a number of major universities (e.g., MIT) in the interest of increasing the overall impact of the function while maintaining the cost at or near current levels.

Second, when appropriate, the internal audit office should focus on processes that may cross departmental boundaries, rather than on reviewing individual departments in isolation. A similar suggestion may apply to OEP as a whole.

Third, auditors' qualifications should be modified. Synergy can be created by filling these positions with auditors who are sensitive to the dual objectives of quality/efficiency and internal control. These objectives need not be at odds.

The independence of the internal audit function should be maintained. Although internal auditors will work closely with others in OEP in order to identify vulnerabilities, the reporting relationship of internal audit will be with the president (or deputy to the president) rather than with the director (or "process manager") of OEP. Independence of the internal audit function is required by the Institute of Internal Auditors Standards for the Professional Practice of Internal Auditing.

Brokering Services

OEP will also serve a brokerage function in order to ensure that services elsewhere within the university are available to client departments. Such services might include, for example, various services provided by the department of human resources; management systems consultation; and research conducted by the department of institutional studies on enrollment, personnel, and facilities data.

Organizational Structure

There are two quite different options for structuring OEP. One option is to structure it as a new department within the presidential area. This approach would signal the importance and permanence of the university's commitment to continuous improvement. The other option is to define an organizational effectiveness process that would tie together functions from disparate offices and departments. A process manager would coordinate the various functions and report to the president (or deputy to the president). This approach has the potential to break down traditional bureaucratic barriers, as opposed to creating a more top-heavy organizational structure.

Fee-for-Service Consultation

Any department may elect to use OEP on a fee-for-service basis. For example, departments requiring management engineering studies may contract directly with OEP for this service. In this case, the client department bears the full cost of the service.

Client Perceptions

Four factors related to client perceptions and relations are important to the success of a performance improvement program. First, client departments and their managers must perceive the process more as an opportunity than as a threat. The current administrative review process has been designed and implemented well in this regard. Second, departments undergoing administrative review must perceive a substantial level of accountability for their performance as assessed by the review process. Thus, a delicate balance must be maintained between creating positive perceptions of the process and insisting upon accountability. Third, there must be a clear incentive for departments to participate in the process and implement the resulting recommendations for performance improvement. The proposed design provides a substantially greater incentive for client departments by introducing consulting services. The implementation agreement reinforces the incentive by making the consulting services conditional on positive action by the client department. Fourth, the program must have early and highly visible successes in order to foster positive perceptions. Therefore, initial reviews and interventions should be selected carefully for maximum impact.

Departmental Versus Process-Based Reviews

As a base of institutional experience with performance review and consultation develops, a shift toward reviewing processes rather than departments may be desirable. Processes might include data systems, enrollment processes, or "the student experience." These processes are sometimes difficult to study, because they are not defined by organization charts. However, process reviews might reveal discontinuities, redundancies, or coordination problems between departments that would not be identified by reviewing each department separately.

Contracting with OEP

The diagnosis phase of the management consulting process will be essentially the current administrative review process, but the prescription and implementation phases will be much more extensive. Typically, the diagnosis phase will be followed by a negotiated implementation agreement between the department under review, the relevant vice president, and OEP. The implementation agreement will specify the contribution that each will make toward addressing the problems and opportunities identified in the review. Thus, in order to receive consulting support from OEP, the client department must be willing to make a firm commitment to address issues that it is capable of addressing.

CONCLUSION

This chapter outlined internal audit and performance management functions, described an administrative review process, and proposed a mechanism for integrating these functions to promote managing for excellence. These functions are less control mechanisms than they are sources of support for organizational analysis, self-reflection, and interdepartmental cooperation and smoother, more effective operations. Internal audit, performance management, and management engineering studies can work together to take advantage of their synergies while maintaining their unique contributions.

These functions are agents for organizational change. The directions for change are based on analyses of information about existing work processes and outputs. The next chapter shows how quality measurements coordinated by the performance management department are used to examine organizational effectiveness, make comparisons with similar operations at other institutions, and suggest areas for improvement.

NOTES

1. The section entitled "Managing for Excellence" was written by Douglas Panico.
2. The section entitled "Internal Audit Charter" was written by Carl J. Singler, Jr.
3. The section entitled "Performance Management Program" was written by Douglas Panico.
4. The section entitled "Administrative Review Process" was written by Douglas Panico.
5. The section entitled "Integration of Functions: Toward an Organization Effectiveness Unit" was written by Jeff T. Casey.

7

Assessing Service Quality

The previous chapter described performance management functions for improving departmental performance. Keys to performance excellence are information and feedback. Information about work effectiveness can indicate the cost of the services provided by one department to another and the appropriate transfer pricing strategy. This chapter is a compendium of service quality measurement techniques and applications. The chapter begins by outlining the process for establishing interdepartmental service agreements—with management engineering as a basis for determining the appropriate fee for a given level and amount of service during the course of the year. In addition to service agreements, a method of cross-charging is to set per-unit prices requiring client departments to purchase products and services on an item-by-item basis. This leads to questions about whether charge-back systems work. So we review the progress of a department that switched from internal subsidization and centrally controlled costs to self-sufficiency through charge-backs. The next section outlines key indicators for evaluating university effectiveness and collecting "benchmark" data to compare input, process, and outcome measures with similar departments in other organizations. Then the chapter describes ways to obtain information from users of university services. Quality means satisfying customers, and having information about customer perceptions can be useful feedback for increasing the value of internal products and services.

FORMULATING A POLICY ON SERVICE AGREEMENTS

This section presents the purpose and methods for establishing internal service agreements.[1] The process starts with a considerable effort to establish a methodology for defining the cost for services provided by various administrative departments (e.g., human resources and financial operations, graphics, mail, facilities operations) to other campus entities with independent income streams (e.g., university hospital, campus businesses run by the auxiliary services corporation, residence hall operations). In particular, the goals were to

1. Establish and document buyer-seller relationships between client and service departments within the university.
2. Promote accountability for provision of services.
3. Determine objective costs of contracted services and budget accordingly.
4. Develop optimal methods for payment of services.
5. Define and establish a businesslike, arms-length relationship characteristic of a purchaser-vendor between providers and clients.

The resulting memoranda of understanding (MOU) process is an important element of the university-wide effort to improve performance, to enhance accountability and efficiency, and to foster a more service- and quality-oriented (provider/client) relationship in the provision of support services. Memoranda of understanding describe the relationships between "service" departments and their "clients." These documents identify services, service levels, quality expectations, and accountability measures, and they provide a mechanism for achieving a "meeting of the minds" between the parties concerning their service relationship.

Memoranda of understanding describe the needs of offices providing and receiving the services, procedures for interaction between parties to the agreement, and methodologies and statistics that support cost development and reimbursement to the area providing the service. The standing committee on MOU is a staff group consisting of representatives from various campus constituencies. The committee is charged with the oversight, expansion, and coordination of the university's MOU process. This committee is essential to the continued development of the MOU process and also plays an important role in the university's budgeting process. Full cooperation from all involved parties is necessary for the committee to fulfill its charge.

The following guidelines ensure an objective, rational, and coordinated approach to MOU development:

1. The cost of providing services to each funding source are to be based on an all-funds analysis (state support, tuition, contributions, grants, and contracts; indirect research cost reimbursement from granting agencies, etc.) carried out by service department personnel and/or appropriate staff groups. Such analyses are subject to review by the committee for consistency and completeness.

2. The all-funds analyses of service departments assume a constant overall level of funding for each service unit until comprehensive, objective engineering and cost analysis quantifies, documents, and obtains agreement from area management that savings can be accomplished through redesign of work processes and/or increased automation. The committee provides recommendations on service departments that might benefit from detailed engineering/cost analyses.

3. Proposed MOU documents are to be negotiated between provider and client departments with assistance (where requested) from appropriate staff. The costs identified in the related cost/engineering study or in the provider department's all-funds analysis (where no cost/engineering study has been completed) will be used as the basis for negotiating the reimbursement amount. The extent to which a particular funding source provides resources through an MOU to support the cost of services provided may need to be resolved as a policy question addressed to the president. A policy resolution procedure is recommended.

4. The committee ensures the consistency of MOU documents with regard to cost and terms and conditions. To accomplish this, the group reviews and, where necessary, requests revisions to all MOU documents prior to execution by the parties and to insure reviews of existing MOU annually to determine whether changes are required.

5. The committee develops proposed MOU budget allocations, working closely with the campus budget office and representatives from service and client departments. The committee provides allocation proposals in relation to the university's budget process, consistent with the dates indicated on the budget calendar (see Chapter 4).

6. The committee identifies and brings to the president's attention policy and/or transition issues that arise in the process of developing MOU. The president provides policy guidance to the group after consultation with appropriate members of the senior management team. The committee incorporates these decisions into future MOU.

Membership

It is recommended that the Standing Committee on MOU be chaired by a senior representative from the finance and management area such as an assistant vice president, controller, or budget director. More than one representative from finance is preferable. Other committee members should represent the major purchasers of services (research foundation, hospital, residence halls, etc.) as well as the larger service providers. Other useful participants would be from performance management and/or management engineering offices.

Ongoing Activity

The committee maintains an ongoing effort to refine and improve the consistency of the costing methodologies used in the MOU process, strengthen the accountability/performance aspects of the process, and conduct process reviews to improve administrative efficiency and make cost/efficiency comparisons to external entities.

Major Challenges

The overriding challenge faced by the committee is to make the MOU process go beyond its initial success in documenting an agreement between parties and as a budgetary tool, by incorporating quality and performance goals into the university's day-to-day operations, making them part of "the way university does business." In order to allow the committee to address this goal, significant time and effort must be expended in putting into place the procedural elements that support the process and bring together the separate client and service units.

Other challenges are to:

1. Continually educate committee members and managers new to the MOU process.

2. Expand the MOU analyses to all major campus revenue sources. This can be a difficult task, as external constraints and campus policies may impede progress toward fully implemented customer/services agreements. For example, should the research enterprise at a major public university pay the full cost of administrative services or is some portion of that cost considered an institutional contribution to research?

3. Develop appropriate linkages between the MOU process and the university budget process. The timing of the outcomes of the committee's work must meld appropriately into the campus budget development process.

4. Integrate performance and accountability mechanisms into the process and ensure that they are meaningful to all involved parties. The MOU documents are intended to identify performance expectations as well as costs to be reimbursed. Performance standards and other accountability mechanisms are necessary to adequately evaluate service.

5. Develop an improved method of assuring annual reviews and updates of existing MOUs. Midyear assessments of cost analysis and service volumes are required in many areas.

6. Develop the role of the MOU committee as a consultative, problem-solving group to ensure the continued development of the MOU process.

The following is an example of an MOU between a service (the office of university affairs providing media, fund-raising, government relations, and conference/special events planning) and a client organization (the university hospital). Keep in mind that the MOU could be between any service provider and an incoming generating unit, such as the center for performing arts, a campus museum, or the business school's executive management center.

Memorandum of Understanding Between University Hospital and University Affairs

A. General Information

1. Description of Services to Be Provided

Enhance the visibility and reputation of the university and university hospital, supporting marketing initiatives and managing the university's internal communications with faculty, staff and students. [Specific internal publications and data bases are listed.]

Responsible for maintaining an active relationship with federal, state, and local elected officials, as well as with local civic, business, and community organizations. Governmental relations will provide assistance to the campus community and university hospital, when communication with elected officials at all levels of government is required and coordinate events involving elected and local officials.

With overall responsibility for fund-raising activities on campus, the development office oversees fund-raising conducted at the university hospital. It provides senior management, prospect research, and cultivation; solicitation, gift administration, and stewardship. Integrate hospital funding opportunities into capital campaign plan and utilize appropriate resources to secure private funding. Included are: corporate and foundation solicitation; planned giving presentations and illustrations; proposal preparation for funding opportunities; assistance from capital campaign consultants; and direct mail expertise.

Provide both service and resources required to produce academic and non-academic conferences, seminars, institutes and events, and, at the same time, organize events that showcase the university to both internal and external constituencies. The office is the management liaison with revenue-producing programs that result in the provision of funding to other university units and student programs.

Provide planning and management services for organizations and associations with university or hospital sponsorship and endorsement, and will assist units within the university and hospital in the development and facilities of educational conferences.

2. Parties to the Agreement

University affairs: Vice president for university affairs, associate vice president for development, associate vice president for public relations and creative services, director of governmental relations, and director of conferences and special events.

3. Terms of Agreement

The effective date of this Agreement is for the twelve-month period ————. It is the parties' intention to continue this Agreement beyond the expiration date noted herein. Therefore, if notice is not given by either party at least ninety (90) days prior to expiration, the Agreement automatically becomes renewed for the following fiscal-year period with the required units and extended dollars to be updated. It is the parties' intention that in lieu of notification, the Agreement will be perpetually renewed on an annual basis.

B. Procedural Requirements

1. Identification of Needs of Department Providing Services

University hospital will designate person or persons to be a liaison to provide basic information regarding new and ongoing projects.

University hospital will supply budget support for all aspects of direct costs.

2. Identification of Needs of Department Receiving the Services

Planning support for budget proposals and frequent updates of planning schedules.

Support for attendance and invitation listings.

Guidance with brochure outlay and appropriate mailing listings.

3. Identification of Interaction with Other Departments

University affairs will provide appropriate communication to all parties involved in special programs and events.

C. Compensation for Services Rendered [Sections are listed here. The actual MOU provides the details.]

1. Definition of Standard Unit(s) of Measurement
2. Determination of Unit Price(s)
3. Estimated Unit/Dollar Volumes of Services for Term. [Appropriate schedules were attached.] Types of Services identified and salary efforts relating to the hospital were determined.
4. Method for Determining Actual Unit Volume(s) N/A
5. Method of Payment/Reimbursement
6. Periodic Monitoring of Status

All persons involved will evaluate the services on an ongoing basis.

D. Measurement of Service Quality

Identification of Method(s)/Procedures for Measuring Service Quality, such as participant comments following events, efficient use of dollars, and degree of satisfaction on part of parties involved with services rendered.

E. Signature Block

(1) Administrator of Delivering Department

Vice President   Date
University Affairs

(2) Administrator of Department Receiving Services

Executive Director   Date
University Hospital

(3) Administrators of Coordinating Departments

Vice President for   Date
Finance and Management

Chief Financial Officer   Date
University Hospital

Expanding the MOU Process

As noted in Chapter 6, the MOU process can be viewed as a way to enhance interdepartmental negotiations—the concept of "getting to yes." As such, the process can be applied to a wide range of transactions, not just transfer pricing between service providers and income-generating departments. Therefore, MOU facilitators need to be trained in ways to create win-win solutions and improved communications.

Summary

The MOU process is a joint effort between provider and supplier departments to negotiate a fair price for services and agree to the type (quality) and amount of services to be provided during the course of a year. This is a negotiation process overseen by a standing committee and based on management engineering studies to help ensure fair treatment and efficient operations. As such, the process reveals considerable information about what is provided, how it is provided, and how it is managed. The client department agrees to a certain level of service, and this remains in effect during the course of the contract, usually one year.

Another approach to transfer pricing is to charge a per-unit fee, such that customers pay on the basis of services used (e.g., letters mailed, brochures and forms printed, personnel used for a special activity). Implementing such a process requires careful planning and communication. There is the assumption that customers can purchase the goods and services elsewhere and that the provider must be competitive with market rates and quality. Moreover, the clients must not have the costs imposed without the ability to plan ahead. Otherwise, unanticipated fees will mean that client departments will not be able to meet their responsibilities. The clients will perceive that the supplier met budget cuts or cross-subsidized other functions by arbitrarily imposing or increasing prices. The following is a case example of instituting self-sufficiency in a graphics services unit.

MOVING TOWARD SELF-SUFFICIENCY: THE CASE OF GRAPHICS SERVICES

An implication of implementing an internal market economy is that service departments should be competitive and self-sufficient, such that their revenues match or exceed costs.[2] However, the process by which subsidies are pulled out of a service function may cause problems for the viability of the function, especially in times of budget cutting. The following case history of graphic services illustrates the point.

A total of $600,000 in state support was removed from the graphic services area during two fiscal years—$150,000 in the first year and $450,000 in the second.

These reductions in support helped the campus service departments absorb resource reductions resulting from budget cuts across the campus. Within graphic services, budget reductions were dealt with by eliminating certain operations, limiting the types of work accepted, and revising the rate structures to include the costs previously paid from university subsidy. Three significant results of these actions were:

1. The area only accepts print jobs that are of an "economically feasible" size. This was an attempt to eliminate smaller jobs where the area could not compete effectively.
2. The area no longer provides graphics design services. The union employees who worked in the design section filed an appeal concerning the retrenchment of this area.
3. The rates were found to be significantly higher than they were and are currently competitive with outside service providers, even though the area is not charged with utilities, fringe benefits, or other costs that are associated with a for-profit enterprise.

After two years, the finances of the operation are in deficit. The area ended the past fiscal year with a loss of approximately $100,000. This loss resulted from the following causes:

1. University dollars previously subsidizing the graphics function were not returned to users. This left users who were already facing their own budget cuts with higher-cost graphic services, with no return of funds to offset the price increase. It is unclear whether the best way for the campus to finance this service is through central support provided to the service area, or through a more "demand-oriented" mechanism.
2. The transition occurred too quickly. The director of graphic services felt that he could create a self-sufficient operation successfully if the reductions in direct support had been phased in over several years, giving him time to improve the operations of the department to help it cope in a more competitive environment. He initiated a Total Quality Management effort in the area, but the effects of TQM generally take several years to occur.
3. Employee management issues: There was discussion concerning the ability of the management of the area to effect the operational improvements/changes necessary to allow a "self-supporting" operation to succeed given the existing set of employees in the area and the union environment.

Several questions remain at this point:
1. *In the short run, how should the existing deficit in the area ($100K) be resolved?*
Options:

a. Deficit should be resolved in the campus services area using a portion of the funds that were removed from the area.
b. Future rates to users should be increased to resolve the current deficit.
c. The deficit should be resolved through the campus budget process.
d. Do nothing.

2. *What steps should be taken to prevent future deficits in the area?*
Options:

a. Rates to users should be adjusted to take into consideration the knowledge gained concerning costs and anticipated work volumes during the recent experience with self-sufficiency.

b. The services offered by the area should be reduced further. This would likely involve either partial or total retrenchment of the printing operation. This area is not currently operating at capacity. Total retrenchment of the printing operation would reduce the scope of the graphics support area to quick copy services and desktop publishing.

c. Identify alternatives to existing services made possible through advances in technology. (Note: these "solutions" generally create their own financial demands.)

One example of this would be the purchase of a machine that allows for digital composition and storage of documents using the campus network. This equipment could cover about 20 percent of the work of the printing area. (Note: the cost of this equipment is approximately $350,000 and vendor would provide financing.)

d. Combination of a, b, c—adjust rate structure, selectively reduce staffing/operations and implement technological solutions.

e. Do nothing.

3. *What is the future of the graphics services area on the campus?*
Answers to questions 1 and 2 above require the campus and the management of the graphics services area to give serious consideration to the area's future. First, the campus needs to decide the extent to which it requires or desires a centralized printing operation. Second, the management of institutional services, which includes the graphics department, needs to develop a long-range plan for the area consistent with the campus vision.

Summary

This case illustrates that an internal market economy may be an ideal that is difficult to achieve. Creating a fair and competitive charge-back process and introducing a fee structure have to be done with an understanding of their effects on client departments. Plenty of communication and planning are necessary to explain the purpose of new fees and provide a way for clients to pay for the services (e.g., by transferring money from the service to the client departments).

The next section begins a review of key measures for tracking organizational performance. Many administrative departments produce reports that indicate the level of activity in the department. This section describes the identification of the important indicators and methods for gathering major reports to produce quarterly high-level records for top administrators.

KEY INDICATORS AND MANAGEMENT REPORTS

Institutions should track the performance indicators relevant to the particular institution. For instance, a research university will care about research funding while a liberal arts college will emphasize enrollment data. Despite institutional differences, Taylor, Meyerson, & Massy (1993) offer a core group of ten indexes covering academic and support areas applicable to most institutions of higher education. These "top ten" include the following:

1. *Overall revenue structure.* This includes sources of revenue and indications of revenue stability and anticipated revenue.

2. *Overall expenditure structure.* This covers where money goes, expenditure trends, and implications for future financial stability.

3. *Excess (deficit) of current fund revenues over current expenditures.* Excess revenues indicate potential for capital investment and other uses for reserves. Shortfalls indicate the need to identify ways to cover the deficits.

4. *Percent of freshmen applicants accepted and percent of accepted freshmen who matriculate.* The first indicates institutional selectivity. The second indicates "yield," an indicator of the institution's attractiveness. The former suggests the amount of control the institution has over student quality and size of the student body. The second suggests how much flexibility the institution has to control the quality and composition of its students.

5. *Ratio of full-time equivalent students to full-time equivalent faculty.* This measures faculty workload and productivity, although analyses by department will be necessary for more precise information.

6. *Institutional grant aid as a percent of tuition and fee income.* This is important to private institutions, and increasingly to public institutions.

7. *Tenure status of full-time equivalent faculty.* This suggests the institution's flexibility in adding faculty to areas of growing student demand, or alternatively to decrease the size of the faculty in underenrolled areas.

8. *Percent of total full-time equivalent employees who are faculty.* This reflects the organization's mission and program mix, suggesting the adequacy of attention given to the academic mission and administrative support areas.

9. *Maintenance backlog as percent of total replacement value of plant.* Many institutions are facing increasing deferred maintenance with insufficient funds available for facilities maintenance and repair.

10. *Percent of living alumni who have given at any time during the past five years.* This recognizes the importance of alumni to institutional support and as a proxy for constituent opinion about institutional performance.

A Quarterly Key Indicators Report

The following is another list of key indicators that are useful for tracking overall university performance. They include data about finances (budget and expenditures), enrollments, fund-raising, health care operations (if relevant to the institution), and other major university activities. The information is provided quarterly in a briefing document for the president and other officers. The document is meant to be a reference throughout the quarter as policy questions arise and decisions need to be made.

1. Revenues by source
2. Expenditures by type
3. Enrollment information
   - Latest semester student head count by division by graduate/undergraduate and percent of enrollment target achieved
   - Revised five-year enrollment plan projections
   - Degrees conferred and graduation rates (by division with comparative data from prior years)
   - New freshmen and transfers (by division and graduate/undergraduate)
   - Student retention data by year (e.g., attrition rate for freshmen entering in the fall, by division)
   - Student ethnicity and gender
   - Origin of students (counties within state, other states, other countries)
4. Health care highlights (with comparison rates for this time last year)
   - Hospital discharges
   - Average length of stay
   - Occupancy rate
   - Clinical practice revenues
5. Human Resources
   - Appointments and terminations by division
   - Origin of employees (counties within state, other states, other countries)
6. Campus Residences
   - Dormitory revenues
7. Fund-Raising
   - Funds raised by source (alumni, community, business), receiving unit, and type (e.g., restricted/endowment, scholarships, building funds/capital projects, unrestricted)
8. Research Funds
   - Grants and contracts by source (government agency, foundation) and receiving principal investigator or laboratory

The quarterly key indicators report not only provides the data for the above items, but also includes a brief narrative summarizing the important results. Here are some examples in a narrative summary.

3. Enrollment Information

Undergraduate retention. The first-year attrition rate for freshmen entering in the fall was 17.1%. The rate for transfers was 27.2% for arts and sciences programs and 6% for health sciences programs. The rates for freshmen and health sciences transfers improved from the previous year. The rate for arts and sciences transfers remained the same.

5. Human Resources

Appointments and terminations. There were 135 appointments to and 114 terminations from the payroll during the month of December.

6. Campus Residences

Dormitory revenues. As of February 15, dormitory revenues were experiencing a collection shortfall of more than $720,000 against projected collections. The dormitory revenue committee has reviewed the billings and occupancy and determined that they are close to projections. The collections shortfall is attributable to slower-than-anticipated collections. Improving the collection of student accounts receivable is the focus of a committee convened by the director of student accounts.

Calendar of Management Reports

In addition to the key indicators, it is possible to collect important departmental reports that are produced regularly. These reports are collected by the performance management department and issued along with the key indicators to the president, provost, and vice presidents. This does not include every available report, but only reports deemed important by the president for top level oversight and management (see Table 7.1).

Summary

This section listed the different key indicators and management reports that can be issued quarterly (or more often if warranted). They demonstrate the scope of top management concern and oversight. In addition, they provide a way to enhance officers' understanding of university operations and changes. As such, they are a valuable tracking, management, and planning tool.

One way to interpret the reports is to examine changes over time. However, a more expansive method is to compare the results to similar units in the same or other institutions. This process is called benchmarking.

COLLECTING AND USING BENCHMARKING DATA

In the spring of 1992, the National Association of College and University Business Officers (NACUBO), in conjunction with the Higher Education Consulting Group of Coopers & Lybrand, launched the NACUBO Benchmarking Project to collect data on administrative and business costs and compile them for comparative purposes (Blumenstyk, 1993). Summarizing the effort, Kempner (1993) wrote:

Table 7.1
Report Calendar

Report	Source	Quarter Issued
Campus financial condition report (revenues and expenses by type and division)	vice president for Finance	All
Student applications and admissions	Institutional Research Dept.	September
Course workload full-time equivalent faculty	Institutional Research Dept.	September
Degrees conferred	Institutional Research Dept.	December
Dental school reports	Dental school administrator	All
Development fund-raising	University foundation business office	All
Residence hall revenues	Residence hall businesses office	All
Distinguished awards	Office of special events	June
Employees headcount details	Institutional Research Dept.	March & June
Enrollments	Institutional Research Dept.	All
Fall actual versus enrollment targets	Institutional Research Dept.	September & December
Student, faculty, and staff gender and ethnicity	Institutional Research Dept.	December

Table 7.1
(*continued*)

Report	Source	Quarter Issued
Financial aid	Office of Financial Aid	December & June
Five-year enrollment plan	Institutional Research Department with Enrollment Planning Executive committee	December
Student retention report	Institutional Research Dept.	December
Hospital reports	Hospital Chief Operating Officer	All
Legal activities	Campus Counsel	All
Library management report	Library business office	September
New hires	Human resources department	All
Sensitive resources (hazardous waste, refuse/recycling)	Campus Environmental Health and Safety Department	All
Utilities consumption	vice president for Campus Services	All

Benchmarking is an ongoing, systematic process for measuring and comparing the work processes of one organization to those of another by bringing an external focus to the internal activities, functions, or operations. The purpose of benchmarking is to provide managers with an external standard for evaluating the quality and cost of their organization's internal activities, practices, and processes. Benchmarking helps an institution to identify where opportunities for improvement may lie, to quantify the magnitude of those opportunities, to identify those institutions that perform a process particularly well, and to adapt that process to aid an improvement effort (p. 22)

Simply put, the purpose is to assist colleges and universities in measuring costs and service levels so that they will have the information necessary to begin a discussion of best practices within institutions that appear to achieve lower costs or higher service levels. . . . An examination of best practices positions an institution to redesign those processes and functions that are operating below an acceptable standard. The results of the study should not be used simply as a comparative report card or to lobby external constituencies for increased funding. The real opportunity lies in using the results as a springboard for positive change in operations (p. 24).

Benchmarking attempts to answer the following questions (Coopers & Lybrand with Shafer & Associates, 1993, pp. 4–5):

- How well are we doing compared to others?
- How good do we want to be?
- Who's doing the best?
- How do they do it?
- How can we adapt what they do to our institution?
- How can we be better than the best?

There are several types of benchmarking (defined in Coopers & Lybrand with Shafer & Associates, 1994, pp. 4–5):

- *Internal benchmarking* is used to analyze the internal practices within departments or divisions of an institution to identify the best internal performance areas and to measure baseline performance.
- *Competitive benchmarking* features an analysis of and comparison to targeted data from a select few, direct competitors or peers.
- *Industry benchmarking* provides an analysis of and comparison to general trends across a much larger group of related institutions. While closely paralleling "competitive benchmarking," industry benchmarking implies a broader perspective. This type of benchmarking can be used to establish performance improvement goals and to identify trends in the overall industry.
- *Best in class benchmarking* looks across multiple industries in search of new, innovative practices, no matter what their source.
- *Vertical benchmarking* seeks to quantify the costs, workloads and productivity of a pre-defined functional area (e.g., accounts payable).
- *Horizontal benchmarking* analyzes the cost and productivity of a single process that cuts across one or more functional areas (e.g., processing a purchase order).

NACUBO's two-year pilot project collects data that allow all these types of benchmarking—with the types of analyses of the total available data set depending on an individual campus's interests. The pilot collected data from 150 colleges and universities. Each institution collects measures of as many as 40 functions, with the measurements designed to be specific to the function yet applicable across organizations. The data include measures of resources input, products output, quality in delivering services, and information on site characteristics. The following is a small sample of functions and measures:

Accounts Payable
- Accounts payable computer costs as a % of total department cost
- Average days payable
- Department cost per voucher processed

- Turnaround time from receipt of invoice to voucher processing date

Admissions
- Admissions computer cost as a % of total department cost
- Departmental cost per applicant
- Departmental cost per accept
- Departmental cost per inquiry
- Number of accepts as a % of number of offers (freshmen and total)
- Number of interviews per applicant
- Turnaround time from application deadline to decision to accept

Alumni Relations
- Alumni association volunteer rate
- Departmental cost per alumni association member
- Percent of membership renewal last year

Career Planning and Placement
- Number of job listings per student
- Departmental cost per student and alumnus receiving assistance

Central Budget Department
- Institutional operating cost per departmental full-time equivalent employee last year
- Percent increase in institutional operating cost last year

Central Stores
- Average turnaround time from receipt of requisition to departmental receipt of goods
- Departmental cost per requisition
- Number of items in inventory

Development Office
- Departmental cost per donor
- Departmental cost per prospect

Facilities
- Average age of facilities
- Building maintenance cost per gross square foot
- Capital renewal/deferred maintenance backlog outstanding as a % of campus replacement value

Other functions include financial aid, general accounting, human resources, information technology, intercollegiate athletics, intramural and recreational sports, and the library.

The cost for participating institutions in 1993 was $6,500 for 40 functions, with lower prices for reduced number of questions per function and fewer functions. Also, university systems were able to negotiate systemwide rates. One system paid for half the cost centrally and then prorated the other half across participating campuses, further reducing the cost to the campus.

Table 7.2 is a sample chart of results for one function, registration.

Uses of Benchmarking Data

Colleges and universities have used benchmarking data to compare their departments to selected other institutions. Individual function managers receive the

Table 7.2
Selected Registration Benchmarks

	A	B	C	D	E
Median days to process grade reports	5.0	5.0	7.0	5.0	11.5
Median days to process transcripts	3.0	3.0	2.0	2.0	2.8
Mean computer costs as a percent of departmental costs	10.6	6.4	8.2	N/A	11.1

A=public research
B=private research
C=public comprehensive
D=private comprehensive
E=liberal arts

From Kempner (1993) p. 26.

data for their department and comparable departments at other institutions. For example, the director of purchasing at one campus of the State University of New York arrayed the data for her department to see how it compared to other SUNY campuses (Kempner, 1993). Wheaton College, a small liberal arts school in Massachusetts, used the benchmarking data with total quality management and business process reengineering efforts across several departments (Kempner, 1993). For instance, they faced the problem of coordinating the information in their financial aid award letters with student bills. These were previously designed from two different perspectives, neither of which considered the needs of the students and family as primary. Consequently, they spent considerable unnecessary staff time answering questions and reconciling differences between the two sources of information. After reviewing the benchmark data, they contacted some similar-sized schools to see how they handled the coordination problem. They found that the other schools had similar problems. Building on others' ideas, however, enabled the school to make larger improvements at a quicker pace than they could have done alone. In turn, they shared their methods and results with the other schools so they didn't all have to "reinvent the wheel."

NACUBO provides each campus with raw data from their institution and others identified by cohort group (e.g., "public research," "private research," and "liberal arts"). At each campus, a study coordinator may provide departments with summary statistics, such as the high, low, median, mean, and standard deviation for each benchmark question. The intention is to identify areas where there is a large deviation from the mean. In using the data, departments need to determine the causes of similarities and differences between their university and other institutions. They need to know whether the results are due to real differences (positive or negative) in the way functions are accomplished or whether inaccurate or incomplete data or differences in question interpretation among participants are causing invalid results for particular benchmarks. Therefore, the results require careful scrutiny and self-reflection.

Efficiency Analysis

The NACUBO benchmark data provide information on relevant departmental inputs and outputs as well as site characteristics. This suggests the possibility of developing efficiency analyses based on input/output ratios controlling for site differences. Burns and Lister (1993) used the 1993 NACUBO data to analyze the efficiency of the 112 college and university libraries in the study. They applied a statistical technique called "data envelopment analysis" (DEA) to measure technical efficiency. The method is based on a linear programming algorithm whose objective function maximizes output subject to a series of constraints and computing adjusted efficiency scores ranging from 0 to 1 (where a score of 1 indicates perfect relative efficiency). The method adjusts library scores for differences in site characteristics such as the school's region and the degree of library centralization. Essentially, the model is the sum of weighted outputs over the sum of weighted inputs (compare Charnes, Cooper, & Rhodes, 1981; Bessent, Bessent, Charnes, Cooper, & Thorogood, 1983; Sexton, Silkman, & Hogan, 1986). The procedure recognizes that different institutions may be operating under different conditions that affect their efficiency in ways that are beyond the control of management. To account for this, stepwise regression is used to develop a predicted score based on site and quality characteristics. An adjusted efficiency score is calculated by subtracting the predicted from the actual efficiency score. After conducting the analyses across the institutions in the benchmarking study, efficiency scores are derived for each participating unit.

The analysis began by selecting variables from the NACUBO list relevant to libraries. After discussion with library personnel, four key input measures were identified: total cost, number of holdings, number of current serial subscriptions, and number of computer terminals with national network access. Four output measures were also chosen for analysis: number of items circulated, number of annual users, number of interlibrary items loaned, and number of interlibrary items requested from other institutions. Six site characteristics were used as controls: number of branch libraries (a measure of centralization), existence of specialized schools (e.g., law, medicine, and veterinary), calendar system (semester or quarter), affiliation (governmental, religious, private), Carnegie classification (e.g., Tier I Research University), and number of full-time equivalent students. Three quality measures were also controlled: percent of library records represented with on-line public access, the average number of hours all campus libraries were open per week during the past academic year, and automation. Categorical variables were converted to bivariate "dummy" variables (e.g., presence of the characteristic = 2, absence = 1).

Note that the study is limited by the variables included in the NACUBO survey. One weakness of the study is that some important variables were lacking. For instance, the NACUBO survey did not measure the number of reference transactions, a variable collected by the Association of Research Libraries.

One finding was that Carnegie classifications indicating a research university and the presence of a law school tended to reduce efficiency scores. Also, state-controlled institutions tended to exhibit higher efficiency ratings. Libraries that provided more hours of service had slightly lower efficiency scores than their counterparts. A comparison of campuses determined most and least efficient schools before and after adjusting for site characteristics and quality measures. Also, for a given campus, it was possible to determine adjustments needed to improve efficiency. For example, to achieve a perfect efficiency score, one campus would need to make the adjustments shown in Table 7.3 in inputs while maintaining the same level of outputs.

Other Sources of Benchmarking Data

Professional associations often collect and publish information about its member institutions (e.g., the American Association for Higher Education, NACUBO in the areas of business office and campus service operations, the Society for College and University Planners in the area of operations and facilities planning, the Council for Advancement and Support of Education in the areas of fund-raising and university development, the Association of Governing Boards of Universities and Colleges, and the American Council on Education's Division of Policy Analysis and Research). This can be a source of benchmarking information about specific functional areas. Do-it-yourself studies can also be conducted. These do not have to be highly quantitative or exhaustive. Rather they can be based on interviews (in-person or telephone) with colleagues at other universities or colleges.

For example, an alumni association board member at one university volunteered to interview alumni directors at ten universities during several upcoming trips taken for personal and private business reasons. The schools were selected by their

Table 7.3
Input Changes Needed for Efficiency Improvement

	Total cost (mill $)	Holdings (mill)	Current Serial Subscriptions (thous)	# Computers with Nat'l Network Access
Current	10.74	4.88	20.60	28.00
Target	9.07	4.14	14.67	23.69

From Burns and Lister (1993), p. 23.

similarity in size, age, mission, and, hence, relevance to the university seeking the information. The board member wrote a report describing the alumni offices (e.g., financial support from their school, dues structure, membership recruitment methods, fund-raising activities, social programs, involvement in university programs, etc.). The report also included a list of trends and comparisons of the target school with the comparison institutions. For instance, the interviews revealed that the target school "has the lowest budget on an absolute basis, as well as when measured per student and per alumni," "has the smallest alumni affairs staff of any school surveyed," and "gives fewer scholarships than alumni associations at the other schools." Trends included: "most schools have separate homecoming and reunion programs," "most schools are shifting from traditional event-based programs toward a service orientation," and "financial services are popular with alumni and can generate significant revenue."

Summary

Benchmarking is an increasingly popular technique driven by the desire of institutions to enhance quality and competitiveness. There are multiple ways of collecting benchmarking data. Using the results requires having an open mind to new ideas that are "'not invented here." Comparative data should not be used blindly. Many factors may account for differences between departments— sometimes factors that are beyond the control of department managers. Also, data do not always speak for themselves. A data point may have different meaning in different institutions (e.g., different ways of calculating full-time equivalent employees), resulting in apples-and-oranges comparisons. Also, circumstances or contextual factors may differ (e.g., unionized shops may have less control over employee time and competence than nonunion shops). Thus, it pays to collect qualitative and quantitative information and be sure of the comparability and relevance of proposed benchmarks. With that as a caveat, benchmark data can be a source of tracking success and seeking ways to improve.

Information about use of resources and outcomes provides information about unit efficiency. However, the bottom line is whether customers buy the services available. Does the university attract the number and types of students it wants? Are funding agencies willing to support faculty research? Internally, are users of administrative services satisfied with the products and services they receive? Do they come back for more or do they look elsewhere? How do their needs and expectations change over time, and what can be done to meet these changes? These questions are dealt with in the next sections on alternative ways to measure customer satisfaction.

CUSTOMER VALUE ANALYSIS

Organizational performance in today's competitive marketplace requires linking customer values to organizational strategies and communicating these strategies to employees in the form of goals and expectations (Adsit, London, Crom, & Jones,

1994). Organizations need to identify what customers value, align organizational responsibilities and effectiveness measures around key value-added processes, and manage employees and work processes to create customer value—a process known as "customer value analysis" (Crom, 1994). This includes collecting measures of customer satisfaction and organization performance. The organization then ensures that employees understand how the performance of the organization is related to customer satisfaction. They can see how accomplishing their goals helps to meet customer expectations.

IDENTIFYING CUSTOMER/SUPPLIER RELATIONSHIPS

This is a needs/gap analysis process that can be applied to evaluate an administrative department's ability to meet customer expectations. The idea for the process stemmed from a general survey on the quality of service provided by the various service departments in the university. The results showed disparities in the perception of the quality of service offered by the departments (the suppliers) and that received by others within the campus community (their customers—students, faculty, and administrators in academic departments and laboratories). The study asked very general questions about the quality of service provided by each department. While it identified the disparity between customer and supplier expectations, it was not detailed enough to indicate the reasons for this gap in each department. The following method provides more detailed, department-specific information comparing customer and supplier perceptions.

The process begins by asking the manager of each unit within the department to identify the unit's customers, rank and rate the quality of services provided by the unit, and list performance constraints that are beyond unit's control. Customers then rank and rate the same set of quality characteristics. Therefore, both customers and suppliers grade themselves on the characteristics that they view as important. The process determines differences between customers and suppliers in the characteristics they deem important and the quality of performance. The data are collected by interviews during which appropriate forms (see Figures 7.1 and 7.2) are completed.

The results are distributed during a focus/feedback group with department managers meeting with a group of volunteer customers. A facilitator presents the results and asks the customers to explain the meaning of the results. The unit managers from the supplier department are given a chance to ask questions. The customers then receive information about the characteristics, ratings, and constraints as perceived by the supplier department managers. After the briefing, the customers leave and the unit managers have a chance to discuss the results further and begin addressing areas for improvement. The group process, therefore, limits opportunities for the unit managers to be defensive or rationalize. Also, the process enhances customers' awareness of elements of the service from the service providers' perspective. This may help customers to be more understanding and have more reasonable expectations. This, combined with steps to improve service

Figure 7.1
Goods/Services Survey

Name: _____   Department: _____

Title: _____   Supervisor: _____
----

(1) What are your major products/services?

    <u>Product/Service</u>   <u>% of Activity</u>

    _____   _____

    _____   _____

    _____   _____

    _____   _____

(2) Do you have competition in the provision of your products/services?

                    Yes_____   No_____

    How does that competition affect you?

_____

_____

_____

(3) What are the key quality characteristics of your products/services that are most important to <u>you</u>?

_____

_____

_____

(4) Who are your major customers?

<u>Customer Type</u>	Product/ <u>Service</u>	% of <u>Activity</u>	<u>Grade</u>
_____	_____	_____	____
_____	_____	_____	____
_____	_____	_____	____
_____	_____	_____	____

Figure 7.1
(*continued*)

(5) Have your customers' needs changed?

Yes_____ No_____

How?

_____

_____

_____

(6) Are you meeting your customers' requirements and expectations?

Yes_____ No_____

For each of your major customers, give yourself a letter grade on how well you are meeting customers' needs: (Indicate a grade next to each customer group listed above. Use the grading system A+, A, A-, B+, B, B-, C+, C, C-, D+, D, D-, F.)

(7) To what extent are there barriers to meeting customers' needs?
Low_____ Medium_____ High_____

Please describe:

_____

_____

_____

(8) Indicate the extent to which each of the following applies to you using the following scale:

never		sometimes		always
1	2	3	4	5

_____ I have the authority to act to meet my customers' needs.

_____ I give my subordinates the authority to meet customers' needs.

_____ I am held accountable for meeting customers' needs.

Figure 7.1
(*continued*)

____ I hold my subordinates accountable for meeting customers' needs.

____ I am encouraged to be innovative and creative.

____ My supervisors demonstrate trust and confidence in me.

____ I demonstrate trust and confidence in my subordinates.

(9) Do you receive feedback on your performance from your customers?

Yes_____   No_____

Please explain:

_____

_____

_____

(10) How often do you receive feedback? (circle the number that best applies)

never		sometimes		always
1	2	3	4	5

(11) How much more feedback do you want?

none				alot
1	2	3	4	5

(12) Identify those university units that provide major goods or services to you:

Supplier	Product/ Service	% of Activity	Grade
_____	_____	____	____
_____	_____	____	____
_____	_____	____	____
_____	_____	____	____

Figure 7.1
(*continued*)

(13) Do these units face competition?

Yes _____   No _____

(14) What key quality characteristics of those units' products/services do you think are important to <u>you</u>?

_____

_____

_____

(15) Are your suppliers meeting your requirements?

Yes _____   No _____

Please explain:

_____

_____

_____

(16) For each of your major suppliers, give them a letter grade on how well they are meeting your needs: (Indicate a grade next to each supplier listed above. Use the grading system A+, A, A-, B+, B, B-, C+, C, C-, D+, D, D-, F.)

(17) To what extent do barriers exist to your suppliers' meeting your needs?

Low_____ Medium_____ High_____

Please describe:

_____

_____

_____

(18) How often do you give feedback to your suppliers? (circle the number that best applies)

	never		sometimes		always
	1	2	3	4	5

Figure 7.1
(*continued*)

```
(19) How much more feedback do you want to give?

            none                                  alot
             1          2          3          4     5
```

(20) Please provide any ideas that you have that may allow
your suppliers to better meet your needs or that might allow
for the better operation of the university in general:

_____ _____

_____

_____

_____

quality, should enhance customer satisfaction in the future. Moreover, the entire data collection and feedback process enhances the participants' sense of community—a realization that they are all on the same team to achieve a common purpose, although each party contributes in a different way.

This process was piloted in several departments—human resources, purchasing and stores, central receiving, and mail. Most of the participants—customers and suppliers—had never had such an experience, and they went out of their way not only to express their thanks, but to indicate an interest in establishing customer/supplier forums on a regular basis.

Data are collected using two forms (see Figures 7.1 and 7.2). The first, the "Goods/Services Survey" is completed by unit managers. The survey recognizes that the managers may be suppliers to some other departments and customers of others. Therefore, the survey serves multiple purposes. It identifies the manager's key customers and suppliers and asks questions about the delivery of services and receipt of other services. The manager then completes the "Customer's Rating" and "Supplier's Response" for each supplier unit. In this way, the process taps multiple customer/supplier relationships at once. Focus groups are then held for each supplier unit with key customers present (as described above). Sample results for one department are shown in Table 7.4.

These results show that the service provider, in this case managers in the central stores department, have a different view of performance and quality. None of the top five quality criteria overlap with those chosen by the customers. While the supplier values the concepts of performance, reputation, and credibility, customers value timeliness, competence, and reliability. They also put responsiveness and courtesy ahead of conformance to rules and communication. After converting the grades to a score on a 5-point scale, the ratings show that the suppliers rate themselves more favorably on their top five categories than the customers rate them on

Figure 7.2
Customer's Rating and Supplier's Response

Supplier: _____

In the spaces to the left, rank-order the top five quality
characteristics that are important to you. Then grade your
supplier on all the characteristics. Use letter grades A+,
A, ..., F.

Rank   Grade

_____   Access   _____

_____   Aesthetics (e.g., product look)   _____

_____   Communication   _____

_____   Competence   _____

_____   Conformance (to requirements)   _____

_____   Courtesy   _____

_____   Credibility   _____

_____   Durability   _____

_____   Features (# of features)   _____

_____   Performance of product or service   _____

_____   Reliability   _____

_____   Reputation   _____

_____   Responsiveness   _____

_____   Timeliness   _____

_____   User Friendly   _____

_____   Other: _____   _____

Supplier's Response

Customer: _____

In the spaces to the left, rank-order the top five quality
characteristics that are important to you in providing the
product or service to your customer. Then grade yourself on
all the characteristics. Use letter grades A+, A, ..., F.

[Form is same as Customer's Response Form]

Table 7.4
Sample Results, Central Stores

Service Provider[1]	Self-Ratings	Customers[1]	Customers' Ratings
Performance	3.4	Timeliness	2.4
Reputation	3.8	Competence	2.6
Credibility	3.6	Reliability	2.7
Conformance	3.7	Responsiveness	2.7
Communication	3.6	Courtesy	2.9

[1]Top five categories--the first category ranked most important.

their top five categories. Data comparing ratings of the same quality characteristics (not shown here) further demonstrate that customers' opinions of the service are not as favorable as customer opinions. The focus group helped to explain to the managers in central stores why customers were concerned with timeliness, competence, and reliability ahead of characteristics such as credibility and reputation. Customers wanted speedy services, not promises that couldn't be met or promises of slow service. The discussion also revealed that the suppliers interpreted "performance" as getting orders delivered. Customers took it for granted that their orders would be filled, but they wanted them filled quickly and accurately.

DEPARTMENT-SPECIFIC CUSTOMER SATISFACTION SURVEYS

Another method for customer input to departmental evaluation is to design a survey that reflects the specific services of a department and collect data from frequent users. Here's an example:

OFFICE OF RESEARCH SERVICES CUSTOMER SATISFACTION SURVEY

At the request of the vice president for research, the university's management engineering office conducted a customer satisfaction survey to establish directions for improving services to principal investigators and reducing administrative overhead costs. The survey, provided in Figure 7.3, was developed with research proj-

Figure 7.3
Research Services Customer Satisfaction Survey

Providing quality service is important to the staff and management of the office of research services (ORS). This survey is designed to solicit your views and opinions. Your time in completing this form is greatly appreciated.

1. Please indicate your position:
   ___ Project Director or Principal Investigator
   ___ Department Chair
   ___ Dean
   ___ Research Assistant/Technician
   ___ Post-doc
   ___ Administrative assistant
   ___ Clerical
   ___ Other (Please specify)_____

2. Please indicate your division/school:_____

3. Please indicate the number of new grant or contract proposals you have submitted through ORS in the last 24 months:
   I have submitted ____ proposals.
   I have submitted ____ proposals through other agencies that did not involve the office of research services.
   ___ I have submitted no proposals (or not applicable)

4. Please rate the availability/distribution of information on the following according to the scale at left, and then indicate the importance of each according to the scale at the right (circle numbers 1, 2, or 3; choose NA for those that do not apply to you):

Availability/ Distribution						Importance	
Good	Fair	Poor			Very	Somewhat	Not
1	2	3 NA	a) Sources of funding	1	2		3
1	2	3 NA	b) Agency forms and program guidelines	1	2		3
1	2	3 NA	c) How to complete the grant application cover sheet	1	2		3
1	2	3 NA	d) How to prepare budgets for grant/contract proposals	1	2		3

Figure 7.3
(*continued*)

1	2	3	NA	e) How to complete a purchase requisition, payroll form, petty cash voucher, travel voucher, etc. 1	2	3
1	2	3	NA	f) Account balances and expenditures 1	2	3
1	2	3	NA	g) Indirect cost rates 1	2	3

5. Please rate the quality of the following services offered by ORS according to the scale at left, and indicate the importance of each service according to the scale at right (again, circle numbers 1, 2, or 3; choose NA for those that do not apply to you):

Service
Quality   Importance
Good Fair Poor   Very Somewhat Not

Good	Fair	Poor			Very	Somewhat	Not
1	2	3	NA	a) Contract writing and negotiations	1	2	3
1	2	3	NA	b) Inquiry assistance and intrepretation of sponsor guidelines	1	2	3
1	2	3	NA	c) Assistance completing grant applications and/or preparing budgets for proposals	1	2	3
1	2	3	NA	d) Inquiries/ consultations on matters of fund availability, expenditure allowability, etc.	1	2	3
1	2	3	NA	e) When necessary, rushing expenditure approvals	1	2	3

Figure 7.3
(*continued*)

f) Assistance/referrals
to other university
departments, such

1   2   3 NA   as payroll   1   2   3

6. Please rate the following aspects of response and communication with ORS and indicate their importance (circle numbers 1, 2, or 3; choose NA for those that do not apply to you):

Response and
Communication   Importance
Good Fair Poor   Very Somewhat Not

a) Timeliness of
assistance in
preparing grant/
contract
proposals and

1   2   3 NA   budgets   1   2   3

b) Timeliness of
expenditure

1   2   3 NA   approvals   1   2   3

c) Timeliness in
responding to

1   2   3 NA   questions   1   2   3

d) Usefulness of
the monthly
expenditure

1   2   3 NA   summaries   1   2   3

e) Computer
access to view
your account's

1   2   3 NA   activity   1   2   3

7. Please indicate in the space below factors that might discourage proposal submission (e.g., indirect cost rates, campus application procedures, etc.):

8. Please feel free to make any comments (below or on the back of this form).

ect directors and their administrative assistants, the vice president for research, and a faculty member in the school of management.

Once finalized, the survey was sent to nearly 1,100 persons on the office of research services internal database. Only 192 surveys were returned to the management engineering department; 78% of the respondents were principal investigators or project directors—the rest consisted of administrators, administrative assistants, and support staff; 38% were from the school of medicine; and about 30% were from the college of arts and sciences (with most of these from the divisions of biological sciences, physical sciences and math, and social and behavioral sciences). There, the sample appeared to capture the major users of research services on campus.

The results showed fairly favorable responses for each service item. However, the client was encouraged to consider the items receiving less favorable responses as candidates for change—especially services rated lower on satisfaction but higher in importance compared to other services. These included information provided on account balances and expenditures, the usefulness of the account expenditure summary statement, and the timeliness of personnel in responding to inquiries. Services that received lower satisfaction ratings but were less important dealt with providing information on how to prepare budgets for grants and contract proposals, information on funding sources, and information on how to complete purchase requisitions. These latter services might be targeted for improvement or possibly elimination if further investigation determines that they are unnecessary or undesirable. (The specific numerical results going to the client are not presented here.) After the survey, the management engineering department continued consultation with the research services department to implement improvements.

CONCLUSION

This chapter described a variety of service quality measurement methods and uses. Work-flow analyses and other management engineering methods are the basis for establishing costs and appropriate charge-backs for inclusion in service agreements and per-unit pricing. Ways to implement charge-backs with minimum disruption were discussed. The chapter reviewed key indicators and management reports for evaluating university effectiveness and collecting benchmark data to compare efficiency and suggest directions for improvements. Finally, the chapter considered ways to determine users' satisfaction with administrative services and products. Customer input should identify the necessary quality of service, while benchmark data should determine ways to decrease the cost of providing that service. The ultimate goal is to be a high-quality, low-cost producer of goods and services. This helps to ensure market share and provides maximum flexibility to the producer in making a profit in a competitive environment. This suggests that quality can be achieved by viewing the university as a mini-market economy, and providing information to adjust to changes in demand, competition, and modes of production.

This chapter continued our discussion of management strategies for higher quality performance (managing for excellence). Part IV considers human resource strategies for organization development. Chapter 8 will describe methods for improving communication and reducing conflict through team building.

NOTES

1. The section entitled "Formulating a Policy on Service Agreements" was written by Daniel J. Melucci.

2. The section entitled "Moving toward Self-Sufficiency; The Case of Graphics Services" was written by Douglas Panico.

PART IV

STRATEGIES FOR ORGANIZATION DEVELOPMENT

8

Building Teams

Considerable work gets done in teams—especially in universities where there are endless committees and task forces. Some team-building efforts are aimed at improving work relationships of such interdepartmental groups that are usually composed of people from different departments who have a common objective as well as potentially different, and possibly conflicting, departmental responsibilities or objectives. Other team-building efforts are aimed at improving work relationships of natural work teams—people who report to the same supervisor and who are expected to work together to accomplish the work of the unit. Team-building methods also vary. Some attempt to build cooperation and improved working relationships by encouraging the group to discuss work processes. The assumption is that if they perceive and understand their patterns of interrelationships, their quality of work and level of cooperation will improve. Other methods try to enhance the work that gets done in the group by holding specially structured meetings to set goals and review progress.

Individual team members make sense of their own and each other's activities on a team by constructing certain types of roles. Studying university presidents and members of their administrative teams, Neumann (1991) interviewed 70 individuals from 8 teams in different institutions. She asked the interviewees to describe their own and other team members' contributions to team deliberations. Qualitative analysis of the transcribed interviews resulted in distinguishing 8 roles: (1) the *definer* who identifies and proposes problems for the group, (2) the *analyst* who explores and maps the team's reality (e.g., elaborates on topics of concern), (3) the *interpreter* who predicts what others (especially those outside the team) are likely to see, (4) the *critic* who redefines the team's reality by expressing and exploring contrary views, (5) the *synthesizer* who orchestrates what the team knows, (6) the *disparity monitor* who gauges what outsiders think (bringing information about what is going on outside the team), (7) the *task monitor* who keeps the team on course, and (8) the *emotional monitor* who is attuned to the emotions that brew and forces the team to confront their feelings (often through humor). This is a cognitive role typology in that it defines the different ways team members think of their own behavior. The same member may enact more than one role. Members share roles. Also, the appropriateness and importance of the role depends on the stage of team development and productivity—for instance, with the definer role especially important at the outset and at key turning points in the group process. Teams develop norms for role enactment that new members must learn to interpret and become a part of. Members observe and learn from each other, thereby expanding their capabilities, appreciating each other's differences, and enhancing the team's effectiveness.

This chapter describes efforts to enhance teamwork among top university managers. First there are sample agendas from planned retreats to discuss university goals and to establish common objectives. Another example is the mission for a facilities users group to work more closely with the people who maintain the facilities. The chapter also describes the formation of a team of top administrators for the explicit purpose of improving interdepartmental relationships.

RETREAT AGENDA

Following is the agenda for a cabinet-level retreat held at the start of the academic year. The agenda explains the scope of the responsibilities. The purpose of the day and a half meeting was to help the university's officers understand the major objectives for the coming year.

Instructions for the team members stated that the presentations were to be brief— no more than 15 minutes—to allow plenty of time for discussion and questions. To be successful, the retreat had to be a *working meeting*, not a "show and tell." Presentations needed to be snappy with handouts. Instead of being exhaustive analyses, the presentations were to generate discussion about the issues on which the president and members of the cabinet should work during the next year and how that work would get done. "Wish lists"—things we would do if we only had the money— were to be avoided. Instead, the format was a series of discussions around decision points and work plans. This was a real working meeting, resulting in a set of concrete action steps for moving forward during the remainder of the academic year.

Session I: Mission Planning

Provost: Academic Initiatives

1. What are the most important academic initiatives you plan to pursue in the next two years?
2. What changes of direction do they entail?

3. What work will be needed during the coming academic year to get them done?

4. What difficulties/issues requiring resolution do you anticipate?

Vice President, Health Sciences Center: Future of the Health Sciences Center (HSC)

1. How will HSC academic programs change over the next 3–5 years?

2. How will patient care services change over the next 3–5 years?

3. What work should be completed during the academic year to move in the planned direction?

4. What difficulties/issues requiring resolution do you anticipate?

Chair, University Accreditation Self-Study

1. What are the most important recommendations in the self-study?

2. What changes of direction are proposed?

3. What new issues are raised that have not been addressed in the university planning process or have been differently addressed?

4. What are the implications of the answers to items 1–3 for the university agenda for the academic year?

Session II: Current Initiatives

Vice Provost for Undergraduate Studies: Undergraduate Initiatives

1. What issues/themes are being addressed this year?

2. What kinds of projects do you believe are the priorities for future funding?

3. What kinds of initiatives, activities, and changes do you believe are priorities for improving the undergraduate experience?

4. What are the implications of the answers to items 1–3 for the university agenda for the academic year?

Chair, Campus Information Technology Task Force

1. What goals should drive the development of information technology and systems at the university?

2. What are the essential elements/characteristics of an information technology system to fulfill those priorities?

3. What work should start this year to begin to move toward the creation of that system? Please be specific here. What are the budget implications?

4. How should we organize ourselves for that work? One or more concrete scenarios would help focus the discussion.

5. What difficulties/issues requiring resolution do you anticipate in the implementation of the university's information technology system?

Vice President, University Affairs: Capital Fund-Raising Campaign

1. What are the implications of the process of conducting a capital campaign?
2. Who will be responsible for doing what in the capital campaign?
3. What work should be completed this year to launch the campaign?
4. What difficulties/issues requiring resolution do you anticipate?

Session III: Workplace Problems and Solutions

Director, Human Resources Department

1. What characterizes this university as a workplace?
2. What can we do to change undesirable characteristics?
3. What is the role of the human resources department in improving the personnel management of human resources?

Session IV: Planning Processes

Vice President, Finance: Budget, Planning and Assessment
Provost and Vice President, Student Affairs: Enrollment Planning Process
Vice President, Campus Services: Capital and Facilities Planning Process
For presentation of each process:

1. What are the elements of the process?
2. What are the overall goals of the process?
3. What are the specific implications of the process this academic year?

For discussion:

1. Historically, what problems and weaknesses has the university had in this area?
2. Does the process as currently described solve these problems?

Session V: Implications of Mission Plans for Service Departments

Panel of Vice Presidents

1. What are the most important implications for support services of the plans for academic development?
2. What other issues must be addressed in order to improve the strength of the university's support services?

3. What should be done this year to move toward that improvement?
4. What difficulties/issues requiring resolution do you anticipate?

Next, the group considered the establishment of an ongoing customer focus group. The goal of this team was to promote working relationships between the customer (principal investigators who use laboratories and other research facilities) and the supplier (campus services).

RESEARCH FACILITIES USERS GROUP: MAJOR GOALS

This group is intended to identify and guide implementation of methods for the improvement of facilities maintenance serving principal investigators and other members of the research community. As a "quality circle," the group will strive toward continuous improvement to meet customer needs. Customer satisfaction is the key criterion of success. Goals for discussion include:

- Facilities maintenance personnel should be more sensitive to the needs of researchers.
- Conflicts and disagreements about methods, costs, and resources should be transparent to the principal investigators.
- Rules and standard procedures should not be adhered to so rigidly that the researchers' needs are disregarded or ignored.
- Costs should be credible (i.e., reasonable in relation to the services provided and the constraints under which the facilities department operates).
- Sources of maintenance support should be reviewed with a complete accounting of available resources (including identification of multiple funds supporting research and indirect cost reimbursements available for allocation).

Here is the agenda for a team-building meeting of the 40 or so senior staff of the campus student affairs department—the people responsible for admissions, student life, residence halls, and the student health service.

Agenda for Student Affairs Team-Building Session

Focus: Developing shared values for Student Affairs.
      Identifying interdepartmental goals.

8:30 Introduction to Retreat: Vice President, Student Affairs, and the Retreat Planning Group.

8:45 Introduction to morning Team Building session: Facilitator (expert in group dynamics).

Purpose (shared experience, common understanding, platform for further discussion).

Participants generate their expectations—list what they would like to happen during the retreat. The facilitator clarifies what will happen (what is realistic).

9:00 Definition of an organizational value.

Group discusses defining elements of an organizational value and agrees on a definition or principal components.

9:15   Subgroup discussion.

Participants break into groups of 5 (predetermined by the planning group to ensure cross-department representation in each group).

Subgroups discuss what are and should be the shared values in the department.

10:00   Establishing shared values.

Total group reconvenes to hear output from each subgroup and synthesize the results.

Identify a single set of shared values for student affairs.

10:30   Break

10:45   Review 12 major Student Affairs goals.

A member of the planning team hands out and reviews goals.

11:00   Subgroups reconvene.

Subgroups are formed (again preestablished by the planning team to ensure cross-department representation; the different mix of people provides an opportunity for participants to work with others in a small group).

The subgroups identify the four goals that have the most cross-departmental implications. For each of these four goals, the subgroup indicates how it offers an opportunity to express the shared values and how departments work together to accomplish the goal.

11:45   Integration of subgroup efforts; identification of four principal cross-departmental goals.

Subgroups report their results; total group agrees on four principal goals.

For each goal, the group agrees on how the goal should be carried out to be consistent with the shared values.

For each goal, the group agrees on relevant departments.

12:15   Review

Group discusses "what we learned" and "value of our discussion for where we go from here."

THE "TOP TEAM"

Now we consider the formation of a team of top university managers. These are people who work with each other frequently, but are often at odds because of resource constraints and conflicting (or, at least, not overlapping) goals. However, they are the key administrators who make the university work. The deputy to the president (the author of this book) led the effort.

Some Background

As the first step in developing a team-building effort among top administrators, the president suggested that I hold one-on-one meetings with the provost and vice presidents to determine issues. The president was concerned that we do more to enlarge the circle of senior administrators who communicate and work effectively with each other. Communication between their offices and the office of the president as well as between VP offices was especially relevant. We wanted people to know that escalating issues to the president's office is a way to avoid later problems, not a way to get in trouble. So an important question was, How can we enhance upward and lateral communication?

Consistent with the above point, if we needed team building, it should involve the people who report to us. We needed to understand the barriers to effective interdivisional working relationships and how they could be overcome.

One of my roles as deputy to the president was to spearhead management systems that lead to more effective internal operations of the university. Toward this end, the university's planning staff (described in Chapter 4) and I had been working on the following initiatives in cooperation with, and sometimes directed by, other departments: a system of management reports, a process for administrative departmental reviews analogous to academic departmental reviews, internal audits, performance management, memoranda of understanding (MOU), a revenue budget, a three-year financial plan, budgeting and priorities committee review of financial plans, departmental profiles, and procurement mechanization. (Most of these procedures are discussed in Chapters 5 through 7.) Our goal was to increase understanding of the issues, ensure adequate documentation of decisions, and be sure these decisions and related actions have the desired effects. We wanted to enhance these procedures. We also wanted better documentation and analysis.

The president, provost, and vice presidents had participated in a team-building experience two years earlier. They felt that it was time to reinitiate the effort, this time with a twist. The goal was to involve their direct reports in the process. Indeed, the intention was to have the group of direct reports begin and guide the effort. Toward this end, these individuals were invited to a team-building planning meeting.

So that this did not begin as a totally unstructured effort, I did some thinking about possible content and process for team building. I also talked to a consultant with whom I worked closely during the last ten years. We came up with the following ideas and presented them to the "team." Our planning meeting began by outlining these ideas. This was just a way to jump-start the effort. The team was free to change this in any way they wanted.

1. Desired Outcomes for Team Building

- A high level of trust among all team members
- The establishment of improved information flows
- Increased communication within and between departments
- Shared sense of team purpose and commitment
- Overall alignment of department and university mission, vision, and goals
- Attention to university-wide goals and objectives versus narrow, parochial departmental perspectives

2. Process Goals

To accomplish these outcomes, the following should happen:

- Create and maintain support structures and mechanisms. Determine what kinds of organizational structures and support mechanisms can be created to ensure the ongoing success of the "team" and the achievement of the university's goals. The MOU process and the research/facilities users' group are examples of recently implemented structures.
- Create a learning organization—one that routinely collects and analyzes information (e.g., management reports and key indicators) and makes changes in line with the information and university objectives. This includes a focus on team learning (i.e., learning about how we relate to, and work with, each other) and individual learning (personal characteristics that influence our behavior toward one another).
- Organization diagnosis and action planning. This will allow the team to arrive at a common understanding of the problems and issues facing the university and our departments and realize that university and departmental success are interdependent.

3. The Team-Building Experience

- The team building should be conducted over time, probably one day per month over 12 to 18 months. This is based on the rationale that organization change occurs slowly, and the team will need time for diagnosis, action planning, change, and evaluation.
- An "action learning" approach will diagnose problems and implement solutions to resolve them.
- The team needs to be guided through the use and application of techniques that promote team learning, and will be shown how team learning supports organization learning. The team, through this experience, becomes the university's first learning team and the model and catalyst for making the university administration a learning organization.
- Issues of trust, communication, and work relationships will be identified, discussed, and resolved.

4. Preliminary Assignments

Prior to the first session, if we agree in the planning meeting that we want to do this, the team will complete the following:

- A learning styles inventory. Feedback of the results of this self-assessment measure will enable team members to understand their own and others' learning styles.
- A team learning inventory. This self-assessment measure identifies conditions that promote or inhibit team learning.

5. Outline of First Session

Again, if we agreed in the planning meeting that this is what we want to do:

I.   Overview
     —Introduction, purpose, agenda, expectations
II. Self Focus

—Learning styles feedback
—Personal action planning

III. Team Focus
  —Team learning feedback
  —Team learning action planning

IV. Organization Focus
  —Organization diagnostic model overview
  —Preliminary diagnosis of organization and team dynamics
    • Identification of work-related problems and issues
  —Review of methods for analyzing issues (work flows, barriers)
  —Establishment of subgroups to examine selected problem areas and formulate an action plan to diagnose and resolve the problem
  —Report to full team on proposed action plan

V. Assessment of First Day's Experience
  —Agree to subgroup action plans
  —Identify between-session learning experiences (e.g., each person keeps a record of incidents that are symptomatic of individual behavior and relationship problems)

6. Outline of Second Session

I. Overview of Agenda, First Day Review
  —Learning styles, team learning

II. Between-session learning activities report
  —Feedback on lessons learned

III. Exercise/simulation for enhancing team learning
  —Short lecture and facilitated experience based on obstacles uncovered in team learning assessment

IV. Subgroup data collection updates and shared learning
  —Reports by teams on problem identification
  —Sharing significant personal, team, and organization learning
  —Feedback from other subgroups

V. Assessment of second day's experience

VI. Formulate action plan and between-session learning activities

7. Subsequent Sessions

• Activities will depend on progress during the first two sessions. Team members will be involved in setting the direction (problems to be solved, issues to be addressed).

Here's the agenda we actually followed for the first team-building meeting:

10:00–11:00 Introductions

              Background—what led up to today

              Purpose—long-term team-building objectives

              Your expectations and concerns

11:00–11:30 Framework for team building—meaning of the "learning organization" and "organizational transformation"

11:30–12:30	Identification of Problems and Barriers—in small group discussions during lunch
12:30–1:00	Review Problems and Barriers—review each group's view of major problems and barriers; derive a single list of priorities
1:00–2:00	Select Area(s) for Next Actions—determine one or more areas for improvement (e.g., focus on individual, interpersonal, team, interdepartmental group, or university level) and discuss possible actions depending on area(s) of focus. Actions to consider include self-assessments on learning style or management style inventories, training in group process, identifying common goals and priorities based on the university's strategic objectives, leadership simulations, etc.
	Determine Method for Designing Next Actions—e.g., appoint a subgroup
	Schedule Regular Series of Meetings—e.g., one every 6 weeks

RESULTS OF INITIAL TEAM BUILDING

The following is a summary of our initial team-building meeting. The summary describes an overarching goal and desired outcomes from future team building, as well as requirements for success.

Overarching Goal and Desired Outcomes for Team Building

We want to create a sense of community and purpose that transcends functional boundaries and unites us to achieve university-wide goals through teamwork, accountability for results, enthusiasm, and a sense of urgency. Desired outcomes include:

- A common, university-wide vision, developed by and shared with the maximum number of community members.
  —World-class focus, with a strong sense of university community
- Clear mission, along with
  —A set of common goals, driven by the mission and vision
  —An emphasis on cross-functional cooperation
  —Clear accountability for action and results
- A supportive culture that is
  —University-wide
  —Performance-oriented
  —Communal and collegial
  —Adaptable and flexible
- A supportive climate that is
  —Integrative and team-oriented
  (overcomes isolation)
  —Accepting of uncertainty and change
  (overcomes chaos)
  —Goal- and achievement-oriented
  (overcomes frustration)

—Promotes high morale
(overcomes demoralization)
—Encourages member trust and respect

Requirements for Success:

- A "top team" with a strong focus and bias for action
- A "top team" working together on common, university-wide problems
- Communication strategy and methods for sharing both strategic and tactical information
- Structures for organization-wide meetings, developing agendas, working together to solve problems, implementing solutions, and collecting feedback
- Team problem-solving and decision-making processes to ensure overall operational effectiveness
- Agreed-to norms and principles of operation
- Systems and resources for support, including automated systems, financial resources, and team rewards
- Increased understanding of the external environment, emphasizing competitive analysis
- Training and development in areas such as team learning, organization learning, and quality processes
- A focus on, and commitment to, personal learning, team learning, and organization learning to promote and ensure necessary growth and change

Next Steps

There were several options for next steps. One suggestion was to start a university forum to review university goals, objectives, strategies, and initiatives. This could be done several times a year and involve top managers along with deans and other key people in the academic sectors. Another idea was to design a series of meetings in which we engage in structured exercises for learning about how we interact with each other and how we can develop a sense of community and team. Of course, this approach could be combined with the forum idea.

What actually happened is outlined next. I began by working with the consultant to develop a plan for the coming academic year.

PLANS FOR THE FALL SEMESTER'S "TOP TEAM" SESSIONS

The following is an outline for four one-day sessions, two during each semester.[1] The sessions focus on (1) individual and team learning styles, (2) conflict resolution, (3) empowering and developing subordinates, and (4) leadership.

This is a combined action learning and team-building project. Action learning refers to a process of learning through experience by working together to solve problems. Team building refers to increasing the effectiveness of the leadership team as we work together to solve cross-functional and university-wide problems.

The major goal will be to create a sense of community and purpose that transcends functional boundaries and unites us to achieve university-wide goals through teamwork, accountability for results, enthusiasm, and a sense of urgency. As a result of the four sessions, the team will be prepared to foster a better sense of community throughout the university.

Major *outcomes* will include:

- Increased levels of trust
- Improved information flows
- Increased communication within and between departments
- Shared sense of team purpose and commitment
- Improved task and relationship effectiveness
- Skills to foster team and organization learning
- Skills in managing organization change
- A supportive culture that is university-wide, performance-oriented, and collegial
- A climate characterized as high in morale, trust, and respect

Session I: Learning Styles

Prior to the session, we will complete self-assessment inventories about our own learning styles and our ability, as individuals and as a group, to learn. A consultant will identify relevant instruments, provide instructions, analyze the data, and present feedback reports as part of the first meeting. The consultant will guide us in learning about organization diagnosis. The meeting will include explaining feedback reports, establishing validity of findings and looking for synergy across teams, and assisting in the determination of priorities for individual and team change. Group discussion will focus especially on directions for team growth and development.

Session II: Conflict Resolution

We will participate in a workshop on managing and resolving conflict within and between departments. The training will be in direct support of building and enhancing personal effectiveness and team learning effectiveness. The training will consist of understanding conflict in the workplace, developing win/win strategies, and learning and practicing skills for managing and resolving conflict.

Session III: Empowering and Developing Subordinates

Here we will examine the extent to which we build and manage effective work teams. Effectiveness includes working cooperatively within a department as well as building networks and alliances between departments. The meaning of empowerment will be discussed within the established rules and systems of the university. Emphasis will be placed on ensuring that administrative work teams understand university-wide goals and strategies and how to contribute to their accomplishment.

Session IV: Leadership Development and Planning for Continued Learning

The final session will consider the role of leadership at the university. We will examine the extent to which we are empowered to be leaders—that is, the extent to which we are willing and able to formulate strategies, request input for decisions from subordinates, make decisions, and monitor results. Our degree of accountability will be examined along with discussion of the support systems available and what we expect from the president, provost, and vice presidents by way of support, encouragement, and reinforcement. The session will conclude with establishing plans for continued team and individual learning.

The content for each of the above stages will reflect our needs during the course of the year and as the stages take place. This may require adjusting the curriculum and the nature of the presentations. As such, the programs will have an element of "just-in-time" training—training that is sensitive to the individuals in the team, their group process during the meetings, and information about interdepartmental activities and relationships that occur during the year.

To secure the services of the consultant to work with us during the academic year, the state required filing a request for proposal (RFP) and inviting bids from potential consultants. Excerpts from the RFP show the nature of the consulting desired consulting services and the desired qualifications.

CONSULTANT TO LEAD TEAM-BUILDING WORKSHOPS FOR UNIVERSITY ADMINISTRATORS

This is a request for proposal for a series of four team-building sessions (outlined above) to be conducted during the coming academic year. The sessions will be for the group of about 35 senior-level managers—all the people who report to the provost and vice presidents and several senior staff in the office of the president. (Deans were not included in the group, since the focus was on administrative services, not academic issues. However, the associate provosts for undergraduate and graduate studies did participate.) The goal is to build a strong, cooperative work team. The project includes preparatory work, running four one-day workshops, and follow-up work. Each workshop is viewed as a separate stage of the project, and the project should be viewed as four separable subprojects. The university will make a decision to continue after each stage depending on the success of that stage and the availability of funds. However, since each successive stage builds on the prior stage(s), the intention is to retain a single consultant who can ensure continuity across the four stages.

Qualifications of the Consultant

Overall, the consultant should have in-depth background and experience in adult learning and individual, team, and organization development. Specifically, the consultant should have substantial (10+ years) experience in designing, developing, and facilitating programs that foster individual, team, and organization change. This includes working with leadership teams in a variety of organizations in bringing about significant organization learning and change. Experience in higher education as a consultant and as a faculty member is desirable. The consultant should have an educational background that includes a master's degree in counseling psychology, and doctoral-level work in graduate training in organization development and adult learning. The consultant should have knowledge of, and experience in, designing and developing performance management systems, leadership and management development programs, curriculum design, and organization development interventions. Specific knowledge in conflict resolution, empowerment, management style, learning style, and team development is required as is experience in administering, scoring, and developing feedback reports on self-assessment and team development instruments.

Expectations of Consultant

The consultant's role in each stage will include the following:

- Facilitation for the overall project
- Detailed design and facilitation of each large team meeting
- Pre- and postmeeting planning and administrative activities
- Ongoing consultation with small groups and/or individuals as needed during each stage
- Administration and reporting of self- and team assessment surveys, as well as other measures

Here is the report of our first meeting of the semester.

REPORT ON A TEAM-BUILDING MEETING

The following is a summary of the major problem areas discussed at our recent meeting. The issues are divided into five categories: information-sharing and communication, structure, systems, goal achievement, and culture.

We divided the group into teams and encouraged each team to meet at least once before the next meeting in three weeks. (I assigned people to teams even if they were not present at the first meeting.) The teams did the following: determine if there are any other barriers to learning that would fall into their category and add them; subgroup or divide the category further, if necessary; clearly define what the "problem" is or the "problems" are; write a one- to two-sentence problem statement for each problem identified; brainstorm the causes of the problem(s); brainstorm actions that might be taken to alleviate the problem(s); and summarize and send a copy of the above to the campus training director in the administration department or to me. These are the barriers to learning:

1. Information-sharing and communication: Different areas are too self-focused—they don't share information. A good means of communication across all constituencies does not exist. Communication is not (must be) a two-way street. There is fragmentation—as a result of lack of communication.

2. Structure: We need to avoid duplication; centralize some of the functions that now exist in each organization. Our overuse of committees is not productive. It is not getting things done. There is a lack of rigorous committee discipline. We need to be more flexible. There is too much administrative bureaucracy.

3. Systems: We lack advanced computer/administrative systems.

4. Goal achievement: Resources are often not applied to effect stated goals. Resources are not managed as well as they could be. Rewards and punishments for achieving or not achieving stated goals are inconsistent. Performance rewards are not as prevalent as needed. The university mission statement is neither clear nor specific enough to inform university activities, particularly those that cross VP units. Cross-VP goal setting, goal achievement, and evaluation is very difficult, if not nonexistent. A focus on consensus in decision-making and an overreliance on it does not lead to accountability.

5. Culture: The institutional culture is not supportive enough of risk taking. We fear criticism. Bosses fight with each other. Managers don't see the urgency of doing better. We don't have a community spirit. There is a lack of understanding and respect between different units. Team building is promoted, but it is difficult to have this transcend down the organization.

The following is a memo written by a team member expressing reactions to the meeting.

Reactions from One Team Member

Thank you for including me in the recent team-building meeting. I found it very useful and look upon it as time well spent. I have thought some more about the future and what I want out of this process. I don't think we need more sessions to air our concerns (once was important but is enough). If we proceed, I would like to have articulated some expected outcomes. I think it might be useful to assign smaller groups of us to address some of the "environmental" issues that were identified. That may be more task oriented than team building, but may have the same outcome. The only drawback to my suggestion is that a group would be considering and discussing issues in "other people's" domains. Perhaps, though, removing domain barriers is part of team building.

After a series of meetings throughout the course of the academic year, here is where we ended up.

TEAM EVALUATION

The following is a summary of our evaluation of top team meetings and activities from our last meeting for the academic year. I'll be in touch with you soon about the date for our next meeting.

Overall, the feeling was that the meetings are worthwhile and should continue monthly (or thereabouts, depending on the work we decide to undertake as a group). We saw value in information sharing and working in subgroups on substantive tasks. We also would like to find ways to incorporate input from the president, provost, vice presidents, deans, and others (e.g., hospital administrators). We could do this by inviting representatives of these groups as new members or guests.

Key Points

1. The top team is considered a valuable administrative structure. It's a productive, informal way to have face-to-face discussions about issues. The top team is also a useful mechanism for informing new people at this organizational level about university processes and colleagues.

2. The top team is ready to go beyond information sharing. The top team wants to work on practical issues that matter to all members, such as our recent work on understanding cross-charges and fees. One way to do this is to do more work in subgroups of the top team rather than in meetings of the whole group. An example is the task force spearheading the implementation of the Visitors Center Committee recommendations.

3. Members would like to take the team to the "next level" by engendering involvement with other university officials and academic leaders (the cabinet and deans in particular). For instance, selected cabinet members and deans could attend meetings to provide their perspectives on current topics, directions for action, and evaluation of progress.

4. The top team needs to clarify its purpose, which will drive its actions, membership, and participation of others in meetings. Membership could be expanded to include representatives from other key campus groups (hospital, academic deans, etc.).

5. The top team should meet about once per month. However, as has been true this past semester, the schedule we follow should be a function of the issues we are working on (i.e., let the work drive the schedule).

Barriers

Several barriers were identified: (1) Our administrative culture does not provide sufficient formal process for working across functional areas. (2) Administrators face many distractions to thinking about policy issues. Working through policy issues is not part of our day-to-day practice/work. (3) There is a problem with a time commitment from team members. (4) There will be potential changes as a result of the new administration.

Enablers

These were identified as enablers: (1) Input is necessary from the deans, VPs, etc. to solve problems. (2) There must be a schedule, work plan, and deadlines—

rigor of process. (3) We must identify who is accountable and responsible for taking action. (4) There will be potential changes as a result of the new administration. (5) There should be more socializing (have the coffee break in the middle of the top team meetings as a way to promote networking).

CONCLUSION

This chapter suggested ways to engender teamwork by helping the team focus on work objectives, goals, and values. Most of the chapter described the formation of the top team group of administrators reporting to the president, provost, and vice presidents. Its purpose was to discuss departmental goals that have interdepartmental implications—that is, initiatives that require input or cooperation from one or more other departments. We saw it as a vehicle to implement and track university-wide goals and objectives and initiatives—issues and programs that touch all the administrative departments, such as diversity, performance management, and recommendations emerging from the university's accreditation review. We wanted to address university culture, to discover the type of university we want to be and what this means for administration and management.

We envisioned that the top team could be a forum to discuss external changes that impinge on the university and what they mean for us. It would give us a chance to analyze the need for change and directions for change. Moreover, it would continue our quest to become a "learning organization" focusing on the processes by which we work together, such as how we resolve conflict, develop our people, and involve our people in decision making. We could serve as a sounding board for the development of new policies and programs and a vehicle for communicating programs and policies. Overall, the top team could be a source of identification with the university beyond our individual departments and functional expertise. That is, we could identify ourselves as members of the university's top team. Our initiatives could improve administrative and management efficiency and effectiveness. We could move toward a culture of openness, learning, and cooperation. The top team could be a way to integrate new administrators, given that the team is an evolving group. Overall, the top team was our investment in ourselves and in the university.

The top team was a successful, albeit sometimes rocky, endeavor. It continued throughout the first academic year and into the new presidential administration. It was neither a panacea for eliminating conflict nor a forum for expressing and resolving all conflict. It did clarify some important issues and helped the group members know each other better. It also served as a useful vehicle for the top team members to meet the candidates in the presidential search and give input to the search committee. As such, it was a source of identification for ourselves and incoming administrators to see the top team as a community focused on common goals rather than members of disparate departments that rarely come together.

The goals of team building must extend below the top administrators. In some respects, we hoped that the top team members would convey the message of teamwork and interdepartmental cooperation to their troops. However, we recognized the importance of training and development for all employees to meet the challenges of the future. This is the subject of the next chapter.

NOTE

1. Edward M. Mone is the consultant who coauthored the section, "Plans for the Fall Semester's 'Top Team' Sessions."

9

Human Resource Development

It is a paradox that institutions of higher education are among the last of major organizations to recognize the importance of staff training. Universities, like other organizations, need to adapt to an ever-changing environment, both in terms of their own maturation and that of support for higher education in general. The ability to capitalize on opportunities requires an organizational culture capable of operating in a more fluid, less-well-defined environment. Universities, particularly public universities, often operate in bureaucracies. However, they also make creative, entrepreneurial decisions. Employee training and development is a key element to change the way business is conducted at the university.

To develop a more active approach to training and development, the president created a campuswide steering committee on training. The goal was to focus the campus's attention to the importance of employee development and to design programs that could be implemented quickly while requiring few resources. We did this by designing the first training month. The program consisted of special events and training sessions open to the campus. The committee published a training resource guide and initiated a month training calendar that is now routinely published as part of the campus newspaper. This effort continued for the next four years and is still ongoing. The committee was chaired by the deputy to the president.

This chapter presents the master plan for employee training and development written by the committee to outline training goals and activities. It can be viewed as architecture for action to enhance employees' readiness to meet changing job requirements and organizational structures.

A MASTER PLAN FOR EMPLOYEE TRAINING
AND DEVELOPMENT

The university's primary goal is to achieve organizational excellence—that is, to become a more flexible organization that is both highly coordinated in its planning and actions and also accountable for the outcomes it produces. In addition, the university wants to increase its ability to effectively use information technologies instead of less-efficient, paper-dependent processing operations. At the heart of its strategy to achieve this goal is continuous training and development aimed at supporting the school's mission and strategic objectives and contributing to sustained excellence in all academic and administrative areas. More specifically, training and development is necessary to change the culture at the university from a by-the-books, bureaucratic mentality to a customer-oriented, flexible organization that encourages continuous improvement in all its services.

BACKGROUND

A report issued by the Work in America Institute, titled "Meeting the Challenge of Change," highlights the changing demands of the American workplace: "workers are being asked to adapt to work places with advancing technologies and leaner work forces of self-supervising teams doing more complicated work. Training for all this has lagged" (cited in Cummins, 1992). Current wisdom tells us that training is important for productivity improvement and competitiveness. Further, training is essential for an organization's continued vitality in tight economic times. This is especially true as the university moves from a bureaucratic, by-the-books, rule-bound mentality to a flexible, fast-acting, customer-oriented environment. From the individual's viewpoint, training is critical to meet these changing organizational demands. In this sense, training becomes a key to employment security and morale enhancement.

Large organizations once offered job security and structured career paths in exchange for employees' loyalty and performance. Today, organizations offer challenging experiences and competitive levels of pay and benefits in exchange for employees' contribution to meeting organizational objectives. Development is not just for advancement anymore (although advancement opportunities certainly still exist). Rather, development is for ensuring that employees understand the needs of the organization and have the required skills for today and the future. Ultimately, this assures the individual's employment security in the current organization or somewhere else. Establishing opportunities for development require creative initiatives and a futuristic perspective to identify, communicate, and develop skill requirements for today and tomorrow.

In a recent *Harvard Business Review* article, Peter Drucker (1992) wrote about the importance of continuous learning to productivity improvement in the service sector. He stated that continuous learning must accompany productivity gains. Redesigning a job and then teaching the worker the new way to do it, which is what [Frederick W.] Taylor did and taught, cannot by itself sustain ongoing learning. Training is only the beginning of learning. Indeed, as the Japanese can teach us . . . , the greatest benefit of training comes not from learning something new but from doing better what we already do well. (p. 78)

Other universities are undergoing transformations and see the importance of individual development to emerging quality-oriented cultures. UCLA's strategic plan for sustaining excellence ("Transforming Administration at UCLA," 1991) states:

a successful new vision must accelerate the shift toward a philosophy where human resources and personnel development are strategic. This requires one indispensable enabling value—namely, the value of each individual, and their diverse contribution, must become the premise and focal point for organizational processes. . . .

organizational goals are subverted by an entrenched culture which accepts attitudes of protecting reputations, posturing for personal gain, avoiding the early surfacing of problems, and withholding sensitive information that is relevant to problem solving. . . .

a broad set of interpersonal and organizational inquiry skills designed to effect change exist and can counter these tendencies. This can help create an inquiry based learning environment that promotes openness on financial, management, planning and implementation issues. (pp. 6–7)

UCLA, along with the University of California system, is attempting to develop a "networked environment," as distinguished from a "bureaucratic environment." This new environment emphasizes the value of the individual, the importance of self-reflection and organizational assessment, and the contribution of an inquiry-based learning environment. Responsibility moves to low operational levels, and education and job opportunities enable employees to achieve sustained performance excellence.

While employee development is important to organizational change, the value of investing in people development may be difficult to justify in organizations that are suffering budget cuts and downsizing. Training is often the first thing to go in these organizations. However, organizations trying to renew their competitiveness and enhance the quality of operations and output depend on employee skill development and knowledge acquisition in technical, managerial, and interpersonal areas.

In the private sector, such efforts occur in fairly munificent environments as compared to the public sector, especially public-sector institutions of higher education. In the private sector, training and development efforts are viewed as supportive of cost cutting and organizational redesign. While less expensive training development mechanisms may be sought, there is the realization that training is important (London, 1989). It fits with the emerging organization culture. Employee development is acknowledged by top executives as vital to quality improvement and customer service. Also, employees are rewarded for their participation in terms of increased pay for increased skills (because of enhanced value to the organization) and enhanced marketability (within and outside the firm). Overall, there is a long history of support for technical and managerial training, and spending money on training even with diminishing resources is often viewed as not just as acceptable, but necessary.

The goals of training and development are much the same in both public and private sectors and in universities as in corporations. Training should be linked to productivity improvement and organizational strategies. The role of training is critical to the continued vitality of an organization, especially in a tight economic environment that demands efficiency and customer responsiveness.

This chapter presents a broad vision to inculcate a continuous learning environment for university employees. Such a goal recognizes that organizational change comes from preparedness, flexibility, and empowerment, such that all employees will be ready and willing to meet the demands of today and the challenges of the future. Continuous learning must become a central building block for organizational change at the university. Facing a constricted financial condition, the institution realizes that investing in its people is critical to its continued viability and future success.

CREATING A DEVELOPMENT-ORIENTED/CONTINUOUS LEARNING CULTURE AT THE UNIVERSITY

To begin developing a more active approach to training and development and to support the activities of the university human resources department, which has primary responsibility for training, the president created a campuswide steering committee on training. The president charged the committee with focusing the campus's attention on training and to begin developing programs that could be implemented quickly and required few resources. The committee planned and implemented the first training month, held in July, less than two months after the formation of the committee. The committee continued its efforts sponsoring similar events each year (four years running at the time of this writing). Through training month and other activities, the committee tried to establish a foundation upon which to encourage employee development and recognition for that development. A description of the first training month and plans for the second one are outlined later in this chapter. These initial efforts provide the foundation for establishing a training and development strategy for the university that could be integrated into the goals and objectives of every administrative and academic department.

These efforts show how the institution began to create a continuous learning environment for its nonacademic employees. The effort began within the context of severe budget constraints and a preexisting culture that often discourages employee development. The goal was a university-wide effort to tie training and development to the missions of the institution, promote career planning, improve current job performance, and provide development for future job opportunities. The process and content of the effort rested on the belief that the continued vitality of a downsizing, and at times beleaguered, organization depends on commitment to employee training and development. Training paves the road toward enhancement of employee commitment to the institution and improves productivity and the quality of service. After reviewing the goals and activities of the training committee during its first year of operation, a plan is outlined for continuing these efforts in tandem with a variety of departmental activities.

Some Recent History

Despite its role as a provider of quality advanced education, the university did not foster the training and development of its nonacademic staff. The service staff, though important, was considered not central to the research and teaching missions of the institution. There was no link between accomplishing these missions and employee training and development. The environment was plagued by decreasing resources, uncertainty about future resources (except to anticipate continued decreases), and the need for cost cutting, restructuring, and downsizing. The small training staff in the human resource department pointed out the benefits for additional training in many areas. While the president understood this need, money was not readily available for investment in additional training resources. Further, there was no history of supporting employee development. The training that did exist was not clearly linked to the missions of the university. No systematic movement of employees between jobs (career ladders) as a means of development existed, and there were few advancement opportunities. The university does not provide a fast-track advancement program for highly valued managers.

There was limited tuition aid for employees. Support personnel were stymied by low salaries and few opportunities for upward and even lateral movement. Also, academic department chairs did not view themselves as managers despite their obvious supervisory role. Interviews with 10 department chairs indicated that the label "manager" was viewed as demeaning to the scholar turned temporary administrator. They tended to shun traditional duties of managing people, often delegating responsibility for appraisal, supervision, budgeting, expense tracking, and other managerial duties to ill-prepared administrative assistants.

The training available depended on state mandates (as a public institution), union agreements (there were three large unions on campus), and technical needs. A small career planning function offered training and career counseling. There was a job posting system that follows civil service regulations. Movement of people between departments occurred as vacancies arose and qualified people applied for them. Employees generally stayed in the same positions for years.

Needs Analysis

Sensing the requirement for increased training, the deputy to the president commissioned a student project under the supervision of the director of the university's center for labor/management studies. Three administrative departments were studied by a group of three masters-level management students. Questionnaires were administered to 200+ employees and their supervisors. The questionnaire asked about type of training received during the past year, the source of this training (e.g., whether on-the-job, classroom training provided by a campus training group, or off-site training), and future needs. Lists of training topics were presented to the respondents. The results showed that employees and their supervisors disagreed about the types of training needed. Employees saw a need for training in computer literacy, writing, and stress management. Supervisors saw a need for administrative and technical ("how to") training. The specific results of the needs analysis were probably less important than the value of the study for increasing the awareness of the need for more employee training across the university.

Change Strategy

The president responded to the results of this analysis. Given the tough economic times and absence of a history of support for employee training and development, the president and his deputy decided to use existing university resources to create a continuous learning culture and provide the needed training. The design effort involved representatives from every major division. They created the presidential steering committee for training and development. As such, the project demonstrated top-level support from the start. The 11 members of the committee were representatives from all divisions and organizational levels (secretaries, assistant vice presidents, and mid-level administrators, all appointed by their vice presidents and the provost). The committee chair was a faculty member with corporate training experience. The president's deputy was responsible for continued oversight of the committee.

First Tasks

The president formally charged the committee with developing ways to increase the importance of employee training and highlighting its contribution to the university's missions. The committee began its work during the late spring by hearing from the university's upper management (the president, the provost, and the five vice presidents) who described their training priorities. The other officers described their training priorities.

The first task of the committee was to proclaim July "training month." Since the committee was formed at the end of May, there was barely one month to plan and execute the effort. The purpose of training month was to increase the salience of training and development on campus. Activities during the month emphasized that employee development was important to the continued vitality of the institution in tight economic times. Also, the goal was to arrange for the delivery of some required training, using July as an occasion to update employees' knowledge in key areas.

Some committee members noted that July was a "slow" month, with many faculty and staff on vacation or on summer breaks—this didn't seem to be the time for a major organizational initiative. Indeed, some felt that having special events during July sent the message that training was not important. If that were true, training month should be at some prime time—such as October or March—when the semester's activities were at their height. However, the president felt that there was no time like the present, and employees were more likely to have available time for training during a relatively slow period.

Activities for the First Annual Training Month

The committee decided during an initial meeting that they should not attempt a major extravaganza during training month since all the campus's employee training needs could not be met in 30 days, and given they had only five weeks to plan. There was no point in raising expectations to a level that couldn't be met logistically. Therefore, a set of limited, feasible activities was outlined to call attention to employee development and provide an occasion for employees to celebrate its importance.

After deciding on the activities and establishing commitment and funding (about $7,000) from the president's office, the following activities were planned:

1. *A kickoff celebration."* An outdoor event was held with booths from 18 campus units that offer some form of training and employee assistance. Training was defined broadly as any activity that provided assistance, support, information, or skills to employees. Units represented included the employee assistance and wellness programs, computer training, safety training, hospital personnel training, the Small Business Development Center, faculty support services, supervisory training, career planning, and employee activities (e.g., crafts).

The celebration day included speeches by the president, deputy to president, and the training committee chair. The president spoke about the importance of employee training to the missions of the university. In particular, he characterized a research university and the need for continuous learning to support sophisticated scientific efforts and provide efficient, high quality services to students and patients.

The atmosphere during the day was festive, with lemonade served in plastic cups with the training logo, which were given to attendees. The event was held in the tunnel between the east and west campuses, making the event convenient for employees and providing a symbol to link the health sciences center to the east and the arts and sciences departments to the west.

2. *Public relations initiatives.* Various PR initiatives announced events and emphasized university commitment. Banners were placed at the campus entrances proclaiming, "July Is Training Month—Invest in Your Future." The president issued a proclamation communicated via the campus electronic bulletin board and in print. A training logo was designed and embossed on various giveaways (cups and note pads).

3. *The university training and development resource guide.* A resource guide was produced to describe departments that provide training. This was sent to more than 200 "responsibility center" managers in administrative and academic departments.

4. *Special training programs.* Three half-day special training programs were offered twice each. Topics included recent developments in budgeting and administration, career planning, and a three-hour overview of a supervisory training program (to whet supervisors' appetites for a more extensive five-day program already offered by the training department). In addition, a special two-hour overview of the supervisory training program was given to the officer team (the president, provost, and VPs) so that they could better understand the type of training available for their managers.

5. *Campus training calendar.* The first of what became the regular publication of a campus training calendar was published in the campus newspaper. The calendar communicated the schedule of all major training departments (those listed in the Resource Guide).

Campus Reactions

The president required that all VPs become involved and encourage their people to take part in July's events. The kickoff had a large turnout (about 800 people including the provost and all the VPs). The six training modules were fully subscribed (60+ people at each one). The training committee received a number of requests for additional training. In general, the committee members were highly energized and wanted to continue their efforts.

Beyond the First Training Month

The president requested that the committee continue its work during the fall semester. They did so, meeting biweekly for sessions that lasted about two hours each. At the first meeting of the semester, the members decided to change their role to that of a *steering* committee. They defined their mission as guiding and facilitating training directions and programs—not as a task force responsible for actually implementing programs.

The priorities expressed by the university's officers in preparing for July were used as input. Specifically, the following programs were developed to meet specific needs.

(1) *Need: Increase Employees' Commitment to the University*

Action: A revised orientation for new employees that can also serve as a reorientation for current employees.

Several VPs felt that employees had little knowledge of the university beyond their own departments and that an extensive orientation program would help broaden their scope of knowledge. We needed a way to ensure that employees understood the scope of what the university is and does.

(2) *Need: Increased Flexibility, Greater Management Depth, and a More Highly Skilled Workforce.*

Action: A "University Professional Development/Certification Program."

A mastery path is a listing of the training and developmental experiences required to achieve mastery on a particular level. Another term might be "job-specific certification." Broad categories of jobs (e.g., clerical, executive assistant, area director) can be identified and mastery paths established. For technical and other unique positions, the training committee can formulate guidelines for supervisors to follow with their subordinates to establish appropriate customized mastery paths. The establishment of a mastery path is relevant to experienced employees, as well as new employees, both of whom can specify a series of learning experiences drawing on the university's training resources and the new certification process.

The success of this approach depends on supervisors meeting with subordinates to agree on the developmental experiences needed to achieve mastery and then to evaluate progress and ultimately attainment of mastery. Achieving mastery might take a year or more. Progress and final attainment are noted in the individual's personnel file. A department or division holds annual or semiannual meetings to award mastery certificates.

This contributes to establishing a continuous learning environment for employees. The involvement of supervisors and subordinates is a vehicle for changing the university's culture, making employee development an important part of every supervisor's job. It also makes self-development an important goal for the university employees.

The following is a three tiered approach to employee training:

Tier I: A university-wide certification process, with certification in areas that are applicable to most if not all the university employees. Drawing on the priorities provided by the VPs, six areas were selected for training:

a. Supervisory training—a sequence of courses in basic elements of supervision such as goal setting, appraisal, feedback, and recognition.

b. Affirmative Action and Equal Opportunity awareness training (covering such topics as selection methods, sexual harassment, and managing diversity).

c. Computer literacy training as needed in one's current job and to become eligible for other desired jobs.

d. Budgeting and administration training to help employees who need to know information about new financial procedures, goal-setting methods, budgeting and other formal processes.

f. Service quality training to increase employees' understanding of how to better serve customers, students, and patients, as well as employees in other departments.

Each of these areas consists of a series of five to six modules to be designed by the administrative department responsible for the function with involvement of the training committee members. This requires coordinated action and involvement of departments across the university. Employees who complete a series receive a certificate of accomplishment and completion that is recorded in the employee's official personnel file.

Tier II: Job-category certification, with certification in areas that are applicable to broad categories of positions (e.g., a supervision curriculum and certification process, a finance and budget curriculum and certification process, etc.). The training committee encouraged internal department-specific training based on the idea of professional development modules to expand professional development to job families (e.g., graphic services). Department managers develop their own training sequence to enhance the professionalism of their own department.

Tier III: Job-specific certification, with certification in areas that are unique to the specific position.

Overall, these three tiers form a mastery path for each individual.

Action: A process and form enabling every employee to have a development plan.

This is an annual process, separate from the performance appraisal (since performance feedback can prompt defensiveness). Supervisors meet with each subordinate to discuss their jointly perceived need for training to do better on his or her current job or to prepare for another job. The supervisor and subordinate mutually establish a training and development plan for the ensuing year that reflects the department's needs and resources and the subordinate's strengths and weaknesses and career goals. Supervisors are encouraged to think of training broadly to include a variety of job experiences and special assignments, job aids, and other ways to instill new skills and knowledge. Such a program includes courses offered to employees by the university or from an outside source. The information is collected in a departmental and university-wide training needs analyses to facilitate planning and coordinating university training resources.

Action: An executive development program for senior management.

The president's steering committee on training and development proposed the university's first leadership development program geared to the needs of upper management. This program commences with a class of 20–25 managers attending five half-day modules, one a month during a semester. The content overlaps with the professional development program described above. Discussions focus on university strategies, ways to increase communication among departments, and ways to accomplish institutional goals. Four modules highlight the skills and attributes important to the university's missions:

The Leadership Challenge: Key Roles for Excellence. Participants explore the skills and competencies required to lead the human enterprise. Emphasis is on eight specific roles—the manager as producer, director, group facilitator, mentor, innovator, broker, monitor, and coordinator.

Leadership Self-Assessment. This activity offers participants the opportunity to complete a formalized "leadership" self-assessment and compare their responses to those of co-workers and relevant others. The data gathering occurs before the class. Results are distributed in the classroom, and the instructor helps the students process the information and develop action plans.

Diversity. Leaders, for "legal" reasons, are required to establish discrimination-free work environments. However, a better reason for promoting the "value of diversity" is that embracing diversity is a primary means of promoting excellence. Also, diversity is a principal mission of the university. This workshop offers practical strategies for promoting diversity in the workplace.

Quality Service. So much has been written about quality, customer service, employee involvement, and total quality management. This workshop provides participants with highlights of applied principles that have been effective in a variety of organizations, an overview of the university's perspective on quality service, and strategies for gaining acceptance of the "quality" message within the participants' department.

Some of these modules require outside consultants, text materials, support staff time, and specialized training materials. For instance, the diversity workshop includes an outside speaker. The entire series costs approximately $8,000, or about $80 per participant per session, or $320 per participant for the entire series.

(3) *Need: Ensure That Managers Understand the Direction in Which the Institution Is Moving and Their Place in This Effort.*

Action: Establish the University Managers' Forum.

Groups of 35–40 managers meet periodically to hear from the president, provost, and vice presidents and have an opportunity to discuss university-wide strategies and actions.

Action: Provide an orientation program for academic department chairs.

This is a briefing for department chairs on essential information regarding their managerial responsibilities, including faculty development, personnel management, union contracts, hiring practices, management research, academic guidelines, functions of various administrative offices including public safety, and assignment of teaching responsibilities.

Implementation Strategy and Facilitating Factors

As these programs were conceptualized, the committee chair communicated the plans to the university's officers during special presentations. Several officers had been regularly receiving copies of the minutes of the training committee meetings. Occasionally, the vice presidents' representatives on the committee were requested to speak to their VP about a particular issue.

During the six-month period that these programs were developed, a new human resource department director was hired. She became very supportive of the efforts of the training committee and involved herself and her people in the design of training programs. She assigned increased responsibility to the training manager who led a subgroup responsible for designing the orientation program for new employees. Also, the human resource department director expressed a desire to spearhead other actions outlined above as a way to reinforce the idea that the human resource department was the institutional home for the training function, while the training committee continued to focus university-wide attention on training and development issues.

Other development-related ideas and initiatives emerged during the academic year. For instance, one department started an experiment with upward feedback (subordinates rating their managers). There was increased attention to total quality management, and the training committee chair was requested to present TQM principles to the officers in their cabinet meeting.

The Second Annual Training Month

The training committee began to initiate plans for the coming summer's training celebration at the start of the spring semester. The theme for the month was "U-Matter" (the "U" referring to university and "you"). The tight financial environment suggested the value of programs that focused on the university's concern for its people. Workshops included topics pertaining to university skills, career development, and personal enrichment. For instance, the university-related training provided an update in budgeting and financial systems for administrative managers and staff assistants, an overview of TQM and operating efficiency analysis, and a review of labor contracts. Events and products included a repeat of the first year's successful kickoff celebration and publication of an expanded training resource guide. A recognition program made awards to departments that implemented special internal training programs for their employees. Communications about training month included a special edition of the campus newspaper and an extensive brochure of special training programs for the month.

Continued Efforts

The training committee, the human resource department, and local departmental efforts progressed as their training missions were strengthened and new goals and objectives emerged. As stated at the outset, we hoped that employee training and development would become an integral part of operating the university. By the fourth year, the theme for the training celebration was "Summer Is Training." The kickoff became an annual tradition with an increased number of departments providing booths and demonstrations and more courses offered throughout June, July, and August. The training director and other campus personnel offered a variety of programs and courses.

One course was called "How to Be a Better Trainer." This was not meant for professional trainers but for any manager who might be involved in developing and delivering a training program for their unit. This was a half-day course offered on three consecutive days. The program announcement read as follows:

How would you rate your presentation skills on a scale of 1–10? If you rated yourself a 7 or less, it's time to strengthen those training muscles! Excellent trainers are not born—they're developed. Find out how you can further enhance your presentation skills to teach, stimulate, and motivate your trainees.

Here are a few more examples of courses:

"Better Business Writing": Currently we live in an information and service society where business and professional writing skills are essential. However, many of us continue to have difficulty putting our thoughts into words. We often become anxious staring down at that blank piece of paper. This full-day seminar will provide the fundamental steps to writing clearer, more concise documents. Learn how to overcome the hardest part of business writing—getting started.

"Men and Women Working Together": By the year 2000, about 75% of all women in the U.S. will be in the workforce. This is an increase of 45% since 1950. With such massive societal change, gender-role confusion is becoming widespread. This half-day course will explore how men and women can expand their gender-cooperation skills to become productive partners in the workforce.

"Preparing Travel Vouchers": The Travel Office offers assistance to campus personnel involved in the preparation of any travel-related vouchers. The guidelines and regulations will be explained, questions will be answered, and assistance in using the correct forms will be given in this two hour workshop.

Some specific future goals and activities of the training committee beyond the summer's events included the following:

1. *Incorporate training and development into individual and responsibility center goals and objectives and performance standards.* The committee felt that each department manager should have a "people plan" that states what will be done to ensure that employees have the knowledge and skills to meet changing job requirements. Managers need to understand changing university goals and take ownership of them. This means interpreting the goals and new organizational culture and identifying the learning required to be successful in this emerging environment. Department-specific training will be necessary and is encouraged by the training committee. A grants program can be established to review proposals and provide seed money to assist in establishing these efforts. Also, each individual should have a development plan that is established jointly with the supervisor and that lists developmental experiences that will occur during the coming year.

2. *Introduce the revamped new employee orientation program, giving current employees a chance to attend as a reorientation to the university.* All employees should have a working understanding of the university's mission and structure. They need to know how the university operates, and how they fit into the operation. They must go beyond their narrow job function to be a representative of the whole institution, contribute to the effectiveness of other departments, and generally be part of a single team. Current employees may need to be reoriented to the university, given the growth and development of new endeavors on campus. New employees certainly require a sense of the whole and knowledge of the resources that will help them do their jobs.

3. *Implement the Professional Development/Certification Program, the Executive Development Program, and a Recognition Award Program for department training efforts and model managers.* The training committee emphasized these programs because they direct employees' attention to the changing organizational culture and provide the resources to enable the change. These programs recognize that training and development is for all employees regardless of level. Further, they acknowledge that individual departments have specific needs for employee development. Managers who step up to these needs should be recognized for their accomplishments and highlighted as role models.

4. *Support other new human resource department initiatives (e.g., retirement workshops and supervisory training).* The human resource department maintained its responsibility for a host of employee training and development activities, principally a valuable series of supervisory training. The human resource department has a central role, along with the university-wide committee, as architect and implementer of training strategy and delivery.

5. *Start the university forum.* As indicated above, the 200+ responsibility managers would meet periodically in groups of about 35–40 to discuss university-wide strategies and actions and better understand the contributions of their departments to the university's mission. The rapid pace of change at the university means that key managers should be informed about evolving directions and goals. Further, they should be communicating with each other in a cooperative spirit that builds networks and alliances among and within departments. The "forum" would be an opportunity to hear from the university's officers, express opinions, and encourage coalescence around a coherent strategy for the university.

Several other programs were more long term in nature. The committee felt they are important, but more time would be necessary to formulate the ideas. Specifically:

6. *Initiate training to support a customer-responsive, quality-oriented administration* (e.g., training in total quality management, group dynamics, and quality control). TQM is becoming a new way of doing business in institutions of higher education, just as it has in large and small corporations. Promoting constant quality improvement is built on commitment to enhanced customer-supplier relationships and a philosophy of participative management. Departments in the university—such as institutional services, student affairs, and the hospital—experimented with TQM principles and structures. Training and facilitation is critical for the success of TQM. Guiding training to support TQM would be an important part of the training committee's activities in the future.

Stanford University initiated a training program for finance department groups that focused on service quality and ways to improve service (Massy, 1992). As such, the training program is integrated with team building and quality improvement goals. Highlighting strategic thinking and empowerment, the training reinforced good service as a priority (e.g., the sessions made visible top management's support for service quality); services were clarified and defined and unnecessary services were eliminated; service skills were reviewed (e.g., characteristics of good and bad service were discussed—aspects such as accessibility, follow-through, and courtesy); communications were examined and improved, including initiating ongoing direct client feedback; and other improvements were suggested and implemented. Overall, team building among group members was enhanced as participants realized the contribution they make to the university.

7. *Select and train a cadre of facilitators who can assist in team building and improved group dynamics.* TQM and allied processes such as committees and task forces (which are ubiquitous in most universities) require facilitators to structure and guide team efforts. This does not require creating new positions. Rather, current employees who desire to expand their interpersonal skills can be tapped to learn the facilitator role. They can then be resources to their departments (and to other departments) to orient employees to TQM, improve communication in committees and task forces, and help managers redesign the structure of their units to enhance efficiency and quality.

8. *Design training for employees to conduct analyses of customer expectations, work flows, human resource utilization, and quality improvement.* The university hospital's director of management engineering was placed on special assignment to the office of the president. He and his staff completed a series of efficiency studies of administrative departments. If we believe in continuous improvement and empowerment, employees, who after all know their departments the best, should learn to conduct these analyses themselves.

9. *Establish a formal training policy for the university.* The training committee worked hard to draft and wordsmith a training policy that was approved by the campus policy committee and the university's officers and ultimately distributed by the president. The text follows:

Providing and encouraging opportunity for continuous training and development is a critical managerial responsibility necessary for improving and supporting skills of staff members both as practitioners and as citizens of the community. The university encourages employees to participate in approved programs and courses that provide personal enhancement as well as those that enable one to improve necessary workplace skills.

Supervisors and their employees should jointly develop the employee's annual plan for continued training and development of skills. The plan is based on the identified needs and expectations of the employee and the availability of approved programs. If training is immediately relevant to the employee's workplace responsibilities, the implementation of the plan may be incorporated into the employee's performance program for the ensuing year. If the desired training is not immediately relevant to work responsibilities, but is important to the personal development of the employee, a written agreement describing the anticipated course work shall be placed in the employee's file, but not included in the performance program. All courses or programs must be approved by the employee's supervisor prior to enrollment.

The recommended amount of time to be allocated annually for training is approximately one hour per week. For example, an employee may participate in several training programs of varying lengths during the course of the year (i.e., 1 hour, half- or one-day programs) or take a 3-credit course (45 hours) during one semester. It is to be expected that employees will use their own time for programs or courses for personal development.

CONCLUSION

The master plan for employee training and development presented here recognized that in order to effect a long-term change in attitude and organizational flexibility, more long-term efforts must be planned and implemented in the near future. The special initiatives would complement the training department's efforts at providing courses in needed skills and knowledge. Also, we recognized the importance of rewarding departments that initiate training to meet local needs.

The efforts described above can be viewed as the start of a major culture shift in the university. It was planned as a deliberate operational change by the president and deputy to the president. New symbols and rituals were almost as important as the content of the training. Training month, the kickoff celebration, a training logo and theme (e.g., "U-Matter"), the speeches and proclamations were all aimed at expressing new expectations. Departments were encouraged to piggyback their training activities with those of the training committee and the human resource department, defining department-specific training as part of the university-wide activities. This legitimized their training efforts and helped to justify devoting resources to training.

Many of the university's nonacademic employees were worried about employment security. They were hesitant to look for new jobs given the paucity of positions in the job market. With increased focus on training and personal development, they would become revitalized and aware that their employment security is directly related to helping the institution become more productive and customer-oriented.

Several of the campus officers continued to voice strong support for the training effort. As one vice president wrote,

I agree that training and skill development is important for efficiency and productivity, and it is also a way to demonstrate the interest and concern that we have for the employees that make the university run. When we invest in them, they know that we care; generally the investment is returned several fold.

This chapter treats employee training as a strategic initiative for organization development. The next two chapters consider issues and methods of performance appraisal, feedback, and managing marginal performance. Better people management is a key to organization effectiveness, and human resource programs contribute to the strategic objective of enhancing quality and cost effectiveness in university administration.

10

Performance Appraisal and Survey Feedback

Bringing about organizational changes requires that people understand new directions and behaviors. They have to know what is expected of them and how well they are meeting the expectations. They need to understand their strengths and weaknesses, and they need to know how well they are doing. That is, performance information, evaluation, and feedback are key to helping people know how they have to change their behavior and what they have to learn in order to meet changing job demands.

Meaningful performance evaluation and feedback are not accomplished easily. Employees feel threatened by rating systems, they are naturally defensive about feedback, and managers avoid facing performance problems. This is especially the case when employees are under pressure to do more with fewer resources. It's hard to tell people who are working harder than ever that their performance is slipping. The focus of this chapter is on providing employees with useful performance information. The chapter begins by outlining a process for a ratingless performance appraisal. The idea behind ratingless appraisal is to encourage supervisors to provide more constructive feedback in a nonthreatening way. The chapter outlines components of the system, what needs to be done to implement it, and answers to questions about how to administer the system. The next section describes a program for upward feedback—subordinates rating managers—as another source of performance information that is especially useful for guiding management development. The last section provides recommendations for developing upward or 360 degree feedback (ratings from subordinates, peers, customers, and supervisors).

A RATINGLESS PERFORMANCE MANAGEMENT SYSTEM

This section describes how to develop an appraisal process that has the following characteristics:

- No ratings and no forced distributions
- Establishment of performance objectives and measurements (quantitative and behavioral performance indicators)
- Input from diverse sources (e.g., 360 degree feedback)
- Periodic (quarterly) reviews and feedback from the supervisor
- Rollout that communicates and models the process throughout the year
- Space on performance reviews for describing objective accomplishments and measurements
- Self-evaluations as source of information and stimulus for periodic and annual reviews and feedback discussions
- An evaluation/tracking process to ensure the system is working as intended (i.e., that managers are given meaningful feedback and annual performance reviews); evaluation methods include employee opinion surveys, work group discussions of the process, and reviews of appraisal content

Goals for the Objectives Setting/Performance Review Process

- Facilitate performance feedback (reduce defensiveness often tied to assigning numerical values to performance dimensions).
- Increase constructive discussion during performance feedback.
- Encourage employee development (link the appraisal to training needed to improve on the current job and development for future needs of the department and institution and the subordinate's career objectives).
- Improve quality of performance evaluations and feedback.
- Ensure fairness (avoid unfair discrimination and recognize value of diversity).
- Generate thorough/comprehensive evaluations that address key dimensions of performance—those behaviors and outcomes important to the department, division, clients, and institution.
- Increase the value of appraisal to the subordinate (focus on behaviors and behavioral change, reduce categorization and labeling, increase desire of subordinate to work with the supervisor to understand and improve performance).
- Capture subordinates' performance goals and objectives.
- Recognize changing departmental priorities and project requirements.
- Have evaluation questions that are meaningful across departments to ensure comparability and usefulness (e.g., in evaluating candidates for transfer or promotion).
- Recognize individual accomplishments and contributions to group efforts.
- Establish a clear/understandable and direct link to compensation treatment and other personnel decisions (e.g., promotion, transfer, managing marginal performers, restructuring).

What's Needed

To do all these, managers need a package with the following materials:

1. A concise overview of the purpose of the process, its key features, an outline of the steps, and descriptions of applications (with several cogent samples).
2. The forms
3. Outline of how the process is tied to compensation
4. Resource tools
   —Guidelines and samples of performance narratives
   —Guidelines for objective setting, measurements, feedback documentation, and development plans
   —University and departmental visions, mission, and values
   —Guidelines for writing and giving constructive feedback
   —Guidelines for defining departmental values
   —Types of objectives and measures encompassing supervisory support, leadership, management skills, technical/professional projects, teamwork, quality, and affirmative action
5. The rollout process would entail:
   —memos and messages from the president and officers
   —pamphlet outlining the process to all associates (if applicable to occupational and management)
   —the "package" (as delineated above) delivered during orientation training to all managers
   —orientation training
   • outline of the goals and principles underlying the process
   • description of process cycle
      a. objectives setting and agreeing on measurements and needed development
      b. periodic reviews and feedback
      c. self-evaluation
      d. narrative evaluations
      e. feedback
      f. compensation review and feedback
      g. how the process will be assessed

Some Questions and Answers

The process needs to address application to self-managing teams and team evaluation and feedback. That is, how do self-managing teams use the process? How do supervisors use the process to help teams set goals, to evaluate team goals, to give teams feedback, and provide team compensation awards?

1. *How do we make sure poor performers are identified and addressed?* The narrative appraisal will be part of a larger system of performance excellence that ties together objective setting, development planning, and periodic performance review and feedback. Marginal performance will have to be identified and dealt with as it is now by addressing issues of capability and motivation, giving direct and constructive feedback, setting realistic goals and consequences, and tracking

performance. The intention of the new process will be to encourage communication about performance between managers and subordinates, provide documentation, and not let performance problems slide.

2. *Do we eliminate both ratings and rankings?* Yes, both should be eliminated. The goal of the new process is to move away from categorizing people toward providing more detailed summaries of performance linked to specific objectives. The ratings (even without forced choice) are a crutch that is highly subjective, likely to be inconsistent across groups (e.g., "exceeding objectives" may mean different things to different managers), and not necessarily backed by solid and well-documented performance information. Encouraging the meaningful review without the rating will focus attention on performance rather than distract attention to a subjective categorization.

3. *How do we handle compensation under this type of system? How do we differentiate and support the compensation?* Compensation decisions should still be made by peer groups of managers discussing their subordinates' accomplishments. They might be called "Performance Review Discussions." In these sessions, each manager will review the material for each subordinate, including (a) the objectives and any changes in objectives during the year, (b) the development plans established jointly with performance objectives, (c) results of periodic review and feedback sessions, and (d) the final appraisal. Points a–c can be covered quickly, with most attention given to d. (Having to recount the subordinate's performance in this way will have the side benefit of encouraging managers to carry out the objective setting/appraisal process seriously during the year and write meaningful annual reviews.)

After all subordinates have been reviewed, the peer managers can determine a fair pay structure based on distinctions between subordinates. Several patterns of results are possible—for example:

- All subordinates may be equally high performers and should receive the same merit treatment.

- The subordinates can be grouped into three or four categories. Demarcations of performance between these categories will determine if the groups should receive substantially different levels of merit pay or whether there should be minor differences between groups. (After groups are established, another decision could be to pay people somewhat differently within groups.)

- The subordinates can be ranked ordered and a decision made about appropriate pay differentials.

4. *How do we address transfer of people, especially if to an organization that uses ratings? Will our people be treated equitably?* Given differences in standards and the subjective way that rating categories are commonly used, the ratings are not always helpful for staffing purposes. The narrative appraisals should provide far more useful information in making staffing decisions about people. Managers from departments using more appraisals will still be able to understand and inter-

pret the narratives. The candidate's strengths and weaknesses should be far more apparent in the narratives than could be conveyed by a single rating and the brief documentation that usually accompanies the rating. The more extensive information about employees should give a selecting manager more confidence in making personnel decisions.

5. *How do we align this system with those used in our extended university community?* Managers in other departments will have no problem using the narrative appraisals. Indeed, they should find them more valuable than the typical rating procedure. Also, it appears that many university departments are moving in the direction of the ratingless appraisal to a more comprehensive performance excellence approach (linking objective setting, development, periodic review and feedback, and annual appraisal). As such, departments using ratings will be out of line.

6. *What about dotted line relationships where there is dual reporting and different compensation systems?* Dual reporting relationships suggest that the employee's managers need to agree on how time will be split. If the work is independent (e.g., totally different projects for each manager), then separate appraisal processes (and commensurate merit treatment) can be carried out independently by each manager. If the work is interdependent, then the managers can agree on how they will work with the employee to set goals, give feedback, and write the final appraisal. The managers may meet with the employee together, or one manager can take the lead, obtaining input from the other manager all along the way.

7. *How do we make sure that motivation is not negatively impacted? How do we ensure that this system will drive performance in a positive way and move the organization forward?* A process that encourages frequent communication about objectives, development, and performance should enhance motivation and clarify linkages to institution and department goals. The process can highlight major departmental goals (e.g., customer responsiveness, quality, awareness of university objectives, creativity, and cost-effectiveness) to ensure they are reflected in the objectives.

8. *How do we address membership on multiple teams? What about the matrix management environment?* This is addressed in response to Question 7.

9. *How do we include customer input? How much should customer input be included?* Customer input is important and should be gathered by the manager before writing periodic performance reviews and the final appraisal. In general, input from multiple sources is important, and managers should be encouraged to contact the employee's subordinates, peers, and other departmental managers as appropriate to obtain information. The employee can be asked to nominate several people who are familiar with the employee's performance, but the manager is free to contact others as well.

If the department has an upward feedback process and the results are used solely for development purposes, managers can use their results in discussions with their bosses. The department might want to address whether the upward feedback process should be used for evaluation purposes as well (if it is not currently). This would provide results to higher managers for use in the appraisal process.

10. *How do we link to leadership continuity and succession planning?* The narratives should serve as ample justification for nominating people to a program for high potential managers and evaluating candidates for promotion. Having a "Far Exceeds" rating says much less than narratives that clarify the individual's accomplishments, experiences, competencies, competitiveness, and need for further development.

11. *Can we provide the forms in electronic process?* Yes. We will have a form that covers objectives, development, periodic review and feedback, and annual narrative appraisal of performance, task evaluation, and work methods. The form has several columns, allowing the manager to write an objective in the left column and link it to performance review and methods of accomplishment in the middle and right columns.

12. *Should appraisals be done for each project, and when a project is completed? How long should they be used as a guideline? What constitutes a project?* Frequent feedback should be encouraged, and feedback during and at the completion of the project is certainly desirable. This "Performance Excellence" process should require a review and feedback several times during the year at designated, regular intervals (e.g., once every three or four months).

The issue of what constitutes a project might best be stated in terms of what constitutes an objective. An objective might be general (e.g., deliver high-quality products on time). Alternatively, an objective can refer to a specific project. In this case, it should include a set of performance standards reflecting how the project will be carried out. So, for instance, a project might be to complete a media package for a particular department on time and in a manner that demonstrates knowledge of the client's needs.

13. *How do we do appraisals on a team, especially a self-managed team?* Separate guidelines for self-managed teams can be established. Generally, the team will be responsible for objective setting and review and for discussing and agreeing to each other's development plans. The team can work in a group to write the appraisals as they discuss their performance and give each other feedback.

Turning to the issue of managers evaluating team performance, a separate process can be carried out (and form completed) to establish the team's goals and review the team's performance. As usual, input would be obtained from multiple sources. The manager would meet with the team as a whole for periodic goal setting and performance reviews.

A team appraisal might occur even if there are separate individual appraisals for each subordinate. This would depend on the extent to which subordinates work on team projects. Teams could include employees from more than one department. Team goals are established and a team award can be given as part of the compensation merit review.

14. *How do we ensure there are no surprises at the end of the year? How often should appraisals and feedback sessions be conducted?* Periodic feedback

should ensure that there are no surprises. Reviews should occur quarterly or every four months.

15. *What is the linkage to ongoing feedback and ongoing development? How do we ensure that managers are held accountable for the development of subordinates? How do we measure the development? How much input should come from the subordinates?* As evident from responses to earlier questions, there should be a complete process that ties together objectives, development, and ongoing feedback.

One of the objectives of a manager's job should be to develop subordinates. As such, managers should be evaluated on how well they accomplish the goal-setting and performance review process and how much attention they give to their subordinates' professional growth and development.

16. *How do we communicate the rollout of this program to the employees?* Rollout should have several components:

- Announcement from the vice president in the form of a memo and/or video message
- Memo/brochure describing the process (this can be used as a brief job aid for later reference)
- Half-day orientation meetings (i.e., training workshop) to discuss the principles of the programs, policies and procedures, expectations, and examples of constructive meaningful narrative appraisals and poor narratives

A video of the training can be made for new entrants to the department.

Summary

This idea of a ratingless appraisal may be new and strange to many organizations and human resource professionals. People want some quantification of their performance—just as they received grades in school. The ratingless appraisal is aimed at bypassing the negative elements of such numeric systems (e.g., grade inflation and reluctance to given negative ratings). The goal is to increase constructive feedback and focus attention in the performance review of areas for development rather than defending a rating. The process outlined above shows that a comprehensive system is needed to make this work. The system has to be tied into other parts of the institution (if implemented in one department). Also, it needs to be linked to the organization's system of making decisions about employees (for instance, decisions about pay, promotion, transfer, and termination). Overall, ratingless appraisals are a way of enhancing the importance of employee development in the organization, increasing managers' responsibility to provide the resources (including feedback) to support development, and empowering managers to accept and use the information.

Supervisors are not the only source of performance information. As the complexity of environments increases, employees need input from different sources for a more precise understanding of their performance and areas for improvement. The next section describes a process for subordinates to rate supervisors.

UPWARD FEEDBACK: A CASE EXAMPLE

This is a report of an upward feedback survey conducted as a university pilot project in the institution's libraries. The university's president hoped to enhance the relationship between the employees and their supervisors. The library was selected because of its range of faculty, professional- and classified-level employees, and its division into units of varying sizes. The library's director of personnel and development managed the project with the help of a professor in the management school and a graduate student assistant.

In most workplaces, including libraries and universities, the evaluation of subordinates has traditionally been performed by their supervisors. However, subordinates have a different perspective than do supervisors and can therefore provide valuable information that might not be available to the supervisor. Increasingly, organizations are using upward feedback surveys to help managers identify areas for improvement.

Both supervisors and subordinates may be threatened by an upward feedback process unless the results are given to the manager anonymously and confidentially. Therefore, in this pilot project, the results for each manager were given only to the manager. Higher management received only aggregate results averaged across managers. Each manager could voluntarily choose to share the results with his or her subordinates and/or bosses or could choose to study the results alone.

Participants

The study participants were 27 first-line supervisors with four or more employees. A total of 90 subordinates completed the survey describing their immediate supervisors. (If there were only three or fewer subordinates, the manager might be able to guess the identity of the high and low scorers, thereby precluding subordinates' anonymity.) Also, participating managers had to have been in a permanent (not provisional or acting) supervisory position to the four or more subordinates for at least six months during the previous calendar year.

In addition, higher-level supervisors were consulted to determine if they wanted to be evaluated by subordinates two or more levels below them or by staff who report to them informally. Also, provisional or acting supervisors were included only at their own request.

Of the evaluated supervisors, 85% (11 of 13) returned their self-evaluations. (One of the supervisors was abroad during the survey period.) Of the subordinates, 78% (90 out of 115) returned ratings of their supervisors. Only 44% (16 out of 33) of the supervisors who were not evaluated by subordinates returned their self-evaluations, suggesting that involvement in the process is lower for supervisors who do not anticipate receiving upward feedback.

Procedure

To insure that the staff were fully informed about the project, information meetings were held with each departmental group. Also, a report describing the purpose and procedures was sent to every member of the library staff.

Each subordinate was requested to voluntarily rate their supervisor on 30 items. The items were developed by the library supervisors in consultation with the consultant. The goal was to generate items that are important to supervisor/subordinate relationships and that reflect the values and goals of the library. Another goal was to keep down the number of items to make the survey easy to complete. Each item was rated on a 5-point scale from 1 = strongly disagree to 5 = strongly agree. No written comments were collected to simplify the process and to avoid having to transcribe written responses as a way of protecting confidentiality. The name of the subordinate did not appear on the survey. Each survey contained a numeric code assigned to the supervisor, so the supervisor's name did not appear on the survey. Subordinates mailed the completed survey to the graduate assistant in the institution of management. All participating managers also completed self-ratings on the same items.

The graduate assistant compiled the data for each manager who was evaluated by four or more subordinates. For each item, the report provided the highest, the lowest, and the mean across subordinates. In addition, to help the managers calibrate their results, the report provided the average self-evaluation across all supervisors and the average subordinate ratings across all managers for each item.

Each manager's report was placed in a sealed envelope with the manager's code on the front. The sealed envelopes were distributed at a meeting of all the supervisors. A member of the university training department attended the meeting to provide information on available training in areas measured in the study.

The graduate student prepared an aggregate report for the library director. The report included, for each item, the lowest, highest, and the mean for the average self-evaluations for the supervisors who were evaluated by their subordinates, the average self-evaluations for the supervisors not evaluated by their subordinates, the average self-evaluation for all supervisors, the average subordinate ratings provided by classified (nonprofessional) employees, the average subordinate ratings provided by professional employees, and the average subordinate ratings across all subordinates.

Results

The mean average subordinates scores across all supervisors are presented in Table 10.1.

Table 10.1
Library Upward Feedback,
Average Ratings

Average Subordinate Rating[1]	Average Self-Rating	Item # in Survey	Item
4.30	4.19	29	Commitment to library goals and values.
4.29	4.56	15	Considers service to patrons important to decision making.
4.28	4.19	25	Overall technical ability and subject knowledge.
4.24	4.36	28	Commitment to patron-centered service.
4.07	4.48	2	Allows subordinates to express feelings and opinions.
4.06	4.41	21	Knows specific operations of supervised areas.
3.95	4.22	24	Explains why decisions are made.
3.94	4.37	22	Supports subordinates most of the time.
3.86	4.23	14	Manages complex projects effectively.
3.85	3.98	5	Communicates library's goals.
3.84	4.44	3	Seriously considers subordinates' ideas for improvement.
3.83	4.12	20	Makes sensible decisions under difficult circumstances.
3.83	NA[2]	23	Supports other staff most of the time.
3.82	4.04	30	Shows problem solving creativity.
3.81	3.88	13	Clearly defines lines of authority.
3.81	4.22	1	Effectively plans and organizes work.
3.80	4.12	27	Overall operational skills.
3.74	4.07	16	Effectively represents staff concerns to higher management.
3.74	4.48	17	Consults subordinates when decisions affect them.

Table 10.1
(*continued*)

Average Subordinate Rating[1]	Average Self-Rating	Item # in Survey	Item
3.67	3.82	9	Provides subordinates with sufficient feedback.
3.66	4.08	7	Gives proper recognition to staff for their contributions.
3.62	4.09	11	Helps to resolve conflicts among staff.
3.54	3.85	4	Motivates subordinates to do their best.
3.52	4.12	18	Gives clear work assignments and adequate instruction.
3.45	4.27	12	Builds teamwork with the unit.
3.43	4.07	26	Overall people skills
3.39	3.60	10	Helps subordinates to identify steps to achieve goals.
3.22	3.70	6	Deals effectively with under-performing employees.

Items reflecting organizational self-esteem[3]

NA	4.58	a	I am cooperative around here.
NA	4.58	b	I am helpful around here.
NA	4.39	c	I am efficient around here.
NA	4.31	d	I am trusted around here.
NA	4.23	e	I am valuable around here.
NA	4.12	f	I can make a difference around here.
NA	3.92	g	I am taken seriously around here.
NA	3.92	h	I count around here.
NA	3.81	i	I am important around here.

[1]Items are arrayed in descending order of average subordinate ratings.
[2]Supervisors did not provide self-ratings on this item.
[3]Asked only for supervisors' self-ratings.

Subordinates' Ratings

The mean average scores of the subordinates as a whole ranged from 3.22 to 4.30. If 5 is taken to be an A, this translated into a range for the mean scores of from C+ to B+. (It was tempting to compare this to the results of a survey of faculty and professional staff recently conducted by the university senate on administrative departments. While these are not necessarily comparable because the methods differed, the overall average grade was C–.)

The three types of employees showed distinct differences. The library faculty were more critical in rating their supervisors (low = 3.05, high = 4.43) than professional employees (low = 3.06, high = 4.44) who in turn were more critical than the classified staff (low = 3.37, high = 4.45).

Supervisors were rated highest by subordinates on (a) commitment to library goals and values (M = 4.30), (b) considers service to patrons important in decision-making (M = 4.29), (c) overall technical ability and subject knowledge (M = 4.28), and (d) commitment to patron-centered service (M = 4.24). These were in the top six for all library employees, suggesting that there was substantial agreement between the three types of employees on what their supervisors do well.

The four items on which the supervisors were rated lowest by subordinates were (a) deals effectively with underperforming employees (M = 3.22), (b) helps subordinates to identify steps to achieve goals (M = 3.38), (c) overall people skills (M = 3.43), and (d) builds teamwork within the unit (M = 3.45). These were in the top seven for all subordinate groups, suggesting that there was also fair agreement among three types of employees on what their supervisors do less well.

Supervisors' Self-Ratings

Not surprisingly, the range of self-evaluation ratings by supervisors (low = 3.60, high = 4.58) was higher than the range for subordinates' ratings. There was some agreement between the supervisors' self-evaluations and the subordinates' ratings for specific items. One item was in the top four for both subordinates and supervisors: considers service to patrons important in decision-making. Both the supervisors and subordinates scored the same two items lowest: helps subordinates to identify steps to achieve goals, and deals effectively with underperforming employees.

Supervisors also rated themselves on nine items designed to evaluate their organization-based self-esteem. Supervisors rated themselves high on most of these items. The lowest ratings on these items suggested that they felt they were not sufficiently appreciated.

Relationship to Strategic Planning

A year before the survey, the library's director and top managers developed a five-year strategic directions plan, which identified four values as the foundation for library management: flexibility/adaptability, cooperation/understanding, intelligence/ingenuity, and commitment to client-centered service. Several of the survey items measured the supervisors' strengths on these values. Specifically, supervisors received high "grades" from subordinates and themselves for the two items that measured commitment to client-centered service. Subordinates gave lower ratings for the two items that measured cooperation/understanding.

Recommendations

The results suggested that the following actions would be beneficial:

1. Work with the human resources department to offer a workshop for supervisors on the issues reflected in the lowest items: dealing effectively with underperforming employees, and helping subordinates to identify steps to achieve goals. Identifying steps to achieve goals is an important step in dealing with underperforming employees.

2. Devise ways for improving supervisors' skills in building teamwork within their units. Since teamwork is one of the strategic planning values (cooperation/understanding), individual departments should do more to develop their teams and understand how to be part of the library overall team effort. Frequent communication about library mission and objectives and special group meetings to discuss important decisions may help foster teamwork.

3. Address the organizational self-esteem items on which supervisors were lowest—items that suggest supervisors' feeling insufficiently valued by their managers and/or the library administration. Top managers should consider ways to recognize and reward first-line supervisors' achievements.

The last section in this chapter (excerpted from London & Beatty, 1993; and London, 1995) describes a more extensive rating process than upward feedback: 360 degree feedback (ratings from subordinates, peers, supervisors, and internal or external customers/clients). Benefits of the process and methods for developing the process are described.

360 DEGREE FEEDBACK

Feedback is a key ingredient to the development of self- and interpersonal insight. 360 degree feedback is growing in importance as a process that contributes to individual and organizational development. The complexity of organizational life for managers indicates the value of having input from people who have different expectations. Managers may have to respond in different ways to subordinates, peers, supervisors, and customers. Rapid organizational changes have forced managers to be attuned to shifting expectations of these constituencies and to the need for continuous development to accomplish these shifts. Subordinates' perspectives are important given that boss/subordinate relationships are a primary part of managing—in many cases, the central relationship for the manager. Other perspectives are likely to be equally important but for different reasons. Peers' viewpoints focus on the manager's contribution to teamwork. Customers' viewpoints demonstrate the manager's responsiveness to the customer and the manager's contribution to customer satisfaction. 360 degree feedback is a way for organizations to call attention to these differing and changing roles.

360 degree feedback recognizes the weakness of relying on supervisors as the sole source of performance review and feedback. Supervisors may avoid evaluating subordinates, for instance, because of low interpersonal trust or the desire to avoid a negative situation. Supervisors are often uncomfortable giving feedback—whether positive or negative. They find giving negative feedback especially difficult because subordinates often become defensive, deny the problem altogether, or blame situational factors beyond their control, including the supervisor's unrealistic expectations and demands (Meyer, 1991). 360 degree feedback highlights the importance of self-assessment and employees' taking responsibility for their own development. The organization provides the rating process, feeds back the results in the form of a computer-generated report, and offers developmental opportunities. Managers must interpret the feedback results and use them to identify areas for improvement.

The 360 degree feedback survey may ask raters to report their observations of the manager's behaviors. This may be a report of the frequency of different behaviors or an evaluation of the behaviors—the extent to which they were done well. As an alternative the ratings may ask raters for their expectations of the manager—that is, what the manager should do (Moses, Hollenbeck, & Sorcher, 1993). Another format is to request two ratings for each behavior: what the manager does and what the manager should do. Asking the rater to evaluate observed behaviors assumes that the behaviors were observed often enough for the rater to recall their frequency and/or evaluate them. Asking for expectations leaves more to the rater's judgment, but does not require that the behaviors actually have been observed. Moreover, ratings of expectations are a way for the raters to communicate what they expect, not simply report their view of what has occurred. Thus, managers can use the information about expectations to guide their behavior in the future. However, they have to evaluate their own competence and behavioral tendencies in light of the expectations, and they have to evaluate the reasonableness of the expectations.

Whether the rating process asks for expectations, reports of observed behaviors, or evaluations of behaviors will depend on the purpose for the process. Ratings of expectations will be important when there are communication difficulties between the manager and the various constituencies. Knowledge of others' expectations may be especially helpful for new managers. Ratings of behavior frequency and quality or favorability will be important when managers are more experienced in knowing the requirements of the job but perhaps lax in focusing on their routine behavior and the effects of their actions. Behavior-based ratings will also be justified when the raters have had ample opportunity to observe the manager's behavior and performance.

Theoretically, asking for both behavioral observations and expectations determines the degree to which there is a performance gap between what is done and how much should be done. However, practically, the two ratings are likely to be correlated. This may occur because raters like to be consistent. So something that is not done well or is rarely done implies that more is necessary, and something done well implies that enough is being done. In addition, using the same method, such as the same type of rating scale, often results in a correlation called common method bias. The consequence is that the additional rating for each behavior does not contribute much added information beyond the first rating regardless of whether the first rating is an expectation or a behavioral observation.

The results of 360 degree ratings are usually provided to the managers for their use in making development plans, possibly as part of a training program (Van Velsor & Leslie, 1991). Part of the process may be training to help the recipients interpret and use the results—for instance, establish development plans. In other cases, 360 degree feedback may be incorporated into performance evaluations for administrative purposes (e.g., merit pay and advancement decisions).

Using 360 degree feedback for development alone, at least at the inception of the process, helps to alleviate concerns about the fairness and accuracy of the data. It does not eliminate the concern, however, since subordinates may still say inaccurate things either to hurt the boss's feelings or to gain favor with ("brown nose") the boss. Also, the organization may have to take pains to convince ratees of the confidentiality of the results—that is, that higher-level managers will not know the managers' individual results. Using the feedback for administrative purposes puts teeth into the process—that is, adds to its importance—but may lead to concerns about the reliability and accuracy of the method.

Managers who are threatened most by the process, generally those who are concerned about the relationships they have with their subordinates or others, are likely to be vocal in expressing their distrust of the process. Several waves of 360 degree feedback solely for development purposes is a good way to initiate the process. As raters and managers become familiar with it, the policy can be changed to incorporate the results into making decisions about the managers rated. In general, managers are more accepting of 360 degree feedback when they believe the organization supports development efforts related to the appraisal dimensions and when the dimensions are perceived to be high priority behaviors in the organization.

Benefits of 360 Degree Feedback

360 degree feedback builds on the value of feedback as a source of information to direct and motivate future managerial behaviors. 360 degree feedback results are affected by interpersonal dynamics of customer/supplier relationships, self-presentation and disclosure, and impression management. Also, 360 degree feedback can be an organizational intervention that raises the salience of behaviors and relationships and increases employees' participation in decisions and development.

While there has been considerable research and theory on performance appraisal (downward evaluation and feedback), little attention has been given to 360 degree feedback.

Similarity and Differences Between 360 Degree Feedback and Performance Appraisal

Performance appraisal (supervisors rating subordinates) and 360 degree feedback may request reports of behavior or judgments of performance. Both use rating scales, and both may be subject to the same biases, such as response consistencies, leniency, halo, and stereotyping (Borman, 1974). The rating scales may be the same for all ratings or may be customized to reflect the unique nature of each type of relationship. For instance, upward feedback is likely to include items that focus primarily on the boss/subordinate relationship.

There are some major differences, however, between performance appraisal and 360 degree feedback. Performance appraisal is conducted primarily for evaluation purposes and has organizational implications, such as pay treatment and opportunities for job assignments, transfer, and promotion. Secondarily, performance appraisal has a developmental component in that performance results should be fed back to subordinates with the intention of determining ways to improve weaknesses and enhance strengths. As such, performance appraisal is useful in development and career planning. 360 degree feedback may also be input to evaluation, but as discussed at the outset of the chapter, it is often used solely for developmental purposes. Managers may share the results with their supervisors if they feel comfortable doing so. Otherwise the supervisors would not have access to the information.

Advantages of Multiple Perspectives

Unlike performance appraisal, 360 degree feedback is not one-sided. 360 degree feedback recognizes the complexity of management and the value of input from different sources. For instance, subordinates are in an excellent position to view and evaluate many supervisory behaviors. Indeed, they may have more complete and accurate information about some behaviors than supervisors have. This is especially likely to be true of information about boss/subordinate relationships—for instance, the extent to which the manager structures the work, provides performance feedback, fosters a positive working environment, provides necessary resources, sends subordinates to training, and generally supports their development. The quality of boss/subordinate relationships is likely to be important to the success of the work group. Similar arguments can be made for ratings from others—peers and customers.

Ratings from multiple sources allow examining the reliability of the information in relation to expected consistency or differentiation of behavior. When subordinates' capabilities and the demands of their jobs are fairly similar, the manager is likely to behave in the same way with most if not all subordinates. In such cases, subordinates should agree in their ratings of the manager. However, when subordinates' jobs and capabilities differ and subordinates' jobs are not interrelated, the manager is likely to behave differently with different subordinates. In these cases, the range of ratings among the subordinates in the work group may be useful feedback along with the average favorability of results.

This applies to peer, customer, and supervisor relationships as well. Peers may agree with each other about evaluating a colleague because they observe the colleague in the same contexts. On the other hand, they may see the manager differently if they interact with the manager for different reasons at different times. The supervisor may also differ from peers and subordinates in opportunity and occasion to observe. Managers may behave differently with these different constituencies because of how the managerial role and expectations differ in relation to each constituency. They may try to create different impressions, perhaps being more concerned about creating a favorable impression in the eyes of their supervisors, who control pay and promotional opportunities as well as resources, than in the eyes of peers with whom they may be in competition for promotion. Relationships with subordinates may be concerned less with creating a favorable impression than getting the work done to some specifications, regardless of the impression behaviors and directives create. Implementing 360 degree feedback, or a portion of it, may alter the importance of others' impressions and reactions to managerial behavior.

Spin-off Benefits

360 degree feedback has a number of potentially beneficial spin-offs for an organization. It calls attention to performance dimensions that might not have been viewed as important otherwise. As such, it is a way to convey organizational values. It may be an intervention to enhance two-way communications, increasing formal as well as informal communications. It may build more effective work relationships, increase opportunities for employee involvement, uncover and resolve conflict, and demonstrate top managers' respect for employees' opinions. It establishes an element of reciprocity between managers and their co-workers as sources of feedback and reinforcement.

Introducing a feedback system may encourage managers to set goals (Locke & Latham, 1990). This may be especially effective if the feedback includes normative information (i.e., a way to compare oneself to the "competition"). This will work well if the average level of performance is high. If it is low, managers may be satisfied with just meeting or slightly exceeding their co-workers' performance level. The more specific the data (e.g., the more it contains prescriptive or behavioral items), the more it is likely to lead managers to set specific and challenging goals. Furthermore, specific feedback will help managers determine the discrepancy between their goals and their performance. When 360 degree feedback is too vague or general (e.g., ratings of characteristics rather than behaviors), goal-setting theory and control theory predict that behavior change will not be likely.

Reactions to 360 degree feedback are likely to depend on an interaction between goals and self-evaluations. Consider managers who believe their performance meets or exceeds their goals, but co-workers disagree, rating them lower than the managers expected. This is likely to be a common occurrence. The organization hopes that the 360 degree feedback will cause the managers to revise their self-evaluations and set goals to improve performance. However, this may not happen. Managers in this circumstance may lower their self-evaluations (and performance goals), try to discredit or discount the feedback from co-workers, try to alter co-workers' opinions via impression management techniques, develop a greater tolerance for discrepancy, or avoid the situation by directing their attention to other issues. Managers seek reasons for the feedback they receive. The managers are likely to make external attributions for the disappointing results when there are no clear alternatives for improving performance (e.g., training). Thus, the effects of 360 degree feedback on future goals require having support to help managers interpret the feedback accurately and consider constructive responses.

360 degree feedback may also contribute to other organizational initiatives to improve the quality of work processes. Quality improvement programs focus on interpersonal relationships between and within groups. 360 degree feedback is consistent with, and promulgates, participative cultures. While managers may be evaluated on group outputs, information about managerial behaviors should help develop and ultimately improve these outputs.

Costs of 360 Degree Feedback

There are some potential costs to 360 degree feedback. There is the cost of time and money for implementation and preparation (e.g., explaining the purpose of the feedback program and training managers on how to use the feedback). It adds complexity to the appraisal administration process, requiring the distribution of forms to the right individuals and analyzing the data, possibly with the use of sophisticated computer programming and outside help. It imposes potential risks to the raters and may generate tension between the manager and others who provided ratings. It establishes expectations that behavior will change. Further, it may set up potential conflict by highlighting the need to be different things to different people. Also, it provides a lot of information to integrate, and greater possibility for selective perception and information distortion. Because ratings are made by others who are significant to the manager, 360 degree feedback imposes increased pressure on the manager's self-concept and goals—making negative information all the more powerful and difficult to deny, especially when raters agree, or easy to distort or perceive selectively, especially when raters disagree.

Designing and Implementing a 360 Degree Feedback Program

This section offers guidelines for implementing 360 degree feedback. There are different ways to design the 360 degree feedback instrument, collect the data, report the results, and use the results. Here we consider the involvement of employees in the development of the items, the content and salience of the items rated, the inclusion of managers' self-assessment, the implementation procedure (e.g., training, the format of the instrument, and instructions), the use of the 360 degree feedback results (whether the results are used for evaluation and/or development), and the format and detail of the feedback.

Item Content and Involvement of Employees in Program Design

Similar to performance appraisal, 360 degree feedback ratings should be made on performance dimensions that are relevant to the job. These dimensions may be derived from job analyses. However, in some cases, managers should be evaluated on desired behaviors, not necessarily those that are typical or part of the current formal job design. For instance, the top executives of the organization may outline the types of leaders they want to reward and advance in the organization. This may be part of an organizational change effort (e.g., to make management more democratic or to increase employee empowerment). These behavioral elements can be captured on the feedback scales. Also, a group of employees may be asked to generate behavioral statements. Such involvement of employees and the link between 360 degree feedback and key strategies of the firm are ways to engender commitment to the 360 degree feedback process, communicate desired behaviors, and enhance the importance and value of the process to the organization.

360 degree feedback ratings are made on a set of items that are likely to be familiar to the raters. The items may be general (for instance, asking about managers' characteristics and abilities) or specific (asking about behaviors that reflect boss/subordinate relationships or peer relationships). The question posed may request an evaluation (e.g., "How *well* does the manager . . .") or an estimate of frequency (e.g., "How *often* does the manager . . ."). The items are likely to reflect elements of leadership, work group relationships, or boss/subordinate relationships that are easily understood and tied to experiences with the manager. They are the sorts of things one would expect to rate or be rated on. That is, they are consistent with organizational and personal values. Moreover, the raters have ample opportunity to observe the behaviors.

Implementation

The 360 degree feedback process itself must be clear, with participants understanding the procedure and purpose of the results. Instructions should be clear. Employee briefings should be provided to explain the reason for the ratings, how the data will be aggregated, and how the results will be fed back. Also, similar to performance appraisal, training should reduce rater biases by making employees aware of the types of errors people make (e.g., leniency, central tendency, and halo—rating all elements of performance alike).

Format

The specific rating format (number of scale points and wording of items) used may not have much effect on rating accuracy, just as it doesn't in performance appraisal. So the number of rating points on the scale may be a matter of the designers' preference. Having a midpoint, as on a 5-point scale, may encourage more central tendency by making it possible for raters to provide middle-of-the-road ratings. A 6-point scale has no midpoint, alleviating this problem. However, raters may be offended that they cannot provide a neutral rating. The more scale points, the more likely there will be variability in the ratings.

Wording of items may be in terms of behavioral frequency, expectations, or evaluations as discussed earlier. Ratings are likely to be more reliable when the items refer to objective or observable behaviors (e.g., meets with subordinates at least once a year to discuss their career goals) rather than individual qualities (e.g., trustworthy, responsive). Ratings of behavioral expectations produce a different type of information—that is, what the observer hopes will happen or judges could happen given the manager's prior behavior. In general, the focus of the items will depend on the purpose of the process—that is, the type of information the organization wants the process to convey to its managers. Of course, items should be clear and not double-barreled such that it is not clear what question they are asking. (An example of a double-barreled item is, "The manager asks subordinates for input in making decisions that affect the department and in setting development plans for employees.")

Requiring Participation

The administration of 360 degree feedback poses several alternatives. Managers may be required to have their groups participate in 360 degree feedback, or participation could be voluntary. Another aspect of participation is discussing results with subordinates after the manager receives the feedback. This may be up to the manager or specified in the operations procedures. Hautaluoma, Jobe, Visser, and Donkersgoed (1992) investigated employees' attitudes about various approaches to 360 degree feedback along with whether the feedback results should be used for development or evaluation. The employees were 222 subordinates and managers from two departments of a large firm in the photographic industry. Employees preferred an approach that incorporated the advantages of a formal policy requiring managers to use the process and a strong developmental purpose with no direct contact between manager and subordinate in discussing results. Also, exemplifying the importance of organizational context referred to above, employees who rated their trust in the institution higher were more likely to perceive benefits of participation. In addition, they recognized that some of the main benefits from a 360 degree feedback process would be producing a sense of participation in important decisions, increasing beliefs of fairness about supervisors' evaluations increasing accuracy of evaluations, and resolving conflicts.

Raters' Anonymity

Care should be taken to ensure raters' anonymity. This means guarding the ratings, probably by having an outside consultant code and analyze the data and prepare feedback reports. Such reports are usually computer generated, particularly if the survey is on an optically scanned sheet, on a computer disk, or on a computer program tied to a local area network or mainframe. Handwritten comments may require typing to disguise the handwriting. Managers should not receive subordinate ratings if there are too few peers or subordinates (e.g., four or less), since this might suggest the identity of the raters.

The importance of anonymity was demonstrated in a follow-up survey several months after 360 degree feedback had been provided to managers. When asked in an interview, "Would you have rated your boss any differently if feedback had not been given anonymously," 24% of the 53 subordinates interviewed stated yes.

Uses of 360 Degree Feedback

The uses of the 360 degree feedback should influence the seriousness with which it is treated and how quickly it becomes an integral part of managing the organization. Some organizations incorporate 360 degree feedback results with performance evaluation. Alternatively, supervisor, subordinate, and/or peer feedback may be viewed as separate performance criteria, and managers may be expected to reach or exceed a given level of results on each. For example, managers may be expected to achieve a certain level of favorable ratings from their subordinates. If managers do not reach this level, they may be placed on a probation or "watch" list, which requires them to show improvement the next year.

Another model is to use 360 degree feedback solely for development. Managers receive a report, but they are not required to share the results with their boss or their subordinates. Guidelines and/or counseling may be available to help support use of the data. This approach emphasizes the importance of development in the organization and may be a way to introduce 360 degree feedback as a part of the organization culture. As suggested earlier, use of peer and/or subordinate ratings for development only is likely to be less sensitive (less likely to put managers on the defensive and cause them to criticize the validity of the data) than use for evaluation. However, use for development only may also decrease the application of the results since there is no requirement to respond to the feedback. A desirable introduction strategy may be a two-step process, using 360 degree feedback for development during the first few years before using it as input to supervisory evaluations and decisions about pay and promotion.

Use of 360 degree feedback is likely to affect employees' attitudes about the feedback process and possibly the nature of the results. In the 360 degree feedback follow-up survey referred to above, 34% of the subordinates believed that they would have rated their boss differently if the feedback had been used for the manager's performance appraisal.

Self-Assessment

360 degree feedback ratings may be accompanied by managers' self-ratings on the same items on which they are rated by their subordinates, peers, and/or customers. The inclusion of self-ratings should enhance a manager's attention to the results and desire to use them to establish directions for development.

While self-appraisals are often used for employee development, performance appraisal research has shown that self-appraisals generally disagree with supervisor appraisals. Disagreement between raters may be due to differences in attributional processes, with self-ratings subject to a strong self-serving bias (for instance, the tendency to attribute negative events to external causes and positive events to internal causes). Providing self-rating results along with 360 degree feedback allows managers to compare their self-perceptions to how others see them. As such, it can force managers to reconsider their self-concepts in light of direct information about others' opinions about them. However, this still allows room for misinterpretation, discounting, or ignoring the results. The inclusion of self-ratings focuses attention on differences and similarities between self and others' perceptions, identifies gaps in perceptions, and requires resolution (rationalization, changing self-perceptions, or altering behaviors).

Frequency of Feedback

A 360 degree rating is likely to be made annually. Motorola's cellular telecommunications division uses it quarterly. Whatever the timing, managers are not precluded from seeking informal feedback. Indeed, the introduction of a 360 degree feedback process may engender managers to seek feedback more frequently, although this hypothesis needs to be tested. The assumption is that over time, employees and managers will become familiar with the 360 degree feedback process and see its effects on managers' development.

Report Format

The nature of the 360 degree feedback report may influence how the results are internalized and applied. Several report formats are possible. One is a narrative statement summarizing the results. Another is a statistical summary with average ratings reported across the items, or perhaps average results for groups of items. Measures of average variation can also be reported to reflect agreement among subordinates (e.g., average range or variance). A more detailed report format would be an item-by-item report. The results might include the mean subordinate rating, the highest and lowest rating, the norm for the department or organization (the average rating for the item across managers rated), and the manager's self-rating. The more detailed the report, the more specific the information for guiding behavior change. However, summarizing the information by averaging items across predetermined factors should produce more reliable and meaningful data. The more detailed the report, the more the interpretation required, and the greater the likelihood that the manager's biases will affect the interpretation. Also, the more detailed the report, the more the managers may focus on results that match their self-perceptions and ignore results that contradict their self-perceptions. Reports that summarize information based on statistically derived factor analyses should provide reliable data without losing distinguishing information.

CONCLUSION

This chapter has run the gamut from describing a process for ratingless appraisals to detailing a method for obtaining anonymous ratings from multiple parties. The objective in all these cases is to provide employees with constructive performance feedback—information they can use to guide their development. The focus, then, is on providing a regular flow of information so that garnering performance data and calibrating behavior and trying to improve performance become part of the organization's routine. Employees get in the habit of both giving and receiving feedback, and continuous learning becomes part of the institution's culture.

The next chapter continues this discussion by focusing more particularly on problem performance—ways to deal with, and hopefully overcome, marginal performance and ways to deal with abusive managers.

11

Managing Problem Employees

Giving constructive feedback to a good performer is one thing. Handling poor performance is another. Poor performance may be a cause of termination. Or the situation may be marginal—meaning that the individual could improve with some coaching and development. As job demands increase with advancing technologies and fewer resources (financial and people) to do the work, the level of expected performance is constantly increasing. While employees may be grateful for their jobs when others are not readily available, they may not be capable of performing at the higher level. Also, they may not have the motivation to work harder, especially after years of unchallenging, routine work.

A compounding problem may be the nature of management. For many employees, the immediate supervisor probably has the most control over the work environment. This is fine if the supervisor is a good manager, one who respects and understands subordinates' needs and capabilities, who empowers them to do their jobs, who involves them in decision making, and who wants to invest in their development. However, as has been widely cited in the press during the last several years, managerial abuse comes in many subtle and not-so-subtle forms, including sexual harassment, discrimination, and just plain poor management. This chapter examines both the problems of managing marginal performance in an environment striving for excellence (in a section from London & Mone, 1994) and generating an organizational culture that does not tolerate abusive managers (in a section from Bassman & London, 1993).

IDENTIFYING PERFORMANCE PROBLEMS

Marginal performers are individuals who are "in over their heads."[1] They are not doing well in their current jobs because of some combination of factors. Individually, they may lack the requisite ability and/or motivation. At the organizational level, their performance may be negatively influenced by ineffective and unsupportive policies, systems, and procedures. Essentially, there is a high degree of incongruence between the job requirements and the incumbent's ability to meet them, and/or the system's ability to support individual performance. Doing "marginal work" means the person is doing the minimum. It does not mean that he or she has clearly failed or acted with insubordination. Marginal performance is more nebulous and subjective than blatantly poor or unacceptable performance. When quality standards are left unnegotiated, the level of desired performance exists in the mind and eye of the beholder—the supervisor—and this results in marginal performance when the supervisor's expectations are higher than those of the subordinate.

Marginal performance may be viewed in terms of the employee's motivation and ability relative to the standards set by the organization. Increased pressures on organizations to reduce costs and improve efficiency have increased the potential for marginal performance. This is made worse when the policies, systems, and procedures are outdated, thereby inhibiting rather than empowering employee performance.

Marginal performance is not a new problem. An early text referred to problem performers as maladjusted, self-centered, emotionally immature or unstable, picayunish, or even disturbed by psychoneuroses (Moore, 1942). This chapter goes beyond Moore's simplistic and negatively biased judgments of marginal performers to provide a more complete view of marginal performance and the situational and individual explanations for it. The chapter considers ways marginal performers interpret, defend, and change their behavior. It also considers how supervisors recognize and enable subordinates to overcome marginal performance.

In the increasingly demanding environment of postdivestiture AT&T, it was not surprising that role expectations and requirements could exceed the employee's competence or desire to perform well. Manifestations of marginal performance included missed deadlines, inaccurate reporting of information, not checking work, inability to function without structure and guidance, unwillingness to make decisions, attributing blame for problems to others, avoiding work, or doing only what was necessary to get by.

Evidence of marginal performance came from several sources. Top executives complained to managers about low-performing work groups and problem subordinates. Employees informed their supervisors that co-workers were not contributing at an equal level. Some subordinates did not live up to the challenge of an especially difficult assignment, making their weaknesses suddenly visible. Excellent performers highlighted the gap between minimal and outstanding performance. Budget cuts and increased competition put pressure on departments to eliminate slack and require a quality contribution from everyone. Performance appraisal methods, such as rating and ranking employees against their peers, increased scrutiny of performance and focused a spotlight on marginal performance.

Marginal performance can arise from *underutilization* (high ability and low effort), *misdirected effort* (low ability and high effort), and a combination of the two (low ability and low effort). Underutilization may be caused by inadequate goal setting, misunderstanding subordinate skills, oversupervision, and/or poor communication between manager and subordinate. Misdirected effort may be caused by a poor job match or changing job requirements. People who lack both motivation and capability experience repeated failure to meet performance expectations. Often their dissatisfaction with work and absenteeism increase as they withdraw from work relationships and activities.

The Psychology of Marginal Performance

Marginal performers, by definition, are not succeeding in their jobs. They may have an incorrect view of the job requirements and of their own strengths and weaknesses. Moreover, they may lack the self-confidence necessary to face the problem and change the situation (e.g., through training, or changing jobs). Consequently, marginal performers may invoke a variety of *defense mechanisms* when confronted with evidence of marginal performance. Defense mechanisms are defenses against anxiety-producing motives. Defenses may result when marginal performance is a product of low job motivation and not wanting to admit disliking the job. Or defenses may result when marginal performance is incongruent with the individual's self-concept as an effective person. The weaker the individual's self-esteem and the lower the individual's ability to understand the environment, the more defense mechanisms are likely to be strong and difficult to break down.

Denial

Marginal performers may refuse to recognize a performance deficit. They repress the problem. They argue that they are doing all they ever did, all that others are doing, or all that is necessary according to their job description. They may argue that to behave differently or apply different performance criteria would be wrong. They may be convinced that the supervisor does not understand the problems they face or what would happen if they behaved differently.

Attributing Blame to Others or to External Events

Marginal performers may recognize a problem, but not view it as a consistent pattern. They have a different logical excuse or reason for each behavioral incident mentioned by the supervisor as proof of marginal performance, and the reasons are attributed to factors external to them or beyond their control. Essentially, they rationalize why the problem occurred in a way that is not threatening to them.

Attributing Marginal Performance to Others

A form of external attribution or "projection," this behavior points out others' flaws. Marginal performers recognize marginal performance in others but cannot recognize it in themselves. They may blame others for their own poor output (for example, saying that one of their subordinates can't do the job). They may be correct, or they may project their own marginality on others when it is not deserved.

Creating the Opposite Impression

Marginal performers may try to disguise their low motivation and/or low ability by creating the opposite impression. (Clinical psychologists term this "reaction formation.") For instance, they may appear extremely busy, working late at night, coming in early, walking quickly here and there so everyone sees how hard they are working. They may create emergencies or treat what could be minor issues as serious problems demanding the supervisor's attention.

Substituting One Goal for Another

The marginal performer may deny or belittle the importance of doing well on the job while working hard at something at which they can succeed—perhaps off the job. For instance, marginal performers may spend considerable time and energy in a volunteer activity that is recognized as important in the community (e.g., leading Boy or Girl Scout troops or becoming active in a local charity). Or they may get involved in a company-sponsored volunteer effort or committee, such as a working parents network. Some work time may be spent on the activity by taking time off for special events or leaving work early for meetings. This provides a rationalization for lower work performance and it provides a vehicle for demonstrating their self-efficacy to themselves and others. It becomes a substitute for work and a way to compensate for low work satisfaction.

Creating Nonwork Problems

Marginal performers may take out their frustration or "displace" it on family members and friends rather than at work, where overt anger is not acceptable. Family problems may become an excuse for marginal work performance. Substance abuse is another way to displace work frustrations. Nonwork problems spill over to the work setting and may be the first evidence that something is wrong on the job. However, they focus the supervisor's attention away from the marginal performance to seeking ways to help the individual overcome personal problems.

Unfortunately, marginal performance may continue for quite awhile, and possibly indefinitely, without being recognized as such. Some marginal performers have repeated tardiness or absenteeism. Others may work long hours, perhaps in hopes that dedication will substitute for performance or as an excuse for inappropriately attributing blame to factors beyond their control. When marginal performance is evident, supervisors will often prefer to ignore it, sometimes due to their own lack of management skills, rather than face the task of giving feedback that they perceive as uncomfortable to do and negative in outcome.

Strategies to Overcome Marginal Performance

An important step for managing performance is to evaluate subordinate performance and diagnose subordinates' competencies, motivation, and job characteristics. Other steps include choosing a performance management strategy and monitoring and evaluating the success of the strategy. Ways to address performance problems depend on whether the problem is motivational and/or ability determined. Each suggests different strategies for correction.

Underutilization

Employees with high ability but low effort may benefit from the following:

Performance feedback. This is honest and direct feedback about the subordinate's marginal performance. Assuming that the subordinate recognizes the problem and wants to change the situation, the next constructive actions are possible.

Training. Identify in-house or external training programs that help the employee acquire needed knowledge or skills.

Rewards. The desire to achieve may be enhanced by clarifying what needs to be done to accomplish goals and highlighting the value of goal accomplishment. That is, provide meaningful rewards for success. One example is giving the supervisor discretion to give "spot" financial rewards (a valued sum of money) soon after an important project is completed and done well.

Creating and highlighting role models. Visibly rewarding excellent performers is a way to designate role models. Another is to become a role model.

Team building and conflict resolution. Improving interpersonal relationships may also enhance motivation by making the work environment more pleasant and productive. A variety of education and organization development interventions might be tried, such as communications skills assessment and training, group meetings for sharing perceptions, and problem-solving sessions.

Counseling. Motivation may be enhanced by helping employees to achieve better insight into their skills and interests in relation to the current job and available opportunities in the company.

Burnout prevention and management. Supervisors can help reduce or prevent subordinates' burnout by encouraging that the work get done during regularly scheduled hours and recognizing employees for meeting performance goals rather than rewarding them for working overtime. Recognizing burnout when it occurs and dealing with it by reducing workload or providing some extra time off are some other ways to manage the problem.

Misdirected Effort

Employees with low ability who try hard may benefit from the following:

Goal setting. People are likely to flounder when goals are unclear or too difficult. Supervisors can set and clarify goals. Also, they can be sure that goals can be accomplished, given the subordinate's capabilities, within a reasonable period of time. This increases the subordinate's insight into the job requirements and expectations.

Coaching. Supervisors should provide suggestions for behavior change. Effective subordinates might be pointed out as role models. Coaching should include frequent performance feedback and reinforcement for desired behaviors. Daily or weekly meetings may be needed to review progress and discuss behaviors and actions.

Delegation. Some managers may have trouble delegating work to their subordinates. Because they are accountable for the work, they may feel they have to do it all, even when they have a staff. Helping managers structure the work, delegate clear tasks, and coordinate the work may reduce the manager's workload and increase the department's productivity.

Temporary assignments for skill development. Movement to a less demanding job or to a job in a related department may help the employee understand workflows and interdepartmental relationships. New insight into how task outputs are used and what customers and suppliers expect may increase work effectiveness once the employee returns to the job.

Restructuring the job assignment. Recognizing that the marginal performer's strengths lie in other directions, the job may be restructured to rely on those strengths. For instance, an account executive who is not sufficiently aggressive for cold sales calls may be able to handle customer inquiries in the sales office.

In addition, training may help conditions of misdirected effort just as it may help underutilization.

Low Ability and Low Effort

Employees in this category may be helped by the following more drastic steps:

Withholding merit pay. Supervisors who ignore or withdraw from confronting marginal performance may feel obliged to provide the subordinate with some merit pay. Doing so, however, will only perpetuate the marginal performance. Not to do so would be to open the door for an assault from the subordinate. This may be one strategy to send a clear message and open the door for discussion.

Withholding cost-of-living pay adjustments. Some compensation systems separate merit pay increases or bonuses from cost-of-living adjustments. However, even the cost-of-living adjustment may be under the discretion of the supervisor. When this occurs, a stronger message would be to withhold both merit and cost of living, indicating that marginal performers' pay will not increase until performance improves.

Transferring or demoting the marginal performer. Sometimes a transfer is not considered first because supervisors avoid sending problem performers to their peers. However, there may be other jobs, possibly on the same organizational level, that would be more suitable for the marginal performer. In large organizations where transfers are frequent, there may be considerable opportunities to find a better job match. Unfortunately, this may be difficult in smaller organizations, or in organizations in which it is difficult to move between units or departments, perhaps because of technical skill requirements. In some cases, the transfer may entail a demotion to find a position the marginal performer is capable of handling.

Outplacement. This implies a voluntary decision to leave the organization, possibly with generous severance pay and assistance in finding employment elsewhere. Some organizations pay outplacement firms to help such employees find jobs that match their interests and capabilities.

Firing. This generally requires proper documentation of marginal performance over time. Performance appraisals during the last three years should reflect the consistently marginal performance, and there should be evidence that the subordinate read the performance appraisals.

Summary

The performance management programs and strategies detailed here can have several profound implications for an organization. They focus employees' attention on their contribution to the organization. This improves their awareness of their own strengths and weaknesses and organizational expectations. It makes performance improvement an acceptable and important topic of discussion among peers and between supervisors and subordinates. Marginal performance is addressed within the context of performance improvement and organizational objectives. The benefit for the individual is increased employment security and a more rewarding and satisfying job. Quality improvement and continuous learning become part of the organizational culture. When marginal performers cannot improve in their current positions, they find better job matches or leave the firm (sometimes voluntarily, sometimes not).

Conveying new performance expectations can be painful, especially if employees expect job security and managers avoid confronting marginal performers. Program development is costly, and it takes patience on the part of executives and human resource managers. Performance management should be viewed as an investment in the organization. Linking performance management methods to strategic organizational objectives ties human resource functions with business functions, positions human resource managers as an integral part of business operations and change, and highlights the human resource development responsibility of all managers regardless of department or function.

The next section is about abusive management—extreme behaviors that can result in a subordinate or work group plagued by uncertainty, anxiety, and fear. It examines the prevalence of the problem and its implications for management development—in terms of both the development of abused employees and the control of the abuser. It describes abusive behaviors, considers some likely antecedents of workplace abuse, examines subordinates' reactions to abuse, and suggests ways organizations can diffuse or prevent these behaviors through management development.

ABUSIVE MANAGERIAL BEHAVIOR

The subject of abuse, while still a societal taboo, has received increased attention of late.[2] Issues of child and spouse abuse are dealt with daily in the news media and the courts. The workplace has not been free of concern, with issues of sexual harassment plaguing the military, government, and business. However, abuse in the workplace goes beyond gender issues to include how all people are treated. While many firms are known for treating their people with respect, honesty, and understanding, and may have formal policies and management development programs to support this reputation, even managers in these organizations are not uniform in their treatment of subordinates. The pressures of restructuring, layoffs, and financial constraints are ripe conditions for maltreatment. Managerial abuse curtails employees' professional growth and development. Abused employees spend time worrying about the abuse. Their "on-the-job development" consists of learning how to avoid and react to the abuse. This section considers the extent of managerial abuse, the forms it takes, ways subordinates respond, and ways organizations can alleviate the problem. As such, it should be a guide for creating management development programs that address the issue. Understanding the causes and consequences of abusive managerial behavior can help abused employees cope and overcome the negative effects of abuse. Also, such understanding is essential in the establishment of development programs and other organizational actions to control and prevent the problem.

Abusive Behaviors

Abusive managerial behaviors move the organization and its people in dysfunctional and destructive directions. In the extreme, managers who abuse subordinates may operate by means of coercion, intimidation, derision, or vindictiveness. Managers who exhibit abusive behaviors may be high in self-confidence and some managerial skills but misguided in terms of what the organization and employees want or need.

Managers who abuse may not perceive their behavior as such. However, their subordinates do. The subordinate may describe the manager as insulting, controlling, spiteful, hostile, rude, offensive, hateful, punishing, vengeful, aggressive, threatening, derogatory, or some combination thereof.

Abuse may occur in the open with multiple subordinates as victims or witnesses or in private with only the manager and subordinate present. In general, abuse may follow a pattern of behavior, and it often does, or it may occur only once. It may result in physical and/or psychological damage, but the defining factor is the occurrence of maltreatment, not its effects.

There are many examples of abusive managerial behavior (Bassman, 1992; Lombardo & McCall, 1984). Abuse may include unrealistically high or unfair expectations and holding hostage needed favors, such as time off. Abuse may take the form of public ridicule and disrespect, overwork (which devalues personal life), over-control, concentration on subordinates' weaknesses, social isolation, threat, and intimidation. It may include deception, unfair or unrealistic demands, abusive language, insults, bribes, criticism, name calling, unjustly withholding a deserved reward (such as a promotion or pay increase), and physical maltreatment. Further, abuse may involve setting subordinates up to fail, blocking subordinates' access to opportunities, unfairly taking credit for subordinates' work, and/or downgrading or demeaning others' capabilities. Abusive behaviors that may have legal ramifications include sexual harassment and discrimination based on gender, sexual orientation, handicap, race, religion, age, or other characteristics unrelated to job capabilities and performance. Pressuring subordinates to drink or take drugs is another form of abuse.

Prevalence of Abuse

The extent of manager abuse of subordinates may be evident from subordinates' descriptions of stress-provoking jobs and employee attitude surveys. A recent study asked 66 employees (all over age 30) for job experiences that caused them stress, made their job more difficult, decreased job performance, undermined relationships with others, and/or caused physical illness. Supervisors were cited along with working conditions and personal/family crises as sources of stress and performance decrement. Managerial behaviors included making poorly planned changes and making unrealistic or unfair demands or work schedules, such as forcing one subordinate to do another's work in addition to his or her own. Data from another 155 employees showed relationships between these negative job conditions and measures of tension, stress, depression, disrupted job performance, injuries on the job, and absenteeism. These relationships were stronger for middle-aged workers (ages 30–53) than for preretirement workers (ages 54–72), and the middle-aged workers reported higher levels of managerial abuse than the older workers. These age differences suggest that experience and maturity may permit older workers to keep job-related threats in their proper perspective, perhaps because they have little alternative to do otherwise, short of retiring. Alternatively, older workers experiencing great stress may have been underrepresented in the sample—perhaps because they have already changed jobs or left the workforce.

As indicated in the previous chapter, upward feedback surveys (subordinates rating their supervisors) are another source of information about the prevalence of abusive managers. An examination of employee attitude survey results in one large company provides another view of the extent of managerial abuse. Survey questions dealing with supervisor/subordinate relationships showed a rate of 5% to 20% of employees rating their supervisor's behavior as "very unfavorable." Questions included "gives credit for work well done," "treats me with respect," and "is accessible." One item, "shows favoritism to some people in our work group," had 17% to 27% of subordinates rating their supervisor "very unfavorable."

Poor supervisor/subordinate relationships in themselves may not constitute abuse, and there could be many reasons for low evaluations that may be beyond the supervisor's control or that say more about the subordinate than the supervisor.

Yet there are obviously many instances of subordinates who are highly discontent with how their supervisor treats them. These attitude survey results suggest that abuse of subordinates is not an isolated or uncommon phenomenon.

Anecdotal evidence of abusive managerial behaviors is easy to come by. We explained the meaning of abuse management to a class of more than 60 part-time students, all with years of work experience. When asked for examples of personal experiences, every student was able to write about at least one instance in which they felt they were abused by a supervisor.

Reasons Why Managers Are Abusive

Reasons for abusive managerial behaviors have their root in the manager's psychological makeup, the manager's social/cultural background, and the interaction among these factors.

Psychopathological Explanations

Psychopathological explanations focus on the abuser's underlying emotional disturbance. Abusive behavior is the symptom of a personality disorder characterized by the inability to control aggressive impulses. The manager may abuse a subordinate due to unmet emotional needs that signify discontent, anger, or irritability; excessively high expectations (an inability to balance the subordinate's own needs and capabilities with the manager's expectations); lack of empathy for the subordinate; or emotional scars from being abused oneself or deprived in one's early career.

Social-Cultural Explanations

This view argues that abuse is positively related to stress or feelings of stress. Accordingly, abuse is not a personality defect or isolated phenomenon but something that can involve "normal" people who may be socialized into abusive relationships.

Managers who abuse subordinates may be similar to husbands who psychologically batter wives, parents who batter children, and children who batter elders. In fact, abusive behavior in the home may be part of a pattern of abusive behavior that includes the workplace. Personal background factors are often used to explain violence-prone personalities of men who batter women. A commonly reported pattern is a strict father and an inconsistent mother who alternated between being lenient (sometimes in a collusive way to avoid upsetting a potentially violent husband) and being strict in applying her own standards of discipline. The batterer's mother may have smoothed everything over for the batterer so as to protect him from his father's potential brutality. A battered woman herself, the mother may have inadvertently conditioned her son to expect someone else to make his life less stressful. As a result, violent and abusive behavior has been learned and rewarded over a long period of time. This could apply to abusive managerial behaviors as well as to the violence-prone husband.

Abusing and putting up with abuse may be due to prior experience with abuse. For battered women, battering was reported to have been present in 67% of the battered women's homes, 81% of the batterers' homes, and only 24% of the non-batterers' homes (Walker, 1984). Abuse begets abuse, a lesson that may apply to the workplace as well as the home. Further, the abuse of alcohol and drugs may correlate with abusive supervision, just as it does with wife abuse.

Stressful Work Situations

Numerous sources of stress may engender abusive management. Examples include limited resources, lack of supportive higher management, threats to the manager's job security, pressure to get results, highly ambiguous task responsibilities, limited influence with higher management, and lack of ability to meet job demands.

Abuse may occur when the manager perceives that the costs of abuse are lower than the benefits. Costs are likely to be perceived as low when, for instance, subordinates are defenseless and/or have little recourse for complaints. The benefits of abuse are likely to be perceived as high if the manager believes the situation demands and even condones aggression. Other benefits of abuse stem from personal gratification—that is, the manager feels more in control and superior.

The costs and benefits of abuse may be interpreted in terms of the perceived risks. Abusive managers are likely to implicitly or explicitly assess the risks of their intended behavior. The risks are likely to be low when, for instance, subordinates are dependent on the supervisor for rewards, work structure, and job security and when managers are rewarded for achieving their goals regardless of the means. In addition, risks are likely to be low when the situation is viewed by others, such as higher management, as difficult (e.g., subordinates are believed to be inept, unqualified, or unprepared) and/or when managers observe others (perhaps their own supervisor) using political or abusive behaviors. Other conditions fostering abuse include cases in which managers are rewarded for being heavy handed or "macho." Managers are not expected to be exemplars of morality or supervisory excellence, and there are no explicit behavioral standards for good or outstanding managerial behaviors. Further, abuse may arise when the manager has little formal basis to control subordinates (e.g., little discretion over valued rewards such as pay), there are no punishments for being abusive, and/or top management ignores whistle-blowers.

The years since the mid-1980s have produced a vast change in the social structure and expectations within many organizations that has increased managerial stress. As organizations become more competitive and lean, employees are expected to do more with less. They have more responsibility and are held accountable for producing more. Simultaneously, they may lose employment security and income (given the declining value of the dollar). This environment may be ripe for abusive management. Workplace abuse may occur because the organization fails to provide alternatives (e.g., exposure to appropriate manager/subordinate role models and training) or clear-cut restraints (e.g., strong personnel policies with clear negative outcomes for abuse).

Social/Individual Interaction Explanations

This view focuses on the personal and situational conditions that influence the relationship between the manager and the subordinate. The manager's learning history, interpersonal experiences, and intrinsic capabilities are predisposing factors contributing to abusive behavior. Under stress, managers who are predisposed to abuse due to their own learning history or coping abilities may feel that they are expending considerable energy on subordinates who offer little appreciation. The manager's resentment lowers inhibitions and leads to abusive practices. Thus, existing conditions and prior social and cultural forces establish the parameters for individual behavior. In the stressful situation, anger turns into aggression, which takes the form of abuse. Feelings of negative arousal (tension, anger, rage) and/or negative attributions ("this subordinate is doing this to upset me") influence aggressive reactions.

Accountability and Self-regulation

Some people impose standards on themselves and apply those standards through self-evaluation and control. Lack of accountability to oneself or others may facilitate abuse or fail to prevent it. Accountability for one's decisions and actions is an implicit or explicit constraint on all consequential acts. People generally seek the approval and respect of those to whom they are accountable and are motivated to protect and enhance their social and self-image. When accountability is absent (for example, when higher management ignores the means of accomplishing a goal), this is tantamount to permission to abuse.

Impression Management

Abusive behavior can be understood in terms of the impressions the abusing manager intends to convey about him- or herself. Impression management includes the behaviors people exhibit and the process of self-disclosure to create and maintain desired impressions. Caring about what others think will be higher when the manager is dependent on the source for feedback and rewards, when feedback is public, and when a formal performance evaluation is imminent. The impression a manager wants others to have of him or her may not conform to the actual impression. For instance, the manager may try to convey an impression of being a strong-willed, "take no guff" supervisor, while the subordinate views the behavior as unrealistic and abusive.

Manager-Subordinate Relationships

Another interactionist perspective requires understanding the relationship emerging between the supervisor and subordinate. Building this relationship is an exchange process that involves both parties, but is usually dominated by the leader. A leader's status, formal authority, and control reduces the need for abuse or manipulative behaviors. However, a manager may wish to gain a reputation for effectiveness, for example, by conveying a hard-nosed, tough managerial style. Further, the manager may claim that inequitable treatment of subordinates is based on differences in job capabilities when in actuality it is based on non-job-related factors such as race, religion, or friendship. Showing favoritism may be abusive in itself, especially if the "out group" subordinates are regularly excluded from opportunities for development, valued job assignments, pay increases, or other rewards.

How Subordinates React to Abuse

The manager's role is central to employees' work experience. People pay close attention to the attributes of those on whom they depend. As such, abusive managerial behaviors can create an overwhelmingly negative experience. Abuse generates negative conditions such as stress and alienation and puts employees at a distance from the supervisor.

Subordinates' reactions to abuse may include aggressiveness or retaliation against the manager (an "eye for an eye" strategy), aggression against others who are defenseless (one's own subordinates, one's family), passivity, withdrawal, increased effort to meet supervisor's expectations, or a combination of these behaviors. Each reaction is likely to lessen the subordinate's job performance, job involvement, organizational commitment, and career motivation.

Learned Helplessness

One reason abuse works is that people are generally obedient to authority. The explanation for this may lie in the concept of learned helplessness. This is a passive response to abuse. It results from a perception that "I have lost personal control over my ability to influence my environment." Learned helplessness occurs when the target believes that the chance of changing the abuser's behavior is very small and there are no opportunities for redress. This is especially likely when the abuser's power is authority-based, as is the case for the supervisor. This is self-perpetuating in that helpless behavior reinforces the subordinates' beliefs that they are helpless, thereby reducing their self-esteem and perceived control over their environment.

Learned helplessness is likely to occur when subordinates view themselves as the cause of the manager's behavior. This further decreases the subordinate's self-confidence. Also, subordinates who believe the abuse is not likely to go away are likely to be more prone to feelings of helplessness. In addition, subordinates who believe that the abuse affects many aspects of their lives are also likely to feel helpless.

Learned helplessness is a type of human depression that has cognitive, motivational, and behavioral components. The inability to predict the success of one's actions leads to perceptual distortions. Such depressed people have negative, pessimistic beliefs about the effectiveness of their actions and the likelihood of obtaining future rewards. The subordinate learns that the manager wants the subordinate to feel helpless.

Some subordinates may fight to restore their lost control. They may file a complaint, threaten to complain, or refuse to comply. These are direct confrontations to the abusive behavior. However, these actions may have negative consequences for subordinates, and subordinates are likely to avoid them except in desperation.

Management development programs that address the occurrence and effects must help employees understand learned helplessness, why it develops, and how it can be negated. Abused employees need to recognize that they aren't helpless and that the organization wants to know about cases of abuse. Also, employees need to recognize more subtle abuse for what it is and be able to counteract it themselves. They can practice establishing plans for themselves, including ways to respond to abuse when it occurs. They identify abuse situations they have experienced and role play alternative reactions. Of course, further support and action may be needed, as described below.

Ways Organizations Can Alleviate or Prevent Abuse

Our discussion of abuse and its possible causes and consequences suggests several different strategies for controlling and preventing abuse. These techniques can be described in management training programs to help higher-level managers recognize and deal with abusive managers in their organizations. They can also be used in development programs to help treat abused managers.

Once abuse is identified, points of leverage for change include psychological treatment, altering behavior through changes in reinforcement contingencies, and changing the situation to eliminate factors that facilitate or exacerbate abusive tendencies and impose policies and remedies that ensure abusive management will not be tolerated. These approaches build on prevalent sound human resources policies and programs, suggesting that strengthening good management practice can help alleviate or avoid abuse.

Employee assistance programs can provide the advice and referral for appropriate psychological treatment—for instance, psychotherapy or counseling. Of course this requires the abusing manager's cooperation and may take considerable time. As with alcoholics, the first step is for the abuser to admit that there is a problem.

Other treatments do not necessarily require that the abuser recognize the problem and cooperate in the treatment. One short-term solution is to separate the abuser from the target(s) of abuse by transferring the manager or the subordinate to another department. The manager can be fired when the behavior is sufficiently documented. Higher-level management can establish policies that make it clear that abusive management will not be tolerated. Whistle-blowing rules can be implemented to protect employees who file complaints.

The organization can adopt new reinforcement contingencies. For instance, a set of desired leadership behaviors can be developed as a way to set standards and communicate expectations. Managers should be clearly informed that they will be evaluated and rewarded on how well they demonstrate these leadership dimensions. Managerial training programs can explain and demonstrate the new behaviors and unacceptable behaviors. Communications programs for all employees can clearly define and give examples of managerial abuse so employees know it when they see it and understand procedures for redress.

Negative feedback to managers about their abusive behavior is not likely to work, especially if the managers are the only ones receiving the information about themselves. Abusive managers are likely to avoid and ignore feedback. Self-insight stems from accurate interpretation of feedback. People who are high in self-confidence and insight engage in frequent self-assessment and self-regulation. Abusers, however, are likely to try to protect themselves from criticism. Indeed, they are likely to deny or avoid negative feedback and try to control the feedback they receive.

Organization development experts can facilitate group and interpersonal interventions that encourage open and honest communication and improve working relationships. Organizational interventions may control and limit abuse. Employee attitude surveys are likely to be effective only when the results are fed back to both the manager and higher-level management and when the results have implications for losing something valuable, such as pay or job level. Another similar intervention is an upward feedback program that gives subordinates the opportunity to evaluate their immediate supervisor's performance. This will only help prevent abuse when the results are incorporated into the formal evaluation and reward system. Unfortunately, subordinates' fear of identification and reprisal may cause them to withhold honest feedback, even when the upward ratings are made anonymously.

The abused subordinate may require treatment as well as the manager. While the manager may be removed from the situation, the subordinate may suffer permanent psychological scars and performance deficits as a result of the experience. Supportive management that reacts quickly and affirmatively to reports of abuse may not be sufficient to overcome or prevent long-lasting damaging effects of abuse. Group therapy and support groups may help victimized subordinates. When abuse affects an entire work group, professional assistance may help the group to discuss the experience openly, share reactions, and encourage employees to attribute the cause of the abuse to the manager and not themselves.

What Don't We Know About Abuse in Management

There is a lot we need to learn about abusive managerial behavior. Abusive situations are the results of complex phenomena that have psychological, social, behavioral, and environmental components. This suggests a number of open questions.

We don't know the incidence of different types of workplace abuse. This includes different forms of abuse, their frequency of occurrence, how they develop, how they are perceived, and alternative individual and organizational reactions. We don't know conditions under which behavior is interpreted as abuse. Abusive behavior that can be attributed to the situation may be seen as justified. In such cases, the cause of the behavior may be viewed as short-term, and the manager will not be blamed. Behavior that cannot be attributed to the situation may be attributed to the manager's inherent character and viewed as unchangeable.

We don't know how impression management affects abuse. What impressions are intended by abusive managerial behaviors? What impressions and attributions does the target of abuse form? What characteristics of the situation, subordinate, and the abusive behavior affect how these perceptions and interpretations occur (i.e., whether subordinates attribute the cause of the behavior to the manager, the situation, or to themselves)? Are the same behaviors interpreted similarly by different subordinates? Do abusive managers have erroneous or faulty perceptions of how others react to their behavior? To what extent do abusive managers recognize the effects of abuse?

We don't know enough about how abusive manager/subordinate relationships evolve. What conditions foster the continuance of abuse or cause one-time negative behaviors, such as insults or rude behavior, to degenerate into long-term abusive relationships? Under what conditions do others (subordinates, the manager's peers, or top management) collude in encouraging or directly contributing to the abuse? When are subordinates or peers willing to blow the whistle? Finally, we need to learn more about organizational policies and practices toward abuse to identify types of responses available to targets of abuse and the effectiveness of these policies and practices in curtailing and preventing abuse.

CONCLUSION

Given this uncharted territory, organizations should be open to management researchers who wish to investigate abusive managerial behaviors. This requires executives to admit that managerial abuse can occur and acknowledge that learning about abuse and taking corrective and preventive actions are needed.

NOTES

1. The section entitled "Identifying Performance Problems" was coauthored by Edward M. Mone.

2. The section entitled "Abusive Managerial Behavior" was coauthored by Emily S. Bassman.

12

Conclusion: Developing a Culture of Continuous Learning and Improvement

This final chapter considers how the policies and programs discussed in the preceding chapters shape the organizational culture of university administration. If change is endemic, what kind of culture is needed to be sure the organization is ready to adapt and, more than that, influence the environment and create directions for change? The chapter begins by considering the meaning of a *learning organization* where team and process management provide flexibility for trying new things. Reflecting on the leadership roles, planning processes, performance management strategies, and means for development discussed throughout the book, we then consider what it takes to make it all work. In particular, we own up to the frustrations and successes, consider underlying explanations for barriers and achievements, and suggest ways to move forward into further transitions and transformation.[1]

BECOMING A LEARNING ORGANIZATION

Reactive and Experimental Learning

Organizations do not change naturally, and universities are no exception. *Inertia* implies a resistance to fundamental reorientations in policy (Hinings & Greenwood, 1988). While this is potentially dangerous, its benefits include greater reliability in product delivery and many economies of efficiency and routine (Miller, 1982). However, when there are a wide variety of competitive threats, inertia will retard adaptation. When such threats are few, however, inertia may encourage a more effective and economical use of managerial skills and resources and allow managers to focus on the most important operations and decisions (Miller & Friesen, 1984).

Miller and Chen (1994) proposed two distinct models of organizational learning, one *reactive* and the other *experimental*. Reactive learning occurs as managers experience the rewards and punishments from organizational performance that drive the perceived need to act (Miller & Chen, 1994). Successful organizations tend to experience tactical inertia. Tactical adjustments (those not involving significant long-term commitments—deemed to have a less permanent impact on the institution) occur when performance problems signal the need to act. Experimental organizational learning is not motivated by performance problems or crises but by provocative information, market diversity, and the desire to seize opportunities. Forces that inspire, rather than threaten, managers to act drive proactive learning and strategic actions (significant investments in capital, people, or structure along with mergers, new alliances, and new services).

Adaptive and Generative Learning

An organization must continually build the performance capability of its members (Morris, 1993). *Adaptive* learners are willing to make incremental changes to enhance existing operations and activities. This works fine as long as things are relatively stable. When they are not, adaptive learning can be dysfunctional by perpetuating behaviors that no longer work. *Generative* learners have learned how to learn. They can effect transformational changes—major shifts in behavior that emerge after self-study and situational assessment (Senge, 1990; McGill, Slocum, & Lei, 1992). Generative learning facilitates organizations making sharp, transformational changes. Generative learners are open, system thinkers who are empathetic, creative, and self-effective. Openness means awareness of a wide range of perspectives. The generative learner suspends the need for control and is open to different values, backgrounds, and experiences. Systems thinkers see connections between issues, events, and data. Empathetic people avoid or reconstruct strained relationships. Creativity is personal flexibility and a willingness to take risks. Self-effective individuals have the feeling that they can and should influence the world. They understand their strengths and weaknesses and recognize that they are able to find solutions to problems and make important things happen.

Learning organizations promote *generative/experimental learning*—that is, "an emphasis on continuous experimentation and feedback in an ongoing examination of the very way organizations go about defining and solving problems" (McGill, Slocum, & Lei, 1992, p. 5). This is in contrast to the usual defensiveness in learning. Argyris (1982) distinguished between "single-looped" learning—the skill to defend ourselves from the pain and threat of dealing with interpersonal conflict openly and honestly—and "double-looped" learning—the skill to recognize and articulate our underlying assumptions and beliefs, even if they are painful to ourselves and others. Single-looped learning results from defensive routines that insulate us from self-examination. The result is "skilled incompetence." Rather than resolve conflict, we contribute to it by suppressing what we are actually thinking, and never communicating the generalizations that underlie our perceptions and behavior. Argyris's concept of "action science" is moving people from single- to double-looped learning. This involves developing skills of reflection and skills of inquiry. Skills of reflection allow us to slow down our own thinking processes so that we become more aware of how we form underlying assumptions and mindsets and the way these influence our behavior.

Building on Argyris's work, Peter Senge (1990; Kofman & Senge, 1993) described the learning organization in his book *The Fifth Discipline*. Senge asserted that managers are natural advocates. They become successful by debating forcefully and influencing others. As they rise to more important positions, however, they confront increasingly more complex and diverse issues that go beyond their expertise and personal experience. They must learn to ask questions. "What is needed is blending advocacy and inquiry to promote collaborative learning" (p. 198). This entails inquiring into the reasoning behind others' views but also stating one's own point of view in a way that reveals one's assumptions and reasoning and invites others to inquire into them. "I might say, 'Here is my view and here is how I have arrived at it. How does it sound to you?' " (Senge, 1990, p. 199). Becoming a double-looped learner takes initiative and courage. It requires a combination of aggressiveness and a spirit of inquiry.

The Need for Continuous Learning

The information age and the advent of more complex computational systems suggest the need for a more skilled workforce and changes in organizational operations and division of labor. However, the greatest roadblocks to change are institutional (Adler, 1992). "Although complex technical systems may demand broader work roles, more decentralized authority, and higher levels of skill, the degree to which the economy moves in these directions will be largely determined by whether firms can free themselves of the structural and cultural sediments of the industrial revolution" (Barley, 1994, p. 183). We need to consider alternative scenarios that bypass or overcome institutional and cultural constraints such as an emphasis on short-term results and managerial values for control. A key will be ensuring the ongoing training of all personnel, including context-specific training that is employer-sponsored and employer-supported training delivered by schools or universities. If universities can contribute to the surrounding community in this way (for instance, serving training needs of local businesses), they should be able to do the same for their administrative staff.

The type of training offered to employees is likely to be related to the organizational culture. Training that focuses on in-group capability will be remembered and bolster self-efficacy if task demands and cultural values support group performance. Training that focuses on individual capability will be remembered and used if task demands and cultural values support individualistic performance (Earley, 1994). Individual-focused training concentrates on how individual employees can perform their work better. It provides employees with performance information based on their own prior performance in relation to the requirements of their jobs. Discussion during the training focuses on the employee him- or herself and how the employee's past performance could be used to enhance success in the future. In contrast, group-focused training focuses on the employee's work group. Employees are told how their respective work units had performed and what the group might do to perform better. Performance is framed in terms of the group's past performance and future capability. Both types of training are needed to support individual performance and team contribution.

Support for Committee Structures

As we indicated at the outset of this book, team processes are important to the operation of universities because of multiple constituencies and norms of consultation. Committee structures and other formal processes arise in organizations facing multiple constituencies. Pressure from public interest groups forces organizations to initiate internal communication and coordination systems to process information and respond to the issues. For instance, according to Greening and Gray (1994), they are likely to develop committees that include members from a variety of functional departments and organizational levels. The committees meet often to address the issues. Moreover, they tend to receive more resources from top management to analyze and develop response to emerging issues. However, large organizations and those led by top management concerned by issues are more likely to have issue-oriented structures. Notably, crises do not necessarily precipitate the formation of additional committees and other response mechanisms, perhaps because organizations likely to face such crises prepare for them beforehand (Greening & Gray, 1994).

Generating Employee Commitment

Different organizational strategies and policies are likely to affect different elements of organizational commitment. There are three dimensions of organizational commitment: *affective* (the employee's emotional attachment to, identification with, and involvement in, the organization), *continuance* (commitment based on the costs that the employee associates with leaving the organization and depending on degree of personal sacrifices and lack of alternatives), and *normative* (the employee's feelings of obligation to remain with the organization) (Allen & Meyer, 1990; Dunham, Grube, & Casteneda, 1994). Each has different antecedents. Job characteristics such as task autonomy, task significance, task identity, skill variety, and feedback are likely to influence affective commitment. Age, tenure, career satisfaction, and intent to leave are likely to influence continuance commitment. Coworker commitment, organizational dependability, and participatory management are likely to affect normative commitment (Dunham et al., 1994).

When Employees Go Beyond the Call of Duty

Organizational citizenship behaviors are innovative and spontaneous activities that go beyond role prescriptions (Organ, 1988). Organizational citizenship behaviors are likely to occur in a context in which social exchange (trust in the supervisor in return for the supervisor's fair decision processes) characterizes the supervisor/subordinate relationship (Konovsky & Pugh, 1994).

Human Resource Systems and Employee Commitment

Arthur (1992, 1994) found two broad categories of human resource systems: (1) *control systems* aimed at cost reduction through reduced direct labor costs, improved efficiency, enforcing employee compliance with rules and procedures, and basing employee rewards on measurable output criteria; and (2) *commitment systems* aimed at maximizing employee commitment (e.g., through forging psychological links between organizational and employee goals—i.e., developing committed employees who can be trusted to use their discretion to do their jobs in ways that meet organizational goals). Commitment systems enhance performance and reduce turnover and enhance the inverse relationship between performance and turnover.

Summary

The once-successful organization facing threats and uncertainties makes tactical adjustments. Administrators in these organizations characterized by inertia are motivated by rewards and punishments. However, experimental organizations are motivated by the desire to seize opportunities. Proactive, generative learning and strategic actions emerge from forces that inspire, rather than threaten, administrators to act. Employee training and development is a key to being prepared for uncertainties, knowing how to learn from changes, and being open to experimentation. Team processes arise in universities because of the multiple constituencies in the university environment. Administrators need continuous developmental experiences in planning and performance management processes. Leadership style and human resource policies and programs support proactive learning and affect employee commitment and citizenship. Leadership trust and investment in employees builds commitment. The next section considers how to make the management systems discussed throughout this book work successfully.

MAKING IT WORK: A PRACTICAL APPROACH TO TEAMS AND PROCESSES

This section offers some ideas about what worked and what didn't. We don't want to give the impression that the development and implementation of the ideas discussed in this book were without barriers. Some were smooth-going; others were frustrating. As should be apparent already, the methods discussed here were not designed as a single system. They evolved. As such, they moved the administration into a continuous learning mode. Each step forward was progress in building a stronger organization and a coherent human performance system. However, for every two steps forward, we took one step backward.

What Didn't Work: Some Problems and Frustrations

Trusting Group Planning Processes

We wanted the planning processes to be dynamic experiences that really drove organizational actions. We didn't want them to be useless bureaucratic exercises. However, admittedly, this was a mixed bag. Getting some of the vice presidents engaged in the planning processes was like pulling teeth. It required meeting with them and their staffs to discuss what they were doing and translate this into plans. We ended up drafting the plans that their staffs should have written. In other cases, departments had long-standing planning processes that fit right into what we were doing on a university-wide level.

One resistant administrator responsible for elements of campus operations felt that working with various committees was useless because his principal goals did not make it into campuswide priorities for funding. For instance, resources for bricks and mortar never won out against scholarships and academic programs. In the hospital, fixing a boiler never won out against a new life-saving machine. So it's not surprising that he felt that prioritizing and planning could seem like hitting one's head against a wall. The only solution was not giving up in informing people about the issues.

There were cases where people's self-interest and protection of their professional territory and careers prevailed over group effort and teamwork. The capital planning council (see Chapter 5) ran into the problem of control. Campus services administrators felt that they were the experts in facilities operations. Their attitude was, "Give me the resources and I'll do my job." Others on the council from the academic sector believed that directions for capital investment should be directed by programmatic initiatives and that the planning process should be a joint effort taking into account program goals and facilities conditions.

In another area, an autocratic, close-to-the-vest administrator admitted to me after submitting the fate of his department to a planning discussion that he was surprised and pleased that the team did the "right thing." A little trust in the consultative process can be a learning experience.

Personnel Issues

As suggested above, management styles were not always conducive to participatory efforts. Management problems, some because of personality conflicts, intervened in effective operations within and between units. Occasionally, people were fired, but usually only after considerable angst and coaching. Also, we recognized that letting someone go was not an instant solution. There was no guarantee that the new person would be any better, no matter how carefully chosen by a search committee.

Systems Issues

The key indicators and management reports were not easy to produce. They were hampered by poor data systems that meant current information was not readily accessible. Data bases on finances, personnel, and enrollments were not always in the shape we wanted for meaningful institutional policy studies. We worked at this over time, bringing attention and resources to ways of improving administrative computing. However, changing technologies and the need to coordinate diverse systems did not reveal simple solutions. Distributed computing (e.g., local area networks linking personal and minicomputers) seemed to be the way to go, moving away from mainframes, but it was not immediately clear how this would work and who would support it for different departments' very diverse systems needs.

Designing Strategic, Integrated Human Resource Systems

As emphasized in Chapter 3 and in many other sections of this book, we view human resources as a strategic tool for accomplishing organizational objectives and bringing about change. Group facilitation (Chapter 8) and employee development (Chapter 9) are areas where the human resource department can take the lead. Unfortunately, the human resource director, by virtue of position in the hierarchy, did not have a seat at the top decision-making table (i.e., the cabinet). Moreover, systems and personnel problems made it difficult for the human resource function to deliver basic services effectively, so it was hard for the department to gain credibility in other areas. This required working in other ways (e.g., the formation of the president's steering committee on employee training and development) to demonstrate the strategic nature of, and commit resources to, programs that could have strategic value, such as human resource development.

What Did Work: Some Successes and Pleasant Surprises

Building Teams

We were skeptical that the top team of administrators (Chapter 8) would be worthwhile, and so were many of the other top team members. However, we found that this and other teams were often a source of innovation and a basis for mutual understanding and cooperation in other contexts. At the very least, the top team helped us get to know each other better. While there was an initial mandate for participation, we believe that we grew to recognize the value of collegial support.

Creating a Continuous Learning Environment

The training committee was a great success. The committee members, representatives of all the provostial and vice presidential areas, were energized by the benefit they provided to themselves and the campus community. "Finally we are doing something for ourselves," was a common feeling. They went all out year after year to produce an exciting training day kickoff and convince employees and managers—even administrators who tended to feel that training took employees away from their jobs—that the university was serious about investing in its people.

Getting More from Less

In many cases, we used existing staff and management interns to develop strategic initiatives. Rather than hire people into permanent positions and create bureaucratic entities, we borrowed people or gave them added assignments to be part of new activities. The training committee and the planning staff were chief examples. This engendered involvement and ownership across departments.

Process Leadership

The finance and enrollment planning processes had leaders who recognized that these tasks were indeed processes that crossed departmental responsibility. They had to be managed in a way that promoted interface between departments to achieve common goals. As a result, administrators' input was sought and appreciated, and people recognized the importance of their individual roles and the need to cooperate.

Summary

Many of the difficulties were attitudinal in nature. People were not always on-board, at least not right away, because they wanted to maintain control and reduce uncertainty. Others were with us from the start. They were flexible, not defensive, and not concerned with politics. (But they were politically sensitive!) Their contributions are recognized throughout this book.

Processes evolve just as plans do. So there was a need for constant revision. We realized that the processes we developed were not set in concrete, and that they would evolve as needs and management styles changed. Moreover, we found that planning is both bottom up and top down. As such, there was opportunity for considerable involvement. We found in the administrative review team (Chapter 6) and in many other instances that people throughout the administration were dedicated, hard working, and wanted to work as a team for the betterment of the university. We almost always won when we gave people credit for their capabilities and extended opportunities for them to show what they could do.

New managerial roles emerged and grew. Administrators became change agents, facilitators, coaches, developers, and experimenters. They began to focus on what they and their staffs needed to do to be successful today and in the future. In the final section, we consider how we anticipated steps for planning and managing transitions.

LOOKING TOWARD THE FUTURE

The change of a university's president is a watershed event. For us, it was a time for reflection about our effectiveness, excitement about what new directions we will take as an institution, and uncertainty, especially for administrators who don't have job security. As we anticipated such a change, the planning staff met to discuss priorities for planning and process. We saw several needs we hoped to move forward in the new administration:

Information availability and management: The administration should develop interactive databases that would help answer policy questions. The technology exists, and we should find a way to fund the necessary hardware and software development. This would allow us to draw on multiple databases from the same platform, and model the likely effects of possible events and different assumptions.

Planning employee selection and development: We needed human resource forecasting and planning to identify the qualifications of people we would need in the future. This would allow us to plan for staff selection and development in a mode that also allowed us to pursue other strategic goals such as increasing opportunities for women and minorities.

Facilities management: We wanted a comprehensive plan for facilities utilization and support. The capital facilities plan (Chapter 5) and the study of research space (Chapter 7) were steps in this direction. However, we felt that we needed to do more to be sure we found the resources to meet our infrastructure needs and developed client-centered facilities management strategies. In addition, we wanted to redress conditions from past budget cuts which managers solved by draining resources from important and, in some cases, essential services.

Student life: The university's concentration on enhancing undergraduate education suggested the need to do more for student retention and quality of life programs. As a planning staff, and as supporters of the enrollment issues forum, we wanted to be sure that these goals continued to be incorporated into university-wide objectives.

Holding the gains: We wanted to be sure that we didn't lose the progress we felt we had made in fostering teamwork and managing critical processes. We hoped to maintain and revise the performance management systems we had developed. We wanted to review these with the new president and seek directions for improvement in line with new administration objectives.

Contributing to organizational assessment: We wanted to be a part of the analysis that the new administration would conduct of existing systems, organizational structures, resources, and goals. Such an analysis was consistent with our desire to create a climate of continuous learning and improvement. Toward that end, we worked with the current and incoming presidents to develop a strategy for an outside analysis. This would provide an objective view of the administration and make suggestions for transition.

Transition as Opportunity for Growth and Development

The organization assessment had to be announced gingerly. We didn't want administrators to feel that the primary goal was to have an excuse for structural and personnel changes. We wanted the assessment to be viewed positively and constructively—not as a break from the participative mode of operating that had been established, but as a way to achieve expert advice and consultation. Here's the announcement memo written by the outgoing president to the cabinet.

Our incoming president has requested that I assist her in securing the services of a management consulting firm to review the status and needs of a broad set of management functions. Such reviews are common when campus administrations change, and several of the large national accounting firms provide services specifically designed to advise incoming campus CEOs.

The scope of the review will include administrative and service functions of the university broadly construed, but excluding the academic administration, program oriented student functions, and health care delivery functions.

The level of the review will be somewhat general because of the large number and size of the units involved. We expect the consultant to take advantage of the copious material already compiled by most units in connection with the many reporting, planning and budgeting exercises we have executed during recent years.

The timing and scope of this project could lead to a misunderstanding of its intent. We know, and the incoming president knows, that there are problems of all shapes and sizes, and that it will take more than a few months of consultant time to fix them. What is needed is an overview independent of the framework in which we have conceived our operations historically on campus. We expect that an experienced management consultant can give advice that will guide administrative action on a strategic level.

Scope of Analysis

Next, here's the scope of work document that outlined the nature of the project. The document was written by the outgoing president with input from the incoming president, cabinet members, and various staff members.

Background

Like other institutions throughout the nation, our university has emerged from a period of harsh budget reductions. This period coincided with unprecedented changes in technology available for management and for the productivity of many institutional functions. Other changes have occurred in the mix of regulation and independence affecting the institution's interaction with its government sponsors and in the relative magnitudes of revenues from state, federal, and private sources.

Now that budgets have stabilized and the campus is looking forward to new leadership, it is time to assess the effects of these changing conditions and to map out a strategy for matching institutional behavior to the new reality in which the university operates.

To begin this process, we are seeking the assistance of a management consulting firm with experience in higher education administration. As described in more detail below, the consultant would not be expected to evaluate or advise on academic issues, but only on those administrative and support functions upon which the changing environments of budget, regulation, and technology have had the greatest impact.

Scope

The review will focus on the administrative and service functions of the university, but exclude the academic administration, program-oriented student functions, and health care functions except as they receive central campus services or impact central campus functions.

Participating offices would include the office of the president, finance and management (which includes human resources), campus services (facilities operations and institutional services), computing and information services, and transaction-intensive functions in the office of student affairs (e.g., admissions and registrar).

The project is expected to take approximately four months, and therefore cannot produce in-depth studies of every office. The university expects to receive objective advice on its administrative effectiveness compared with current national norms in higher education. The rationale for retaining a management consultant is to gain access to national experience of other comparable universities and to benefit from a fresh perspective.

Objectives

The major goal of this project is to provide management information to assist the new president in formulating long-term plans for strengthening university management and the first short-term steps needed to carry them out.

The consultant will evaluate broadly the status and effectiveness of the university's support services, functions and processes. The evaluation will include, but not be limited to: organization of functions, use of relevant technology, responsiveness to client needs, reporting relationships, span of management control, size of units, measures of effectiveness, and interfaces and communications among and within units.

The consultant is expected to view the university's operations in the context of its environment and identify broad strengths and weaknesses not only of the individual functions, but especially how they work together. The consultant will recommend ways to improve the management and coordination of the various functions.

Method

Self-examination during the budget cutting era produced much data regarding performance of various university functions. The consultant is expected to assess the adequacy of these data, and where appropriate use them as the basis for review and evaluation.

The evaluation will address the adequacy and effectiveness of the university's overall administrative operations and the critical processes, process linkages, and information flows that span organizational "boundaries." Examples of these processes include but are not limited to: budgeting, accounting, facilities project management, procurement, hiring, student registration, admissions/financial aid. Most of these functions are well documented.

In performing this work, the consultant will

1. Review and analyze university and unit documentation, data and performance measures including, but not limited to, planning materials, mission statements, goals and objectives, annual reports, status reports on major projects, self-study materials, organization charts.
2. Interview appropriate campus personnel.
3. Compare resources, organization, processes, and technical infrastructure with other universities where possible.

The consultant's report will:

1. Address the following questions concerning the university's current organizational effectiveness:
   a. Is the university responding effectively to the needs of its primary constituencies, including students, faculty, and support staff in their various roles?
   b. Do the university's organization and processes encourage the teamwork and communications necessary to conduct campus business, execute campus priorities and achieve organizational objectives?
   c. Are the university's critical administrative and support processes well coordinated and executed?
2. Identify broad strengths and weaknesses of the university's organization and processes.
3. Offer one or more alternative strategies that will build on the strengths and correct the weaknesses identified above.

Consultants for Organization Analysis

Management consulting firms, often the higher education consulting arm of one of the major accounting firms, offer assistance to new university presidents in assessing the campus administration and offering recommendation for change. One such firm advertises that they will assess the management environment and leadership capacity of the organizations, answering questions such as: What are the strengths and weaknesses of the current senior administrative leadership? Does the management environment foster openness and collegiality? Does it encourage initiative, innovation, and prudent risk taking? They also examine elements of the "management infrastructure"—for instance, answering: Are the institution's priorities reflected in the allocation of resources? Are planning, budgeting, and performance assessment systematic and well integrated? Does the institution reward good management and penalize mismanagement? Do the organizational structure and operating practices maximize efficiency and effectiveness?

Maintaining a Sense of Team

In an effort to set the foundation for the new administration and ensure a team focus as input to the new administrators, the university affairs department held a one-day summer retreat. The agenda, presented below, suggests the importance of taking the new president's perspective in evaluating whether the department is doing the right things right.

University Affairs Summer Staff Meeting Agenda

Theme for the Day

To ensure we have a sound, team-oriented foundation for university affairs operations.

Modules

I. Major Department Activities and Goals

A professional and staff member within each department will make a 10-minute presentation describing what's happening in the department, why, and how it is going. The presentation will have three components:

a. Describe three principal activities that contribute to key university objectives such as enhancing the image of the university.
b. For each of the principal activities, state how you rely on other departments within the division.
c. Mention efforts that have been especially successful in building a sense of teamwork within the department and/or between departments within university affairs.

This presentation is to be given as if it is a briefing for our new president. The audience is to take the role of the new president and ask probing questions. Ten minutes will be allowed for questions after each presentation. (Each department will need to meet in advance to select presenters and develop a method to help them get the presentation ready.)

Presentations will be from development, the foundation, media relations, publications, alumni affairs, and conferences.

II. How We Work Together

The group will divide into five or six subgroups. The members of each group will be preassigned to ensure good cross-departmental representation. The subgroups will discuss the following questions:

a. What problems do we face in working together as individuals?
b. What obstacles or barriers do we face in building effective relationships between departments within university affairs?

III. Areas for Improvement

The group will break into different subgroups (again with predetermined members to ensure a mix across departments). The focus will be on what we can do differently to enhance work relationships within and between departments. Each group will be asked to do the following:

a. Generate at least three areas for improving work relationships between two or more individuals.

b. Generate at least three areas for improving teamwork within and between departments.

c. Generate one or more actions for improving teamwork within the division as a whole—that is, specific actions that can be taken at the divisional level to improve work relationships and work effectiveness.

IV. Department Commitments

Departmental groups meet to determine department and individual commitments. In particular, determine what will be done differently to promote teamwork within the department and between the department and other units in university affairs.

CONCLUSION

Our story ends with the anticipation of further change. Recall several of the themes that we outlined in the first chapter—that organization development is evolutionary, that employee development is critical to meeting changing environmental conditions and expectations, that work is a process, and that cooperative teamwork is essential to effective work processes. The examples and initiatives described in this book are not meant to be copied exactly. Rather, they are models for creating change. We hope they will incite new ideas and a willingness to experiment with administrative teams and processes.

NOTE

1. The first section of this chapter, "Becoming a Learning Organization," was adapted from London (1995).

References

Adler, P. S. (Ed.). (1992). *Technology and the future of work*. New York: Oxford University Press.

Adsit, D. J.; London, M.; Crom, S.; & Jones, D. (1994). Relationships between employee attitudes, customer satisfaction, and departmental performance in a customer service organization. Unpublished manuscript, State University of New York at Stony Brook.

Allen, N. J., & Meyer, J. P. (1990). The measurement and antecedents of affective, continuance and normative commitment to the organization. *Journal of Occupational Psychology, 63*, 1–18.

Anderson, R. E., & Meyerson, J. W. (Eds.). (1992). *Productivity and higher education: Improving the effectiveness of faculty, facilities, and financial resources*. Princeton, NJ: Peterson's Guides.

Argyris, C. (1982). *Reasoning, learning and action: Individual and organizational*. San Francisco: Jossey-Bass.

Arthur, J. B. (1994). Effects of human resource systems on manufacturing performance and turnover. *Academy of Management Journal, 37*, 670–687.

Arthur, J. B. (1992). The link between business strategy and industrial relations systems in American steel minimills. *Industrial and Labor Relations Review, 45*, 48–56.

Barley, S. R. (1994). Review of "Technology and the future of work." *Administrative Science Quarterly, 39*, 183–186.

Barrett, K., & Greene, R. (1994). "No one runs the place": The sorry mismanagement of America's colleges and universities. *Financial World*, March, 38–52.

Bassman, E. (1992). *Abuse in the work place: Management remedies and bottom line impact*. Westport, CT: Quorum.

Bassman, E., & London, M. (1993). Abusive managerial behavior. *Leadership & Organization Development Journal*, 14(2), 18–24.

Bessent, A. M.; Bessent, E. W.; Charnes, A.; Cooper, W. W.; & Thorogood, N. C. (1983). Evaluation of educational program proposals by means of DEA. *Educational Administration Quarterly, 19*, 82–107.

Blumenstyk, G. (1993). Colleges look to 'benchmarking' to measure how efficient and productive they are. *Chronicle of Higher Education.* September 1, A41–42.

Borman, W. C. (1974). The rating of individuals in organizations: An alternative approach. *Organizational Behavior and Human Performance, 12*, 105–124.

Brockner, J.; Tyler, T. R.; & Cooper-Schneider, R. (1992). The influence of prior commitment to an institution on reactions to perceived unfairness: The higher they are, the harder they fall. *Administrative Science Quarterly, 37*, 241–261.

Broque, E., & Lin, P. (1994). Incorporating academic planning in the development of deferred maintenance priorities. Paper presented at the SCUP-29 Annual Conference, San Francisco.

Bruegman, D. C. (1992). Needed: Changes in management focus. *NACUBO Business Officer*, March, 40–42.

Burns, S., & Lister, J. (1993). An application of data envelopment analysis to compare operating efficiencies of university and college libraries. Unpublished manuscript. Available from Dr. Thomas R. Sexton, Harriman School for Management and Policy, SUNY-Stony Brook, Stony Brook, N.Y. 11794–3775.

Charnes, A.; Cooper, W. W.; & Rhodes, E. (1981). Evaluating program and managerial efficiency: An application of data envelopment analysis to program follow through. *Management Science, 27*, 68–69.

Chatman, J. A., & Kehn, K. A. (1994). Assessing the relationship between industry characteristics and organizational culture: How different can you be? *Academy of Management Journal, 37*, 522–553.

"Communicating financial data: A conversation among independent college officials" (1993). *NACUBO Business Officer*, November, 36–40.

Coopers & Lybrand with Barbara S. Shafer & Associates (1993). *Benchmark 92: Operating benchmarking for quality improvement and cost management in higher education.* Vol. I: Using benchmarking and related methodologies, July.

Coopers & Lybrand with Barbara S. Shafer & Associates (1994). *Benchmark 93: Operational benchmarking for cost management and quality improvement in higher education.* Vol. I: Using benchmarking and related methodologies, April.

Crom, S. (1994). *Creating value for customers: Integrating processes and learning new behaviors.* Lexington, MA: Rath and Strong.

Cummins, H. J. (1992). Preparing the front-line workers. *Newsday*, May 10, p. 59.

Drucker, P. (1992). The new productivity challenge. *Harvard Business Review*, November–December, pp. 69–79.

Dunham, R. B.; Grube, J. A.; & Castaneda, M. B. (1994). Organizational commitment: The utility of an integrative definition. *Journal of Applied Psychology, 79*, 370–380.

Earley, P. C. (1994). Self or group? Cultural effects of training on self-efficacy and performance. *Administrative Science Quarterly, 39*, 89–117.

Falk, D. S., & Miller, G. R. (1993). Budget cutting: How do you cut $45 million from your institution's budget? Use processes and ask your faculty. *Educational Record*, Fall, 32–38.

Greening, D. W., & Gray, B. (1994). Testing a model of organizational response to social and political issues. *Academy of Management Journal, 37*, 467–498.

Hartley, J.; Jacobson, D.; Klandermans, B.; & Van Vuuren, T. (1991). *Job insecurity: Coping with jobs at risk.* London: Sage.

Hautaluoma, J.; Jobe, L.; Visser, S.; & Donkersgoed, W. (1992). Employee reactions to different upward feedback methods. Presented at the Seventh Annual Meeting of the Society for Industrial and Organizational Psychology, Montreal.

Hinings, C. R., & Greenwood, R. (1988). *The dynamics of strategic change.* Oxford: Basil Blackwell.

Kaiser, H. H. (1992). Increasing productivity in facilities management. In R. E. Anderson & J. W. Meyerson (Eds.), *Productivity and higher education: Improving the effectiveness of faculty, facilities, and financial resources.* Princeton, NJ: Peterson's Guides, 95–101.

Kelly, E. (1993). Restructuring: The collegial process. *Inside Tulane, 12*(11), 1–4.

Kempner, D. E. (1993). The pilot years: The growth of the NACUBO benchmarking project. *NACUBO Business Officer, 27*(6), 21–31.

Kofman, F., & Senge, P. M. (1993). Communities of commitment: The heart of learning organizations. *Organizational Dynamics, 22*(2), 5–23.

Konovsky, M. A., & Pugh, S. D. (1994). Citizenship behavior and social exchange. *Academy of Management Journal, 37*, 656–669.

Locke, E. A., & Latham, G. P. (1990). *A theory of goal setting and task performance.* Englewood Cliffs, NJ: Prentice-Hall.

Lombardo, M. M., & McCall, M. W. (1984). *Coping with an intolerable boss.* Greensboro, NC: Center for Creative Leadership.

London, M. (1995). *Self and interpersonal insight: How people learn about themselves and others in organizations.* New York: Oxford.

London, M. (1989). *Managing the training enterprise.* San Francisco: Jossey-Bass.

London, M., & Mone, E. M. (1994). Managing marginal performance in an environment striving for excellence. In A. K. Korman (Ed.), *Human dilemmas in work organizations: Strategies for resolution.* New York: Guilford, 95–124.

London, M., & Beatty, R. W. (1993). 360 degree feedback as competitive advantage. *Human Resource Management, 32*, 353–373.

Massy, W. F. (1992). Improvement strategies for administration and support services. In R. E. Anderson & J. W. Meyerson (Eds.), *Productivity and higher education: Improving the effectiveness of faculty, facilities, and financial resources.* Princeton, NJ: Peterson's Guides, 49–83.

McGill, M. E.; Slocum, J. W., Jr.; & Lei, D. (1992). Management practices in learning organizations. *Organizational Dynamics, 21*(1), 5–16.

McGuinness, A. C., Jr., & Ewell, P. T. (1994). Improving productivity & quality in higher education. In *Priorities*, No. 2, Fall. Washington, DC: Association of Governing Boards of Universities and Colleges, 1–10.

McKenna, B. (1993). TQM coming soon to a campus near you: TQM is taking the higher education world by storm. Is it an idea to embrace or one to scorn? *On Campus, 13*(2), 8–10. Washington, DC: American Federation of Teachers.

Melan, E. H. (1993). Quality improvement in higher education: TQM in administrative functions. *CUPA Journal*, Fall, 7–8.

Meyer, H. H. (1991). A solution to the performance appraisal feedback enigma. *Academy of Management Executive, 5*, 68–76.

Miller, D. (1982). Evolution and revolution: A quantum view of structural change in organizations. *Strategic Management Journal, 19*, 133–151.

Miller, D., & Chen, M. J. (1994). Sources and consequences of competitive inertia: A study of the U.S. airline industry. *Administrative Science Quarterly, 39*, 1–23.

Miller, D., & Friesen, P. H. (1984). *Organizations: A quantum view*. Englewood Cliffs, NJ: Prentice-Hall.

Moore, H. (1942). *Psychology for business and industry*. New York: McGraw-Hill.

Morris, L. E. (1993). Learning organizations: settings for developing adults. In J. Demick & P. M. Miller (Eds.), *Development in the workplace*. Hillsdale, NJ: Lawrence Erlbaum Associates, 179–197.

Moses, J.; Hollenbeck, G. P.; & Sorcher, M. (1993). Other people's expectations. *Human Resource Management, 32*, 283–298.

Neumann, A. (1991). The thinking team: Toward a cognitive model of administrative teamwork in higher education. *Journal of Higher Education, 62*(5), 485–513.

Organ, D. W. (1988). *Organizational citizenship behavior: The good soldier syndrome*. Lexington, MA: Lexington Books.

Peterson, C. R., & Beach, L. R. (1967). Man as an intuitive statistician. *Psychological Bulletin, 68*, 29–46.

Price Waterhouse (1993). *Improving audit committee performance: What works best*. Altamonte Springs, FL: The Institute of Internal Auditors Research Foundation.

Ruffer, D. G. (1994). The University of Tampa: A case of administrative reinvention in a private university. Presented at the AAHE 9th Annual Conference on Assessment and Quality, San Francisco.

Senge, P. M. (1990). *The fifth discipline: The art and practice*. New York: Doubleday.

Sexton, T. R.; Silkman, R. H.; & Hogan, A. (1986). Data envelopment analysis: Critique and extensions. In R. H. Silkman (Ed.), *Measuring efficiency: An assessment of data envelopment analysis*. San Francisco: Jossey-Bass, 71–105.

Seymour, D. (1993). *The IBM-TQM partnership with colleges and universities: A report*. Washington, DC: American Association for Higher Education.

Stuelpnagel, T. R. (1989). Total quality management in business—and academia. *Business Forum*, Winter, 4–9.

Taylor, B. E.; Meyerson, J. W.; & Massy, W. F. (1993). *Strategic indicators for higher education: Improving performance*. Princeton, NJ: Peterson's Guides.

"The Future of Colorado State University: The Context for Planning." (1992). Fort Collins: Colorado State University.

"Transforming administration at UCLA: A vision and strategies for sustaining excellence in the 21st Century." (1991). Office of the Chancellor, University of California, Los Angeles, September.

Van Velsor, E., & Leslie, J. B. (1991). *Feedback to managers, Vol. I: A guide to rating multi-rater feedback instruments*. Report 149, Greensboro, NC: Center for Creative Leadership.

Walker, L. E. (1984). *The battered woman syndrome*. New York: Springer.

Index

About the Author and Contributors

MANUEL LONDON is Professor and Director of the Center for Human Resource Management, Harriman School for Management and Policy, State University of New York at Stony Brook. He spent 12 years at AT&T in a series of human resources and training positions as a manager and researcher. His recent books include *Developing Managers*, *Change Agents: New Roles and Innovation Strategies for Human Resource Professionals* (winner of the 1989 Book Award given by the American Society for Personnel Administration) and *Managing the Training Enterprise*, and *Career Growth and Human Resource Strategies*.

EMILY S. BASSMAN is Director of Telecommuting and Job Sharing for Pacific Bell.

JEFF T. CASEY is Associate Professor of Management and Policy at the State University of New York at Stony Brook, where he also holds a joint appointment with the Department of Political Science.

TAMMY FELDMAN is the firm economist at Skadden, Arps, Slate, Meagher & Flom, a major corporate law firm.

EDWARD M. MONE is an organization development consultant in the chief financial officer organization of a global corporation.

DANIEL J. MELUCCI is the associate vice president for finance and management at the State University of New York at Stony Brook.

DOUGLAS PANICO is Director of Performance Management at SUNY-Stony Brook.

CARL J. SINGLER JR. has held the position of Director of Internal Audit at the State University of New York at Stony Brook since 1974.

EMILY THOMAS works at the State University of New York at Stony Brook as university planning coordinator and assistant to the vice president for health sciences for policy analysis.

ISBN 0-275-95246-0

90000>

EAN

9 780275 952464

HARDCOVER BAR CODE